Islands of Holiness

Islands of Holiness

RURAL RELIGION IN UPSTATE NEW YORK, 1790–1860

Curtis D. Johnson

Cornell University Press

ITHACA AND LONDON

First published 1989 by Cornell University Press.

International Standard Book Number 0-8014-2275-2
Library of Congress Catalog Card Number 88-43436
Printed in the United States of America
*Librarians: Library of Congress cataloging information
appears on the last page of the book.*

*The paper in this book is acid-free and meets the guidelines for
permanence and durability of the Committee on Production
Guidelines for Book Longevity of the Council on Library Resources.*

FOR LITA,
as always

Contents

Maps

Chart

Preface

Islands of Holiness examines the evolution of the religious life of an upstate New York county in the years 1790 to 1860. In these years religious excitement swept the Empire State—the western half of New York has been described as "burned over" by waves of religious enthusiasm—and Cortland County shared in this experience. The economic and demographic similarities between Cortland and the surrounding counties suggest that its religious patterns may be typical of rural regions elsewhere in New York.

The most dramatic development in this seventy-year period in Cortland County's religious history was the replacement, by midcentury, of the corporate church structure of the early nineteenth century with modern organizational forms. This transition affected gender relations, individual rights, church discipline, attitudes toward wealth, and nearly every other public aspect of religious life. The chief catalyst for this transformation was the New Measures theology preached by the local disciples of Charles Grandison Finney. The result was that individualistic notions of salvation and sanctification prevailed over the older communitarian ethos.

I accumulated many debts in the course of this investigation into the religious life of Cortland County. John Modell, Russell Menard, John Howe, Arthur Johnson, and William Flanigan all encouraged the study in its early stages through perceptive questions and conceptual suggestions. A special debt is owed to George Green, not only for the numerous hours he spent critiquing my scholarly work but also for his wise counsel and support. In

xi

addition, I thank Elizabeth Faue, David Howard-Pitney, Melissa Meyer, Clark Miller, Edward Tebbenhoff, and William Wilcher for their contributions to this project.

In the past several years, new avenues of research have both expanded and focused my historical inquiry. Much of the credit for this transition goes to Ronald Hatzenbuehler, Judith Wellman, Joan Jacobs Brumberg, David Brumberg, and the members of the Washington Area Seminar on Early American History at the University of Maryland. These individuals pointed out ways to strengthen my analysis and suggested new areas of inquiry, which provided fruitful results. Two anonymous reviewers for Cornell University Press deserve special credit. Their critiques of an earlier draft led to significant revisions, which greatly enhanced the quality of the final book.

Several organizations have contributed financially to my research. The University of Minnesota Graduate School provided a Doctoral Dissertation Special Grant and the Shevlin Fellowship. The University of Minnesota's Computer Center and History Department absorbed most of the expense of computer time. Special thanks go to President Robert Wickenheiser and Mount Saint Mary's College for a President's Pride Summer Research Grant to underwrite the cost of a 1986 research trip to New York State.

Organizations and individuals facilitated the gathering of primary documents and rare secondary works. The staff of the Wilson Library of the University of Minnesota was particularly helpful, as were the staffs of the George Arents Research Library for Special Collections at Syracuse University, the Presbyterian Historical Society in Philadelphia, and the American Baptist Historical Society in Rochester, New York. I am indebted to the staff of the Department of Manuscripts and University Archives at John M. Olin Library of Cornell University for allowing me liberal use of the collection of Cortland County church records. I also recognize Shirley Hepple and the Cortland County Historical Society for sharing rare documents from the community's past with me. A special debt is owed to Leonard Ralston, who graciously shared with me his machine-readable compilation of all state and federal censuses of Cortland County from 1825 to 1875. This volume would have been much more sparsely documented had it not been for his generosity.

With patience and good humor, Nancy Eyler and Judy Ott typed the manuscript with its numerous changes and revisions. Trudie Calvert's thoughtful copyediting and stylistic suggestions significantly improved the final version of the manuscript. The maps were adapted from Leonard Ralston's "Cortland County Codebook" and were prepared by the Public Relations Department at Mount Saint Mary's College.

Finally, my wife, Lita Anna Johnson, more than any other individual, made the completion of this manuscript possible. From my days as a graduate student, she has served as editor and critic, challenged my thinking, and offered the encouragement needed to bring the project to a successful conclusion.

CURTIS D. JOHNSON

Emmitsburg, Maryland

Abbreviations

ABHS	American Baptist Historical Society, Rochester, New York
CCHS	Cortland County Historical Society, Cortland, New York
CUA	Cornell University: Department of Manuscripts and University Archives, Ithaca, New York
CUMMN	Cornell University: Department of Maps, Microtexts and Newspapers, Ithaca, New York
PHS	Presbyterian Historical Society, Philadelphia, Pennsylvania
SU	George Arents Research Library for Special Collections at Syracuse University, Syracuse, New York

Islands of Holiness

Introduction

The role of evangelical churches in American society has been subject to much debate among historians. Fundamentalists and conservative evangelicals have argued that America's Judeo-Christian heritage was established at Plymouth and Massachusetts Bay, endured through the eighteenth and nineteenth centuries, and only recently began to suffer the ravages of "secular humanism." Those of a more liberal persuasion have contended that the Founding Fathers envisioned a secular, not a religious, republic and that their goal was a pluralistic, not an orthodox Christian, society. The political traditions of George Washington and Thomas Jefferson were to be upheld through the principle of separation between church and state.

Scholars have long sought to define the historical relationship between church and society, religion and government. They have focused not only on the events of 1620 and 1787 but on the long periods of time between momentous occasions. William McLoughlin's powerful *Revivals, Awakenings, and Reform* contends that evangelicalism was central to American self-definition, at least until the late nineteenth century. Donald Mathews's *Religion in the Old South* and Eugene Genovese's *Roll, Jordan, Roll* argue the importance of evangelicalism to antebellum southern society and, in particular, to the maintenance of support systems within black communities under slavery. A number of recent monographs, notably Paul Johnson's *A Shopkeeper's Millennium* and Mary Ryan's *Cradle of the Middle Class,* have concluded that evangelical Protestantism provided a bulwark for northern society against the chaos

1

created by commercialization and industrialization. The organizational instrument was the revival; the chief benefactor was the emerging middle class.

Although scholars have examined antebellum religion in many locales, upstate New York has undergone particularly intense scrutiny, largely because of Whitney Cross's *The Burned-over District*. Cross's classic work argued that upstate New York was unique in the intensity of the revivalism experienced there and in the variety and number of bizarre social experiments and new religions originating within its borders. The region had been "burned over" with almost every religious, social, and political enthusiasm of the Jacksonian era. Cross found an explanation for this phenomenon in the economic and demographic conditions in upstate New York in the 1820s and 1830s.[1]

Since 1950 Cross's ideas have been reworked from many perspectives. Paul Johnson's study of the 1831 revivals in Rochester emphasized the social disorganization that accompanied early industrialization and how Charles Grandison Finney's revivals helped create a new social order that benefited the rising bourgeoisie. Mary Ryan, Joan Jacobs Brumberg, and Nancy Hewitt have examined the impact of changing gender roles, evolving household structure, and female benevolence on upstate New York religion. Judith Wellman and Linda Pritchard have used the tools of contemporary social science to evaluate the accuracy of Cross's contentions.[2] Scores of books, articles, and dissertations have been written on the Mormons, Millerites, Antimasons, com-

---

1. Whitney R. Cross, *The Burned-over District: The Social and Intellectual History of Enthusiastic Religion in Western New York* (Ithaca, 1950), esp. pp. 75–109.

2. See Joan Jacobs Brumberg, *Mission for Life: The Judson Family and American Evangelical Culture* (New York, 1984), and "Benevolent Beginnings: Volunteer Traditions among American Women, 1800–1860," in *Women, Volunteering, and Health Policy: Historical Perspectives and Contemporary Viewpoints* (New York, 1982), pp. 1–16. Nancy A. Hewitt, in *Women's Activism and Social Change: Rochester, New York, 1822–1872* (Ithaca, 1984) divides Rochester female voluntarists among "benevolent" women, "perfectionists," and "ultras," depending on their social, geographic, and religious origins. Judith Wellman analyzed three New York towns and found the basic arguments of *The Burned-over District* to be correct but in need of refinement, which she provided. See Wellman, "The Burned-over District Revisited: Benevolent Reform and Abolitionism in Mexico, Paris, and Ithaca, New York, 1825–1842" (Ph.D. dissertation, University of Virginia, 1974). Linda Pritchard, "The Burned-over District Reconsidered," *Social Science History* 8 (Summer 1984): 243–65, questions the uniqueness of the burned-over district.

munitarians, and other groups specifically linked to New York's Burned-over District.

Despite the contributions of Cross and the numerous social historians succeeding him, much remains to be discovered concerning pre–Civil War American religion generally and upstate New York religion specifically. In this book I will (1) examine religion in a rural nineteenth-century environment, (2) reemphasize the importance of ideology, both in encouraging revivals and in shaping the divergent evangelical responses to the central events of that era, (3) explain the impact of wealth and gender on the spread of evangelical values, (4) outline the place of evangelicalism within an upstate New York community, and (5) demonstrate how church relations with the larger society changed over time.

Scholarly attention to religion in the antebellum period generally falls into two categories: community studies of urban areas and general cultural analyses either of a multistate region or of the entire United States. Religion in rural communities has been neglected.[3] Yet before 1860, the Burned-over District, like the United States in general, was overwhelmingly rural. The result of this imbalance is that historians know relatively little about the religious-social environment that helped shape the ideology, behavior, and worship style of most American Christians before the Civil War.

Cortland County, New York, is an excellent place to study rural religion. Located in the Burned-over District, Cortland experienced economic and demographic development typical of west-

3. Studies of the religious aspects of community life have tended to focus on cities, as can be seen by Carroll Smith-Rosenberg's study of New York, Marion Bell's monograph on Philadelphia, and Nancy Hewitt's book on Rochester, New York. Mary Ryan's investigation begins in rural Whitestown but shifts attention to Utica. Anthony F. C. Wallace's portrayal of Rockdale is an exception to the rule, although the central theme is with typically "urban" problems of evangelicalism, socialism, and industrial relations. See Carroll Smith-Rosenberg, *Religion and the Rise of the American City: The New York City Mission Movement, 1812–1870* (Ithaca, 1971); Marion L. Bell, *Crusade in the City: Revivalism in Nineteenth-Century Philadelphia* (Lewisburg, Pa., 1977); Hewitt, *Women's Activism;* and Anthony F. C. Wallace, *Rockdale: The Growth of an American Village in the Early Industrial Revolution* (New York, 1980). Rural religion is studied in Wellman, "The Burned-over District Revisited," and Randolph A. Roth, "Whence This Strange Fire? Religious and Reform Movements in the Connecticut River Valley of Vermont, 1791–1843," 2 vols. (Ph.D. dissertation, Yale University, 1981).

Map 1. Cortland County within New York State

ern New York and much of the northern United States (see Map
1).[4] The majority of Cortland County residents lived on farms or
in hamlets throughout the period from 1790 to 1860. Like many
locales in the Burned-over District, Cortland County was settled
in the 1790s. The early economy centered around subsistence
agriculture. In the 1810s and 1820s, the county experienced a
heavy population influx. As population density increased and a
market economy evolved, small villages grew up to service the
maturing agricultural sector (see Map 2). By 1860 these villages

4. Linda Pritchard, in "The Burned-over District Reconsidered," esp. Table 4,
p. 255, establishes the typicality of Cortland County's experience. Pritchard created a ten-category typology of economic development for western New York and
the upper Ohio Valley. In western New York, the most common level of development was the mixed economy with fifteen counties, including Cortland, falling
into that category. Mixed-economy counties were the third most common category in the 152-county region.

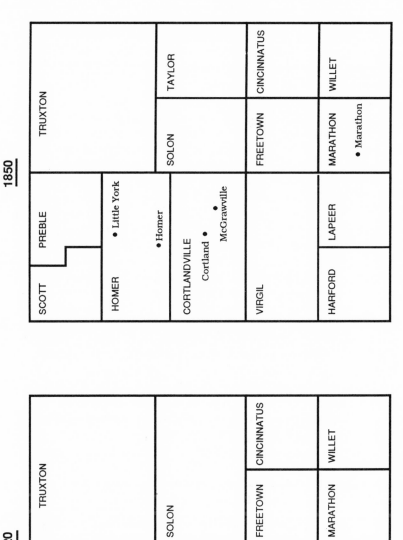

Map 2. Cortland County in 1820 and 1850

were the locus of political power within the county.[5] Cortland County, however, remained rural, its inhabitants, both villagers and country dwellers, dependent on the agricultural sector.

Cortland County's religious history parallels that of both the western half of the Empire State and much of the northern United States in the antebellum period. New England missionaries laid religious groundwork in the early 1800s, after which a dedicated Yankee laity sought to spread religion throughout the county. Revivals began in the mid-1810s, peaked in the early 1830s, then gradually declined until a brief spurt of religious enthusiasm occurred in the late 1850s. The national pattern of religious enthusiasm was similar.[6] As in many other locales, religion in Cortland County was dominated by the Congregationalists, Presbyterians, Baptists, and Methodists. Together these groups consistently accounted for over 80 percent of church accommodations, and here, too, Cortland County appears to be typical.[7]

The vast reservoir of primary documents relating to Cortland County provide an additional reason for its selection. Together, Cornell University and the Cortland County Historical Society hold partial or complete records for twenty-three local congregations. Federal and New York State manuscript census records are virtually complete from 1825 to 1875. Leonard Ralston of the State University of New York at Cortland has transcribed all existing county censuses from 1825 to 1875 into machine-readable form. Information on local voluntarist societies is plentiful, and newspaper coverage after 1825 is nearly continuous.

This volume reasserts the importance of religious ideology,

5. Village populations can be found in *Census of the State of New York for 1855* (Albany, 1857) and *Census of the State of New York for 1865* (Albany, 1867). Additional information on villages and hamlets for 1855 is in John H. French, *Gazetteer of the State of New York* (Syracuse, 1860), pp. 251–56. For the state population in 1860 see U.S. Census Office, *The Eighth Census of the United States, 1860* (Washington, D.C., 1866). Occupational data on household heads were obtained through the use of Leonard Ralston's computerized censuses.

6. The evangelistic cycles of America's major denominations illuminated in H. C. Weber's *Evangelism: A Graphic Survey* (New York, 1929) are very similar to those in Cortland County.

7. Pritchard has shown that both in New York and in the nation these four denominations were dominant in 1850, although by 1860 the Roman Catholics had passed the Congregationalists to assume fourth place in accommodations at both state and national levels. See Pritchard, "The Burned-over District Reconsidered," Table 2, p. 249.

even at risk of being out of step with much of the rest of the historical community. Since 1950 scholars of New York religious history have generally given less weight to theological ideas than to the social origins of various religious viewpoints. Whitney Cross maintained that the Burned-over District's uniqueness originated in the peculiar economics and demographics of western New York after the War of 1812. According to Cross, extreme religious and social behavior, usually referred to as "ultraism," occurred in areas that were heavily populated by literate Yankees and were moving from the frontier stage of development to economic maturity.[8] In recent years, social and economic factors have received the lion's share of attention in analyses of the sources of religious ultraism. Such studies consider class, gender, social status, occupation, birth rate, and life cycles of participants in detail but neglect the ideological universe in which the historical actors lived.

Emphasizing social, economic, and demographic factors to the neglect of political and religious ideology is a serious mistake. Recent scholarship has shown that republicanism affected aspects of American life from gender politics, to class relations, to the choice of alcoholic beverage.[9] Political independence and a devotion to republican values triggered a general reevaluation of religious ideas as well. William McLoughlin has shown how traditional Calvinism and its theory of election was incongruent with the experience of individual freedom and how the resolution of this conflict was at the heart of the Second Great Awakening.[10]

Religious innovation reached dramatic proportions in the Burned-over District partly because there was an unusual degree of freedom to develop new religious ideas and institutions. Unlike Massachusetts and Connecticut, New York did not establish Congregational churches by law. Settlers in western New York, unlike newcomers in the eastern half of the state, did not have to con-

8. Cross, *Burned-over District*, esp. pp. 75–109.
9. Linda K. Kerber, *Women of the Republic: Intellect and Ideology in Revolutionary America* (Chapel Hill, 1980); Mary Beth Norton, *Liberty's Daughters: The Revolutionary Experience of American Women, 1750–1800* (Boston, 1980); Sean Wilentz, *Chants Democratic: New York City and the Rise of the American Working Class, 1788–1850* (New York, 1984); W. J. Rorabaugh, *The Alcoholic Republic: An American Tradition* (New York, 1979).
10. William G. McLoughlin, *Revivals, Awakenings, and Reform: An Essay on Religion and Social Change in America, 1607–1977* (Chicago, 1978), pp. 98–106.

front the social hegemony of Dutch Reformed and Episcopal congregations.[11] The land west of the Catskills was a religious *tabula rasa* on which the local devout could write. But what was to be written? Reflecting a spirit of republicanism and personal independence, these settlers were not content simply to reproduce the religious institutions farther east. Western churches would be built in accordance with democracy and common sense. These principles raised certain questions: What is the proper function of the church? Who should be allowed to join a local congregation? If church membership is restricted to those who have experienced "saving grace," should individuals seek salvation? Should the church promote situations in which salvation is likely to be found? Once in a local fellowship, how should a believer relate to the rest of the world?

These questions brought a variety of responses. The ideological skirmishes fought in Cortland County reflected the battles elsewhere in the Burned-over District. At least three responses were offered to the question of what was the proper function of the church. Those who financially supported evangelical churches but refused to join and those who belonged to nonevangelical groups (such as the Universalists) argued that the function of the church was to maintain social order and encourage public morality. Others, principally the members of evangelical congregations, contended that the church's chief goal was to lead individual souls to salvation. Still others were influenced by perfectionist thought and announced that the church was to purify and redeem society. There was equal disagreement on other questions. Calvinists debated Arminians on whether God or individual sinners determined who would be saved or damned. Formalists (Congregationalists and Presbyterians) disagreed with antiformalists (Baptists and Methodists) over whether the church should focus on individual piety or also be concerned about social issues. In time, those who sought to promote the salvation of their neighbors were fighting coreligionists who believed that any human effort regarding redemption (other than waiting for divine grace) was equivalent to blasphemy. This mixture of ideas and beliefs was further seasoned by a variety of in-migrants ranging from Catho-

11. Edwin Scott Gaustad, *Historical Atlas of Religion in America*, Rev. ed. (New York, 1976), pp. 7, 14, 27.

lics and Episcopalians to Free Will Baptists, Seventh Day Baptists, Christians, and Adventists.[12]

This book explains the interaction of wealth and gender within evangelical congregations. Until recently, historians examining aspects of antebellum religion have generally fallen into two camps. The impact of wealth on pre–Civil War religion has generally been the domain of male historians interested in social control theories such as John Bodo, Charles Cole, Charles Foster, Clifford Griffin, Anthony F. C. Wallace, and Paul Johnson. Not surprisingly, the investigations of gender relations in nineteenth-century evangelicalism have been dominated by feminist historians including Nancy F. Cott, Barbara Epstein, Joan Jacobs Brumberg, Nancy Hewitt, and Mary Ryan.

Here the two strands of scholarship join in one central argument. Women were key figures within the major revivals before 1840. Churches in this period were not particularly wealthy, needed the skills and financial resources of women, and adhered to deep religious values. After the collapse of church discipline in the mid-1840s, wealthy men no longer had to fear the authority of the traditional church, and many began to join local congregations. With the wealth these men brought, congregations no longer needed the relatively minor contributions of women, and females were pushed to the background. Male commercial values replaced religious values. Men gained social control by removing religious leadership and influence from the realm of domesticity.

This study portrays the role of evangelicalism in a typical up-state New York environment. Although a majority of Cortland residents probably identified with one denomination or another, no more than a third of the adult population actually belonged to an evangelical church. Even so, these churches were the center of religious activity in the county. They sponsored and drew support from the various religious societies and benevolent organizations. The churches were the battlegrounds where ideological and theological controversies were fought. The county's congregations can be seen as religious interest groups that were small in size but, because their members were well-organized and highly moti-

12. One outgrowth of the religious debates was Joseph Smith's founding of the Church of Jesus Christ of the Latter Day Saints. See Klaus J. Hansen, *Mormonism and the American Experience* (Chicago, 1981), pp. 21–22, and Richard L. Bushman, *Joseph Smith and the Beginnings of Mormonism* (Urbana, 1984), pp. 51–59.

vated, greatly influenced the county's religious, social, and political life.

Understanding rural religion involves much more than congregational history, however. One must also investigate the religious societies that gave financial support to various congregations, reform organizations that grew out of evangelical social concerns, and women, who made up the majority of the members and who quietly made the churches function effectively.

Finally, *Islands of Holiness* explains how Cortland County's religious institutions changed in the span of a lifetime. Clearly, the relative influence of the denominations varied greatly over time, and the relationship of the churches with society and their own members was far different in 1860 than in 1805.

These changes can best be understood by viewing the evolution of the county's religious institutions between 1790 and 1860 in four distinct but overlapping periods. The first, from 1790 to 1815, was the foundation period, when missionaries entered the county, the first evangelical churches were created, and individual denominations displayed characteristics that would shape religious life for years to come. The second stage occurred from 1812 to 1843. These years were marked by rapid growth, both in the county's population and in church membership. During this time the county experienced its most intense period of revivalism. The third era, covering the years 1826 to 1846, was one of crisis, as the county's evangelical churches were disrupted by internal turmoil. The final stage, from 1846 to 1860, was one of retreat; evangelical churches no longer exhibited the intense religiosity of earlier years.

PART I

FRONTIER CHURCHES,

1790–1815

1

Adapting to the New York Frontier

At the end of the American Revolution, present-day Cortland County was a small portion of Montgomery County, which stretched from a line a few miles west of Schenectady to Lake Erie. More specifically, Cortland County was a small part of a center section of Montgomery County called the Military Tract, land that had been reserved for revolutionary war soldiers who had protected New York's western frontier from Iroquois attack in the early 1780s. By the time the state government fulfilled its promise to grant land to war veterans, many had sold their land certificates to speculators, who in turn sold the notes to land-starved New Englanders who wished to seek new opportunities in central New York.[1]

By the late 1780s, thousands of Yankees were abandoning the overpopulated New England countryside, passing over the well-settled lands of the Hudson River Valley, and entering what appeared to be a "new Eden." Some New England migrants eventually reached a relatively inaccessible area of the Military Tract now known as Cortland County. In 1791 Joseph Beebe and Amos Todd and his wife traveled by canoe up the Tioughnioga

1. Herman C. Goodwin, *Pioneer History, or Cortland County and the Border Wars of New York* (New York, 1859), pp. 103–11. David M. Ellis, James A. Frost, Howard C. Syrett, and Harry J. Carmen, *A History of New York State* (Ithaca, 1967), pp. 151–54; E. Wilder Spaulding, *New York in the Critical Period, 1783–1789*, New York State Historical Association Series, 1 (New York, 1932), p. 282; Dixon Ryan Fox, *Yankees and Yorkers* (New York, 1940), pp. 180–81; David M. Ellis, "The Yankee Invasion of New York," *New York History* 32 (January 1951): 3–17.

River and established their farmsteads on the flatlands just north of the present village of Homer.[2]

In the first decade the residents faced problems typical of the edge of white settlement. Forests had to be removed because it was difficult to achieve a minimum level of subsistence until enough farmland had been cleared to produce a year's provisions. In desperate cases, families lived for weeks on a diet of turnips and salt or boiled and ate roots found in the forest. After the first year, they began clearing the woods in earnest. If he had no other work to do, the average farmer could remove trees from no more than ten acres a year. But the pioneer's time was consumed by such tasks as providing his family with food and erecting buildings and fences. The lack of a market for any agricultural surplus served as a disincentive for clearing land quickly, and settlers rarely cleared more than three or four acres a year. The longer-range goal of creating a large farm was the task of a lifetime.[3]

Once the earliest migrants had cleared enough land to permit small-scale agriculture, they began to channel their energies into improving their common economic situation. Their efforts were rewarded, and by 1800 subsistence farming became easier. Two gristmills had been built in Homer so farmers no longer had to travel out of the county to Geneva, Onondaga Hollow, or Chenango Forks to have their wheat converted to flour. Within the county, farmers cooperated in road improvement projects, which greatly facilitated local transport. Roads were cut through the dense forests, including one connecting the settlers of Homer and Virgil with the state road. Outside markets were still beyond the reach of county farmers, but at least it was easier to visit the local blacksmith or mill operator.[4]

The agricultural system created in the 1790s was similar to those evolving on the Kentucky frontier or in backwoods Pennsylvania, but the political and religious systems created by the county's earliest white settlers had a distinct New England flavor. Displaced Yankees made up the greatest portion of Cortland

---

2. Goodwin, *Pioneer History*, pp. 93, 147–52; Bertha E. Blodgett, *Stories of Cortland County for Boys and Girls* (Cortland, N.Y., 1952), pp. 46–49.

3. Goodwin, *Pioneer History*, pp. 140, 249–50; Ellis et al., *History of New York State*, pp. 164–65.

4. References to gristmills and road building are found in Goodwin, *Pioneer History*, pp. 175, 219–20, 250, 254.

County's eighteenth-century population. Of the 118 adult male settlers coming to the county between 1791 and 1799, the place of origin is known for 78 or approximately two-thirds. Massachusetts was the former home of 31, Connecticut of another 16. Of those for whom information is available, 71 percent came from New England, with only 19 percent from New York and 10 percent from New Jersey and Pennsylvania.[5]

It is thus not surprising that the earliest political institutions resembled those of New England. In the early 1790s, Montgomery County was subdivided and present-day Cortland County became the southern part of Onondaga County. In 1808 the southern towns of Onondaga County were carved off to become Cortland County. Local government began when the town of Homer was organized in 1794, and the first town meeting was held in April 1796. In that session, townsmen were chosen to serve as supervisor, town clerk, assessor, collector, overseer of the poor, commissioner of highways, constable, overseer of highways, and fence viewer. Positions such as town clerk, assessor, and constable were the same as in New England.[6]

Despite similarities to New England town meetings, Homer's political affairs diverged from the Yankee pattern in several ways. It is significant that of the Yankee moral guardianships, the positions of selectman, watchman, tithingman, and constable, only the last was a town office in Homer. Either the memories of past social control or the difficulties of maintaining such control on the frontier dissuaded settlers from creating many positions for the enforcement of moral sanctions. As in New England, peace was maintained in Homer partly through economic regulation. Fences were to be constructed according to exact measurements set by the town. Hogs could "run at large without yokes or rings," but the keeping of cattle was subject to a one dollar fine. Some regulations in Homer would have seemed strange to fifth-generation inhabitants of New England towns. For instance, the town officials believed the indigenous wildlife endangered local live-

---

5. Ibid., pp. 147–265.
6. The modification of Yankee culture in a New York setting is discussed in Ellis, "Yankee Invasion," pp. 13–17. I have discovered no comprehensive list of New England town offices, but some are mentioned in Michael Zuckerman, *Peaceable Kingdoms: New England Towns in the Eighteenth Century* (New York, 1970), pp. 116, 158, 165–67, 202.

stock. Bounties of fifty cents were given for fox pelts, and panthers brought ten dollars each. Overall, the forms of the New England town were kept but were altered to meet the exigencies of the frontier.[7]

Protestant religion was a central feature of New England town life, and, not surprisingly, Cortland County residents quickly created a religious presence in their new community. The first religious services were conducted in 1793. The settlers' understanding of church doctrine and practice garnered from their Yankee past was vital, for with the exception of an occasional visiting missionary or minister, they had no clerical resources. Through the middle and late 1790s, lay-led services were held on a regular basis. Sabbath worshipers were from varied denominations, and though they shared a common orthodoxy, differences over issues of doctrine and practice provided an impetus for intense, protracted, and apparently positive discussions at Sunday meetings. Late in the decade, the devout were numerous enough to consider formal organization.[8]

Two factors combined to make formal church organization a much more difficult task in central New York than in New England. First, the emptiness of the region (Homer had 3.1 persons per square mile in 1800; the neighboring town of Solon had 1.9 persons per square mile) meant that a congregation had to draw members from a wide geographic area. At the turn of the century, a church in Solon needed the support of every adult within five miles to meet basic expenses—assuming that the county's residents would freely offer such support.[9]

Second, New York disestablishment meant that obtaining financial support from the general population would be much

7. Early town meetings in Homer are described in Goodwin, *Pioneer History*, pp. 166–70.

8. Ibid., pp. 170–71; James H. Hotchkin, *A History of the Purchase and Settlement of Western New York, and of the Rise, Progress and Present State of the Presbyterian Church in That Section* (New York, 1848), p. 420.

9. The 1800 census data are found in U.S. Census Office, *Second Census, Return of the Whole Number of Persons within the Several Districts of the United States* (Washington, D.C., 1801). The town of Homer at this time included the military tracts of both Homer and Virgil, each ten miles square. The town of Solon included the military tracts of Solon and Cincinnatus, each also ten miles square. On early boundaries, see Horatio Gates Spafford, *A Gazetteer of the State of New York* (Albany, 1824), pp. 114, 234, 493, 539; *Census of the State of New York for 1855*, p. xix.

more difficult than in Massachusetts or Connecticut. In New England one hundred years of statutory evolution had led to a fairly coherent relationship between church and state by the 1790s. Each household head contributed to the support of the "regular" or Congregational church in each town. At the town meeting, the eligible voters would discuss the condition of the meetinghouse, the minister's salary, the church's financial allotment, and other parochial business. The town provided the financial base for the Congregational church and supervised its material concerns. Dissenters could have their share of the church revenue applied toward the support of their sect, providing they followed specified procedures. A dissenting religious group had to request incorporation as a religious society from the state legislature. Once incorporation was accomplished, each sectarian could register with the town clerk as a dissenter and have his tax directed to his religious society, which would provide for the financial and material concerns of the dissenting church. The system may not always have promoted "piety, religion, and morality" to the degree the devout desired, but it gave Congregational churches and registered sects a financial base. Every household head paid taxes to contribute to the support of one church or another. A similar system existed in Connecticut.[10]

In Cortland County, Yankees discovered that it was much harder to foster religion under New York's 1777 constitution, which separated state and church. In the Empire State, no public funds could be used to support a sect or denomination. In 1784, however, the legislature enacted a series of laws that allowed religious bodies to incorporate. Any local fellowship in the state could create a religious society that would supervise the construction and use of the meetinghouse, help select the minister and establish his salary, and govern other material affairs of the congregation. If a religious group wished to build a house of worship, it must have an incorporated religious society that would own the property and oversee its use.[11] In New York, religious societies could do everything they did in New England. The key

10. John D. Cushing, "Notes on Disestablishment in Massachusetts, 1780–1833," *William and Mary Quarterly*, 3d ser. 26 (1969): 169–90. For a full treatment of this issue, see William McLoughlin, *New England Dissent, 1630–1833: The Baptists and the Separation of Church and State* (Cambridge, Mass., 1971).

11. Ellis et al., *History of New York State*, p. 195.

difference was the nature of financial support. In Connecticut and Massachusetts, 100 percent of the taxpayers contributed; in New York, the societies had to scramble for volunteers.

Homer's religious community took the first step toward church formation by creating the Religious Society of Homer in 1799. The primary goal of the society was financial, not spiritual: it was to take on traditional functions of the New England town, not the New England church. As in Yankee town meetings, membership and voting privileges were restricted to men who were financially able to assist in group projects. Once organized, the all-male organization quickly assumed the tasks mandated by New York law and New England tradition. In addition to providing land for the meetinghouse, raising funds for ministerial support, and making plans for the eventual construction of a church, the society assumed the quasi-governmental task of educating the town's children. Schoolhouses were provided in Homer, and the town was divided into nine educational districts, each of which the pastor visited regularly.[12]

The records of the Homer Religious Society reveal its secular orientation. The 1799 minutes begin: "Activated . . . by a sence of duty . . . we will form ourselves into a Society."[13] Supporting religion apparently was considered a civic responsibility, not a reflection of evangelical zeal, and there were no religious criteria for joining the society: It would "admit any Person of lawful age a member of this Society [with no other requirement] than that he or she become Obligated by Covinent to contribute annually toward defraying the expenses of said society."[14] No creeds, doctrines, or guides to Christian behavior can be found in the Homer society's record book.

In later years, when religious societies were linked to individual churches of specific denominations, the same pattern of doctrinal laissez-faire existed. A minimal religious commitment was crucial to the success of such societies for most members were not particularly devout. The vast majority never joined a church. Of the members of the Homer Religious Society between 1799 and 1821,

12. The institutional structures created between 1799 and 1805 are recorded in the First Religious Society of Homer, Minutes, 1799–1856, Accession No. 6236, CUA. See also Hotchkin, *History*, p. 420.
13. First Religious Society of Homer, Minutes.
14. Homer First Baptist Society, Minutes, 1810–75, Accession No. 6253, CUA; First Religious Society of Homer, Minutes.

only 43 percent had joined a church in the county. Only 24 percent of those who joined the Homer Baptist Society between 1810 and 1819 had joined a local congregation by decade's end.[15] In short, the Homer Religious Society and its successors became a haven for men of the minimalist perspective, those who believed religion was good for the community and ought to be supported financially but were unwilling to make a commitment to any particular set of religious beliefs or code of behavior through church membership.

The foundation of the Religious Society of Homer in 1799 only intensified controversy among the more committed religionists. A religious society was not enough: a church was needed. But how was a church to be organized and from what denomination would the pastor be called? In New England, law, tradition, and popular inclination dictated that the choice be the Congregational church. But in New York, the government was theologically neutral, and church organization and denomination were determined by popular choice.

For two years, the Religious Society argued and debated these questions. One reason for the delay in forming a congregation was that society members were unwilling to depart from the New England consensual ideal. Had the issue been put to a majority vote, there is little doubt what the outcome would have been. Of the forty-one members of the society in 1799, over half can be traced to their state of origin. All of these were from either Connecticut or Massachusetts, so it is likely that the Congregationalists had the numerical advantage. They also had the support of the Reverend Seth Williston, the local Congregational missionary. Yet other opinions were heard and had to be respected. John Miller, founder of the Sunday services that began in 1793, was a devout Presbyterian and lobbied for a church of that polity. John Keep, a society member, was a Baptist and no doubt wanted to organize under those auspices.[16] Unlike New England, on the

15. The percentages were calculated by matching the two societies' membership lists against those of local evangelical congregations.
16. Society members are listed in the First Religious Society of Homer, Minutes. State origins come from Goodwin, *Pioneer History*, pp. 147–265. The roles of Seth Williston and John Miller are explained in Hotchkin, *History*, pp. 420–21. John Keep was a charter member of the Homer (later Cortland) Baptist Church. See Cortland First Baptist Church, Record Book, October 3, 1801, Accession No. 6239, CUA.

New York frontier no religious group received preference. Religious doctrine was to be decided on the basis of reason and Scripture, not by social custom, legal prescription, or even majority vote. Even before the first church was formed, a variety of beliefs flourished in Cortland County.

The search for denominational consensus ended in 1801. Christian unity and the retention of the consensual ideal were deeply held values that were not easily disregarded. The impasse was broken, according to local religious histories, by nothing less than divine intervention. One morning in the fall of 1801, Dorothy Hoar said to her husband, "I have lain awake all night praying for direction as to the method of forming a church. God has heard me and this is the way: Do you go and collect the names of all who are willing to take part in organizing a Congregational Church here, and invite all others who choose to unite with it."[17] The Religious Society followed Dorothy Hoar's strategy, and a Congregational church was formed in October 1801. But the Homer Congregational Church was not the first to be organized in the county. The Homer Baptists officially organized on October 3, 1801, nine days before the Congregationalists.[18]

Despite the establishment of a Congregational church, the Religious Society had to make some concessions to denominational diversity. Clearly, the bulk of the society's efforts and resources went to the Congregationalists. In 1802 a Congregational minister was called and the society pledged an initial annual salary of $300 for his support. Land was donated for a commons in the village of Homer, and the Congregational church, as in New England, would preside over the green as a symbol of village and religious unity. Nevertheless, on November 24, 1801, the society voted "that the Baptist in this society should have their share of the present meeting House according to what they Paid"; shortly thereafter, the Baptists began to use the meetinghouse once a month. In time, lots were given to the Baptists, Methodists, and Episcopalians and churches of those persuasions flanked the Congregational one on the village green. By 1838 the churches on the green had become the dominant feature of the village of Homer,

17. Quoted in Philemon H. Fowler, *Historical Sketch of Presbyterianism within the Bounds of Central New York* (Utica, N.Y., 1877), p. 421.
18. Homer Congregational Church, Minutes, October 12, 1801, Accession No. 6236, CUA; Cortland First Baptist Church, Record Book, October 3, 1801.

a testimony to a New England consensual ideal adapted to the religious diversity of New York.[19]

Despite its diversity, early religious life in Cortland County was based on orthodox Protestantism. By 1815 four major denominations had established churches within the county lines. Exactly how many churches belonged to each religious body is hard to verify because early records are sketchy and sources occasionally contradict each other. The Baptists appear to have been the most ambitious, forming seven and possibly eight congregations by 1815. The Congregationalists were not far behind with four or five local fellowships. The Presbyterians had no more than two religious communities. The Methodists had formed at least two churches. Because it is impossible to know the number of separate stops on the county's Methodist circuits, there is no way of knowing how many household gatherings existed. The only exception to the pattern of orthodoxy was a small band of Universalists near Cortland Village that began to meet informally in 1808.[20]

Like most migrating peoples, the Yankees filtering into central New York in the 1790s attempted to model their new society after the communities they remembered. Usually they had to modify their ideals to fit the realities of a new environment. The government no longer placed one denomination in a preferred position: religious groups prospered only if they gathered public support for their doctrine and practices. Financial aid was no longer guaranteed: churches survived only if citizens could be persuaded to join religious societies that underwrote church expenses. The population base was much smaller than in New England so church survival depended on high levels of commitment from the sparse population. Clearly, there would be a diversity of denominations, and those that would prosper would be the ones that could function best in the free market of religious ideas.

19. See Herbert Barber Howe, *Jedediah Barber, 1787–1876*, New York State Historical Association Series, 8 (New York, 1939), pp. 52, 63–64, and illustrations between pp. 50 and 51 and pp. 58 and 59; First Religious Society of Homer, Minutes, November 24, 1801, December 6, 1802.

20. The early Universalist meetings are mentioned in Blodgett, *Stories of Cortland County*, pp. 222–23, Henry P. Smith, *History of Cortland County* (Syracuse, 1885), p. 272, and *History (in part): All Souls' First Universalist Church, Cortland, New York: First 100 Years*, 1937, pp. 28–29.

2

The Development of
an Island Mentality

Religion in Cortland County between 1790 and 1815 was dominated by a strong sense of separation between church members
and the rest of the frontier community. This separation was so
pervasive that churches no doubt saw themselves as "islands of
holiness" in the midst of an evil and hostile world. To church
members, the spiritual universe was divided into two camps: the
"godly" and the "world"; these groups could also be called "evangelicals" and "nonevangelicals." There is no uniformly accepted
definition of *evangelical,* but the term always implies that each
individual needs to experience the saving grace of God in Jesus
Christ through a conversion process known as the New Birth,
after which the individual begins an ongoing personal relationship with God.[1] To join a Congregational, Presbyterian, Baptist,
or Methodist church one had to profess having experienced
the New Birth. The biblical injunctions to fellowship with like-
minded believers, the cultural expectation that the "redeemed"
would join a church, and the flood of new church members after
each revival suggest that most evangelicals joined a church. If they
did not do so, their salvation was held suspect by their fellow
believers. It is clear, then, that those who were members of one of
Cortland County's four major denominations were evangelicals;
those who were not members can be viewed as nonevangelicals.
The latter group included persons with no religious affiliation

1. Donald G. Mathews, *Religion in the Old South* (Chicago, 1977), pp. xvi–xvii.

and those who supported evangelical churches financially by joining a religious society but never sought or experienced the New Birth.

Religious separatism did not originate on the New York frontier, of course. The evangelical denominations operating in Cortland County all brought a tradition of separateness with them. The Congregationalists traced their tradition back to John Winthrop's 1630 declaration that "we must consider that we shall be as a city upon a hill, the eyes of all people are upon us," which established the Massachusetts Bay Colony as a righteous example for England to emulate. The Presbyterians, who worked closely with the Congregationalists under the Plan of Union, no doubt absorbed much of their fellow Calvinists' perspective. As New England dissenters, the Baptists and Methodists had an even stronger separatist tradition, seeing themselves not only as spiritually removed from the world but also as distinct from their fellow Protestants. Baptists objected to the practice of pedobaptism (infant baptism) found among the state-supported churches of New England. The Methodists, originally a group of pietistic reformers within the Anglican church, had become a separate denomination by 1800 and, like the Baptists, objected to the advantages the Congregationalists received from New England state governments. Decades of church-state controversy led the dissenters even further toward separation for they were "set apart" not only from the world but from their coreligionists as well.[2]

On the New York frontier, the message of separateness reverberated throughout the records of local ecclesiastical units. The Madison Association, to which most of Cortland County's Baptist churches belonged, continually echoed this message when communicating with its client congregations. In 1811 the association's circular letter stated that "Christians are to distinguish themselves from the rest of the world, by their sobriety, regard to religion, and shunning even the appearance of evil." In 1814 and 1823 the association stressed the importance of conducting church affairs "in gospel order" so that "the church may appear like a CITY on a hill, that cannot be hid."[3]

2. Sydney E. Ahlstrom, *A Religious History of the American People*, 2 vols. (Garden City, N.Y., 1975), 1:192–99, 359–61, 396–402, 441–42, 552–53.
3. *Minutes of the Madison Baptist Association*, 1811, p. 9; 1814, p. 10; 1823, p. 7. For another example, see *Minutes of the Cortland Baptist Association*, 1831, p. 13.

Although the phrase "city on a hill" does not appear in existing county Congregational and Presbyterian records, the importance of the church's separation from the world is evident. Church covenants emphasized a godly walk within a hostile environment and the necessity of not identifying with the unregenerate. The Virgil Congregational Covenant, for example, required members to "renounce the service of the devil, slavery of sin and the love of the world."[4] Like the Baptists, Congregationalists and Presbyterians saw themselves as a unique people.

The drive for separation was so strong and fear of worldly contamination so great that some early congregations were suspicious of other churchgoers, even when they were from the same or a closely allied denomination. Some groups, such as the Truxton Congregational Church, would not accept letters of transfer from another church as a basis of membership. Incoming Congregational transfers had to be examined just like recent converts. The Homer Congregational Church would accept letters of transfer from sister churches in 1804 but, despite the Plan of Union, refused Presbyterian letters of transfer until 1810.[5]

The system of church organization brought from New England reinforced evangelical solidarity against the perceived surrounding wickedness. The evangelical churches organized in the early nineteenth century can be described as corporate churches. They were not merely collections of individual believers but were organic entities in which members submitted their individual wills to the higher authority of the collective body. In matters religious— which constituted most of life—the church, not the autonomous individual, defined proper behavior.

The supremacy of the corporate church was impressed upon each new member at the time of entry into the congregation. To be admitted, all Calvinist initiates had to "own the covenant," a contract by which incoming and current church members bound themselves to walk in holiness and godliness as revealed in the Scriptures. The affirmation of the covenant was a significant act. Through these vows, both newly accepted members and pillars of

4. Virgil Presbyterian Church, Church Book of Virgil, Covenant, Accession No. 6234, CUA.

5. Truxton First Presbyterian Church, Record Book, Articles of Practice, Accession No. 6241, CUA; Homer Congregational Church, Minutes, April 27, 1804, October 25, 1810.

the church renewed the pledge to remain separate from the world and to be faithful members of their chosen holy community. In addition, all entering members had to assent to the congregation's Articles of Faith and Practice and agree to submit to the collective authority of the church. Local Methodists held similar standards, for like the three Calvinist denominations, they disciplined and expelled those who violated group norms.

Once in the church, the individual yielded many rights to the will of the group. Not only did congregations maintain jurisdiction over each member's religious beliefs and behavior (the ecclesiastical domain), but they upheld their right to oversee each parishioner's conduct outside of church (the public domain). As a result, broken commandments, quarrels with relatives and neighbors, and worldliness all fell under the purview of church discipline committees. Between 1801 and 1819, Cortland County fellowships spent nearly as much time prosecuting charges of wrongdoing in the public domain as they did in dealing with ecclesiastical misdeeds such as nonattendance, heresy, and other violations of the covenant, articles of faith, or church practice (Table C.1).

The all-encompassing power of the corporate church obligated members to follow a strict code of behavior that left little room for personal discretion. Keeping the Sabbath holy in early nineteenth-century Cortland County was no mean task. The Cincinnatus and Solon Congregational Church Articles of Practice laid out the most specific instructions on Sabbatarian duties: "The lords day is profaned 1 by travelling 2 by visiting 3 by worldly conversation 4 by reading newspapers & such books as are not religous 5 by unnessary walk a broad 6 by admitting into the house such persons as are then profaning the lords day without reproving them 7 by every such attention to food and dress and the concerns of the family as might have been done before or left undone till after the sabbath."[6] Other churches may not have been as specific, but their expectations were generally the same. For example, Sister Higgins received a visit from a Homer Baptist discipline committee for having visited on the Lord's Day.[7]

6. Cincinnatus and Solon, Union Congregational Church, Record Book, Articles of Practice, Accession No. 6235 (pt. 1), CUA.

7. Cortland First Baptist Church, Record Book, February 19, 1825, June 17, 1826.

The congregation's jurisdiction spread into other areas of life. Among Baptists, the decision as to whether a young man had the "gift" of preaching belonged to the group, not to the individual involved. Preaching to any gathering without the authorization of one's congregation would result in church discipline.[8] Members of the county's evangelical churches were not to bring fellow members before the civil courts. All legal issues between members of the same congregation were to be handled internally. To do otherwise could lead to excommunication.[9] Generally, the Christian walk was one of utmost seriousness. In some fellowships, absence from public worship had to be explained to the rest of the congregation the following Sabbath.[10] The purpose of such strictness was to maintain the purity of the church. One member's sin would eventually stain the entire body, diluting the church's ability to redeem sinners. To withstand the onslaughts of the world, the church needed to be strong.

Although the "city on a hill" mentality and corporate church organization came with the migrants from New England, local conditions contributed to separatist thinking. Those who sought to build churches on the New York frontier faced numerous difficulties. As long as church members were a distinct minority among county settlers, conducting religious services required enormous effort, and even the survival of one's local fellowship seemed problematic. It was easy to develop a sense of despair. The local congregation might seem an island of holiness in the midst of geographic and spiritual isolation. For the vast majority of Cortland County churches, the struggle to maintain the most basic functions reinforced a sense of aloneness and a need for solidarity in a hostile world.

Most frontier congregations were small, with church members

8. This principle was overtly stated in the Cortland First Baptist Church, Record Book, December 15, 1832. For a discipline case involving one who violated this rule, see Solon First Baptist Church, Minutes, February 11, 1819, Accession No. 6248, CUA.

9. For examples of cases involving this principle, see Truxton First Presbyterian Church, Record Book, June 20, 1821–October 30, 1822; Truxton Baptist Church, Record Book, August 21, 1830, February 26, 1831, July 23, 1830–October 23, 1830, Accession No. 6242, CUA.

10. Cortland First Baptist Church, Record Books, April 20, 1805; Cincinnatus and Solon, Union Congregational Church, Record Book, October 26, 1822; Virgil Presbyterian Church, Church Book of Virgil, January 9, 1821.

clearly a minority in the community. Of nine congregations known to exist in 1810, only two had more than forty members, and only 9.5 percent of the county's adult population belonged to a church. The revivals of 1812–13 raised this figure to 17 percent by 1814 (Table B.1). Not only were religious fellowships small, but they struggled to exist. With the exception of the two Homer churches, which were located in the most populous and prosperous town in the county, local churches had to overcome much adversity. Finding acceptable clergy was always difficult. Congregationalists and Presbyterians insisted that their pastors be formally educated, but only the Homer church had sufficient resources to compensate professional clergy. There were more pulpits than ministers to fill them, and frontier churches often went for years with no established clergyman, drawing on lay resources and sympathetic nearby pastors. The plight of the Virgil Congregational Church in 1805 was not uncommon. Communion could be served only twice a year, and the pastor who oversaw the congregation was the full-time minister of the Homer Congregational Church, ten miles distant.[11]

Baptists, who called preachers out of the local parish, were better able to provide quantity, but the quality of such men was not guaranteed. Sometimes those called to the ministry eventually became community pillars, such as Alfred Bennett, pastor of the Homer Baptist Church from 1807 to 1832. In other cases, the congregations made unfortunate selections. The Virgil Baptist Church minutes note that the church was founded in 1813 and indicate that Elder Powers was the first minister. Powers "was a very exceptable preacher. His labors were owned and blessed of God," but he "was led away by his appetite for Alcoholic drink but finly came back and confesed his wandering." In 1814, the Scott Baptist Church had to call a council of nearby churches to discipline Aaron Town, who had served as lay preacher to the fellowship. The council found Town "Repeatedly Guilty of the excesive use of Ardent Spirits" and excluded him from the church.[12]

The Methodists had a different way of supplying preaching to a

11. Virgil Presbyterian Church, Church Book of Virgil, October 1, December 3, 1806.

12. See Hezekiah Harvey, *The Memoir of Alfred Bennett* (New York, 1852); Virgil Baptist Church, Minutes, Introduction, Accession No. 6244, CUA; Scott Baptist Church, Record Book, March 26, 1814, Accession No. 6237, CUA.

sparse population. Instead of asking parishioners to travel great distances to hear a minister in a central location, they sent circuit riders to preach to people where they lived. One preacher could serve many "congregations." Although no Methodist had to go without clergy, significant problems still existed. Circuit riders visited only every two weeks, usually on weekdays, when most people were working. They were always hurrying to the next appointment and had little time to talk about parishioners' personal needs, to discuss theological questions, or simply to socialize.[13]

Even if a minister could be found to fill a vacant pulpit, other obstacles plagued the struggling congregations. Small congregations had trouble raising money to pay the pastor's salary. Larger churches in the most economically developed part of the county, such as the Baptist and Congregational churches in Homer, had relatively few difficulties in this regard. Smaller congregations, especially those in cash-poor regions dominated by subsistence agriculture, often had trouble obtaining clergy. The Scott Baptist Church is typical. Brother Jonathan Anthony, a lay preacher, was hired in 1808. Soon his duties were increased to two-thirds time and then to full time. Late in 1810 Anthony resigned because it was not "profitable" for him to continue. A new lay preacher was selected, and visiting ministers from neighboring churches continued to provide the sacraments occasionally. In 1814 the Scott Baptist Church hired an ordained minister at one-fourth time at a salary of $30 annually.[14]

Another problem was the geographical dispersion of church members. In 1804 the Homer Baptist Church had members living as far north as the present-day town of Scott and as far south as Virgil, a distance of at least twelve miles.[15] One local historian noted that in this era "women not rarely went on foot six or seven miles to hear the gospel."[16]

Finally, it was difficult to find a suitable place of worship. Eventually small congregations concentrated in small geographic

13. L. D. Davis, *The History of the Methodist Episcopal Church in Cortland* (Syracuse, 1855), p. 31.

14. Scott Baptist Church, Record Book, 1808–14.

15. Harvey, *Memoir of Bennett*, p. 69; Cortland First Baptist Church, Record Book, 1803–05; *Centennial Anniversary, First Baptist Church, Cortland, New York*, 1901, pp. 8–10.

16. Smith, *History of Cortland County*, pp. 411–12.

areas and people did not have to travel far to worship, but few churches were large enough to finance the construction of a meetinghouse. As usual, the Homer Congregational Church and the Homer Baptist Church did not face this problem. The former completed its house of worship on the village green in 1805; the latter dedicated its church building six years later. For other congregations, the chief barrier was inadequate membership, and, as a result, only one more worship house was built until the early 1820s. Congregations needed sixty adult members (unless they were located in Homer or Cortland village, where they could get financial support from nonmembers) to guarantee adequate funding for church construction. Lacking sufficient membership, most of the early fellowships had to improvise. Individual homes, schoolhouses, and gristmills were common sites for Calvinist meetings. Methodists met in open fields and barns, as well as the above-mentioned places, and once held their preaching service in a distillery.[17] Such improvisations served temporarily, but each religious group longed for a worship place of its own. Most did not realize their dreams until the 1820s and 1830s (Table B.2).

By 1815 many significant patterns in Cortland County's religious history had been established. Congregationalists, Presbyterians, Methodists, and Baptists maintained an orthodox evangelical hegemony over the county's religious life. The dominant organizational form was the corporate church. Each religious group saw itself as a "city on a hill" that must keep itself separate from the all-encompassing, contaminating world. This separatist mentality was reinforced by frontier loneliness and the obstacles encountered in maintaining religious communities in a sparsely settled region. A small band of believers meeting in a poorly lit

17. For the distillery incident, see Davis, *History of the Methodist Church in Cortland,* pp. 59–61. It is not known when all of Cortland County's worship houses were built, but most seemed to begin construction when they had sixty or more members. See individual church records; Hamilton Child, *Gazetteer and Business Directory of Cortland County, N.Y. for 1869* (Syracuse, 1869), pp. 91, 97, 106; Goodwin, *Pioneer History,* pp. 190, 255; Blodgett, *Stories of Cortland County,* pp. 117, 222; Smith, *History of Cortland County,* pp. 225, 316–17, 327–28, 366, 385–86, 403, 426; *History: All Souls' First Universalist Church;* Hotchkin, *History,* pp. 416–28; Fowler, *Historical Sketch of Presbyterianism,* p. 422; Davis, *History of the Methodist Church in Cortland,* pp. 65–77; and David W. Van Hoesen, *History of the Presbyterian Church of Preble, N.Y.* September 26, 1915, CCHS; *Cortland Standard,* August 10, 1938, cited in Cincinnatus and Solon, Union Congregational Church, Records, 1938.

barn or schoolhouse could easily believe their fellowship was an island in a howling wilderness. Few could see, midway through the century's second decade, that the frontier era was coming to a close. Soon the county, and with it the evangelical churches, would undergo drastic change.

PART II

GROWING CHURCHES,

1812-1843

3

The Triumph of Arminianism

The decades between 1812 and 1843 were the most tumultuous thirty-year period in Cortland County's cultural history. In this short span, the county experienced rapid population growth, evolved from subsistence to commercial agriculture, and settled into the stable lifestyle characteristic of a mature rural nineteenth-century economy. At the same time, the county was swept by popular crusades ranging from temperance to abolitionism. For many, the most important change came in the realm of religious ideology as the Calvinist theory of election was shattered by the Arminian doctrine of free will. By the mid-1840s, Cortland County churches, sharing in the county's general growth, had expanded in size and number. The Methodist congregations, as bearers of the Arminian message, had grown most of all.

The transition from subsistence to commercial farming, which provides the economic backdrop to the Arminian conquest, began in 1815. Cortland County residents, like citizens elsewhere in the region, were infected by a new sense of optimism that spread throughout New York. The state government was committed to building the Erie Canal system linking Buffalo to the Mohawk River. The economic advantages from the canal appeared to be limitless. Not only would "Clinton's Ditch" create an all-water route connecting northern Ohio farmers with New York City markets, the canal would help farmers in western New York break out of the subsistence economy imposed by high transportation costs. The canal was expected not only to bring economic growth to the boom towns near its path but to create prosperity throughout the western half of the state. Optimistic economic predictions resulted in an influx of easterners into the area. During the 1820s, western New York was the fastest-growing region in the United States.[1]

Cortland County benefited from canal mania in the 1810s and 1820s. Western New York's northern tier of counties, where the canal was being constructed, was the initial focal point for the migration, but as land was purchased in northern communities, the would-be farmers began to spread farther south. Cortland County, well south of the Erie Canal, experienced rapid population growth.

In 1814, the year the British set fire to Washington, D.C., Cortland County was still in the frontier stage of development. Of the county's six towns, only Homer had a population density over thirty persons per square mile. The southern and eastern towns averaged only fifteen persons per square mile. The county's population of 10,900 inhabitants was impressive when compared to earlier censuses but paled in comparison to the canal counties of Madison, Onondaga, and Cayuga to the north.[2]

After the Treaty of Ghent had been signed, waves of in-migrants entered the county. Between 1814 and 1820, the population grew 7.2 percent annually, bringing the total to 16,500 residents. During the 1820s, the growth rate was more subdued (3.7 percent yearly) and by 1830 Cortland had 23,800 inhabitants. This population influx quickly ended the county's pioneer days. By 1820 the county's population density had risen to 35.3 persons per square mile, and six of Cortland's ten towns had densities in excess of thirty. Five years later, only Willet remained sparsely settled.[3]

By the 1830s Cortland County was no longer growing rapidly but was experiencing the slow, steady growth of a mature economy. From 1830 to the Civil War the annual growth rate was a minuscule 0.3 percent.[4] Reduced economic opportunity was a

1. Cross, *Burned-over District*, p. 56.
2. *Census of the State of New York for 1855*, p. xxxiii. The square miles of each town are given in Thomas F. Gordon, *Gazetteer of the State of New York* (Philadelphia, 1836), p. 416.
3. *Census of the State of New York for 1855*, p. xxxiii; Gordon, *Gazetteer*, p. 416.
4. *Census of the State of New York for 1855*, p. xxxiii; U.S. Census Office, *Eighth Census*, 1860.

major reason for the declining rate of population increase. The amount of land available for new residents had shrunk dramatically. In 1820 slightly less than one-fourth of Cortland's improvable acreage had been cleared. By 1835 unimproved land was half gone, and ten years later two-thirds of the improvable land had been developed.[5] Not only did fewer migrants enter the county, but young native residents tended to leave. No longer could youth reasonably expect their fathers to grant unimproved parcels near the family homestead. Children born after 1800 soon learned that if they did not possess land by the early 1830s, their chances of ever owning their own farm were slim unless they moved west. As a result, the cohort group born between 1801 and 1810 declined 29 percent between the 1830 and 1840 federal censuses. The corresponding drop for the 1811–20 cohort group was 33 percent.[6] The period between 1830 and 1835 was the first in county history when out-migration exceeded in-migration.[7]

While canal euphoria gripped many parts of the state during the 1830s and communities fought over the next Erie feeder line, Cortland County residents had a much more sober assessment of the "great ditch." A feeder line was unlikely in the hilly Cortland terrain, and without direct access to the canal system the canal would remain, at best, a mixed blessing.

Cortlanders did benefit from the canal system in some very tangible ways. Finished goods were easily imported from distant mills and factories. Farm families could buy many items they used to produce at home, thereby freeing them to concentrate on agricultural production. A dramatic example of this shift in pri-

5. Improvable land is defined as the largest amount of land ever denoted as "improved land" on a federal or state census. For Cortland County, the largest number of improved acres was recorded in U.S. Census Office, *Twelfth Census of the United States, Taken in the Year 1900*, vol. 5 (Washington, D.C., 1902), p. 290. Antebellum figures on the county's improved land appear in U.S. Census Office, *Fourth Census, Book One, Census for 1820* (Washington, D.C., 1821); *Census of the State of New York for 1835* (Albany, 1836); *Census of the State of New York for 1845* (Albany, 1846).

6. The decline in the size of cohort groups is based on age data found in the U.S. Census Office, *Fifth Census, Enumeration of the Inhabitants of the United States, 1830* (Washington, D.C., 1832), and U.S. Census Office, *Sixth Census, Book One, Enumeration of the Inhabitants of the United States, 1840* (Washington, D.C., 1841).

7. This conclusion is drawn from the comparison of county population data and the analysis in Richard A. Easterlin, "Population Change and Farm Settlement in the Northern United States," *Journal of Economic History* 36 (March 1976): 46–75.

orities can be seen in the production of homemade cloth. In 1810 Cortland County was trapped in a subsistence economy, and the majority of settlers wore homespun. Following completion of the canal, the cost of importing finished cloth dropped significantly, and the per capita production of homemade cloth fell from 12 yards in 1810 to 4.7 yards in 1845.[8] Similar patterns occurred with other products. By the 1830s local newspaper advertisements told consumers that general stores were filled with manufactured articles, almost all of which were produced outside the county.

Although the canal lowered the prices of many goods, it had a negative impact on local agriculture. Wheat was a major agricultural product before the completion of the canal even though much of the county's soil and terrain was not ideally suited to grain production. Once barges of Ohio and Indiana wheat and flour began to travel from Buffalo to Albany, Cortland farmers realized that they were at a severe disadvantage. Not only did western farmers have more fertile land, but the all-water voyage from the Great Lakes to the Hudson River cost less than the thirty-mile trip from Cortland County to the Erie Canal. Thus the Cortland wheat farmer had already lost the price war before he and his wagon full of grain rolled into the streets of either Syracuse or Ithaca, the two nearest towns in the canal system.

After 1825 the western farmers' comparative advantage in small grain production forced increasing numbers of Cortlanders into raising livestock. By 1845 three-fourths of the county's agricultural acreage was employed as pastures, meadows, and grazing land.[9] Fortunately for the county farmers, the Erie Canal was too slow and western producers too distant to get butchered cattle to market. The only way to get beef to urban areas was to drive the cattle there. Here Cortlanders had a tremendous advantage over their western counterparts because they were so much closer to the eastern seaboard cities.

Despite the shift from grain to livestock, Cortland farmers (81 percent of the population in 1840) slipped financially behind farmers to the north. In Cayuga and Onondaga counties, both straddling the great canal, per capita personal wealth rose 36 and

8. Horatio Gates Spafford, *Gazetteer of the State of New York* (Albany, 1813), p. 50; *Census of the State of New York for 1845.*

9. *Census of the State of New York for 1845.*

144 percent respectively between 1820 and 1835. This increase was caused by rising land values and new industries made feasible by lower transport costs. By contrast, per capita wealth in Cortland County fell from $108 to $96 over the same period.[10]

In comparison to the northern tier of counties in western New York, urbanization in Cortland County proceeded at a lackluster pace. Along the Erie Canal, the boom towns of Buffalo, Rochester, Syracuse, Rome, Utica, Seneca Falls, and Auburn sprouted up. When the feeder systems were developed, Ithaca, Elmira, and Oswego grew rapidly. In some places, Syracuse, for instance, unique natural resources such as salt gave momentum to a shift from an agricultural service center to a manufacturing city. Even more important, locales such as Buffalo, Rochester, and Utica were at key transportation break points that made them logical sites for a host of enterprises. With neither direct access to the canal nor unusual resources Cortland villages would not be chosen by outside manufacturers as sites of factories. Instead, the county's villages continued to function as service centers for the agricultural economy. The few manufacturers and craftsmen operating in the county never produced much more than could be consumed locally. By 1835 only 13 percent of the county's population lived in villages or hamlets. The largest urban communities were Homer village with one thousand residents and Cortland village with nine hundred.[11]

Cortland County's most progressive citizens were not content to let the area remain an agricultural backwater in a rapidly industrializing region. If farmers in other communities had advantages because of better transportation, Cortland County farmers could

10. For a discussion of the impact of new modes of transportation on land prices, see Roberta Balstad Miller, *City and Hinterland: A Case Study of Urban Growth and Regional Development* (Westport, Conn., 1979), pp. 96–97. Miller notes that transportation improvements did not bring universal prosperity but instead caused the value of land to rise rapidly near transport and to increase gradually in more distant towns. The process described is roughly analogous to what happened to per capita wealth in Cayuga, Onondaga, and Cortland counties. The impact of western competition on New York agriculture is described in ibid., p. 61. Per capita wealth was calculated from data in Spafford, *Gazetteer* (1824), pp. 93, 134, 375, and Gordon, *Gazetteer,* pp. 378–79, 416–17, 586–87.

11. Village and hamlet data are based on the number of dwellings listed for each locale in Spafford, *Gazetteer* (1813), pp. 208, 277, 300, 314–15, 319, and Gordon, *Gazetteer,* pp. 414–16. Population figures are based on the number of dwellings times five. County population figures come from *Census of the State of New York for 1855,* p. xxxiii.

compensate by making their operations more efficient. In June 1833 the *Cortland Advocate* urged the formation of an agricultural society to promote the latest scientific farming methods. Five years later the Cortland County Agricultural Society was organized.[12]

The county's most serious problem, however, was not farming methods; it was the lack of efficient transportation to the outside world. By the mid-1830s, local newspapers were agitating for a railroad connecting the county to Syracuse to the north and Binghamton to the south. Such a "thoroughfare," the editor of the *Cortland Republican and Eagle* contended, would "enable [the county] to enter . . . in competition with those along the line of the Erie Canal."[13] But despite local boosterism, Cortland County would not obtain rail access to outside markets until the mid-1850s, and large manufacturing enterprises did not enter the county until the decade before the Civil War. Even then, the county's strongly agricultural economy was not significantly diluted. As of 1860, the county ranked fifty-fifth out of sixty New York counties in manufactured value per capita.[14]

By the 1830s, canal era exuberance had been replaced by a more cautious estimate of the county's future. The lack of adequate transportation meant the county's farmers had to struggle to compete. Industry was out of the question until a railroad could link the county to outside markets. Cortland County had become a mature agricultural region, the sort of place Whitney Cross argued was likely to support Burned-over District enthusiasm.[15]

The growth in the size and number of Cortland County churches paralleled the expansion of the county's economy. In 1815 approximately fifteen congregations were sprinkled throughout the county's hills and woodlands. Most struggled financially, and only three had a religious society to help defray expenses. By 1845 the number of local fellowships had grown to

12. *Cortland Advocate*, June 20, 1833; *Cortland Republican and Eagle*, September 25, October 9, 1838.

13. *Cortland Republican*, November 24, December 22, 1835, January 5, 1836; *Cortland Republican and Eagle*, July 5, August 23, December 20, 1836, March 26, June 11, 1839.

14. U.S. Census Office, *Eighth Census, 1860*.

15. Cross, *Burned-over District*, pp. 75–76.

forty-eight (all but four of them evangelical).[16] The vast majority had worship houses and were supported by religious societies. Congregations were not only more numerous but much larger than before. In 1814 the median size was 35 adult members; by 1843 the median had risen to 115 adult members. But the county's church population was growing in relative as well as absolute terms. In 1810 only one Cortland adult in ten belonged to a church. By 1845 more than one-fourth of the county's adults had joined a local congregation (Table B.1).

One reason for this increase was that the county's population doubled. Many newcomers had experienced "saving grace" and had joined an evangelical church in their former community. Most of them brought letters of recommendation and dismissal from their previous fellowships. With rare exceptions, Cortland congregations treated these letters as evidence of ongoing faith and membership in good standing, accepted the new residents as full communicants, and notified their former congregations of completed transfers.

Between 1815 and 1843 more than twenty-three hundred individuals joined local Baptist, Presbyterian, and Congregational churches by letter of recommendation. Larger congregations, such as the Congregational and Baptist churches of Homer and the Presbyterian church in Cortland, could expect more than eleven in-transfers every year. Over 60 percent of county churches added at least three members by letter per year.

The primary reason for church growth, however, was religious conversion. For every transfer into a Baptist, Congregational, or Presbyterian church between 1815 and 1844, two new members entered by examination, profession of faith, and/or baptism. Religious revivals were essential to this conversion process. Although there is no universally accepted definition, nineteenth-century religious commentators in western New York agreed that revivals were events at which numerous people professed to a "conversion experience," in which they were "saved," and subsequently applied for church membership.[17] Revivals were not

16. *Census of the State of New York for 1845.*
17. Ministers of the period usually defined revivals in quantitative terms. In 1855 Cortland Methodist minister and local historian L. D. Davis used a numerical basis for his definition of a "revival of religion": "Let us inquire what constitutes a

universally appreciated, however. Many evangelicals would have preferred a slow, steady rate of growth with a relatively constant number of converts each year so that initiates could be educated and absorbed with a minimum of disturbance. But evangelicals knew from experience that few converts trickled into a church over an extended period of time; they generally came in droves or not at all.[18] Cortland County churches followed this boom-and-bust cycle. Large numbers of converts flowed into their congregations in 1812–13, 1816–17, 1820, 1826, 1831–34, 1838, and 1843. With a few exceptions, churches had little religious excitement in other years.

The waves of religious enthusiasm that washed over Cortland County occurred at roughly the same time as revivals in other parts of western New York. Regionally 1816 was "the year without a summer." Many New Yorkers interpreted this meteorological anomaly as a "sign of the end of times," a warning to seek redemption before the apocalypse arrived.[19] In 1826 Charles Grandison Finney led a series of protracted meetings in the villages of central New York. Five years later he gained national prominence with his promotion of the Rochester revivals.[20] The 1843 revivals in Cortland County were part of a much larger awakening, prompted mainly by the Millerites, that covered much of western New York.[21] Cortland County's peak revival years parallel those in Oneida County.[22] Apparently, these events were linked to much larger processes occurring throughout the Empire State.

---

revival of religion? Dr. Barnes describes it thus: 'Let many sinners turn simultaneously to God. Let conversions to Christ, instead of being few and far between, become numerous, rapidly occurring, and decided in their character, and you have all that is usually meant when we speak of a revival. It is the conversion of a number of individuals from sin to holiness, and from Satan unto God.' Revivals of religion, then, are times of spiritual awakening, in which the church is quickened, wanderers reclaimed, and sinners saved" (*History of the Methodist Church in Cortland*, pp. 122–23). The Reverend James Hotchkin, chronicler of the Presbyterians in western New York used a similar quantitative definition in 1848 (*History*, p. 121).

18. Fowler, *Historical Sketch*, p. 281; *Minutes of the Cortland Baptist Association*, 1840, p. 12.

19. Michael Barkun, *Crucible of the Millennium: The Burned-over District of New York in the 1840s* (Syracuse, 1986), pp. 107–12.

20. William McLoughlin, *Modern Revivalism: Charles Grandison Finney to Billy Graham* (New York, 1959), pp. 27–30, 53–58.

21. David L. Rowe, *Thunder and Trumpets: Millerites and Dissenting Religion in Upstate New York, 1800–1850* (Chico, Calif., 1985), pp. 39–49.

22. Mary P. Ryan, *Cradle of the Middle Class: The Family in Oneida County, New York, 1790–1865* (Cambridge, 1983), p. 79.

Historians are of a divided mind on the social origins of revivalism. The largest school of thought sees economic, social, and cultural change as central to the revival process. Within this interpretive framework, there is considerable variety. Some, William McLoughlin being the foremost example, contend that in the early nineteenth century American society was moving from a traditional community-oriented worldview to one that valued independence and self-reliance. Accordingly, Protestantism with its Calvinist base had to be revitalized through Arminian theology to fit the new cultural milieu.[23] Other historians, including Paul Johnson, Anthony F. C. Wallace, and Paul Faler, argue that revivalism grew out of class tensions created by the new industrial order.[24] Feminist historians such as Mary Ryan and Nancy F. Cott note that women both promoted and responded to the evangelical message in disproportionate numbers and suggest that the revivals grew out of changing gender roles and styles of household organization.[25] A smaller but important interpretive school posits that the primary impetus for revivals came from the churches themselves, not the surrounding culture. John Hammond and Terry Bilhartz are among those who contend that revivals occurred because evangelical churches considered mass conversion important and promoted religious enthusiasm to achieve it.[26]

All explanations of revivalistic behavior can be subsumed into a larger framework. In any cultural context, mass conversions will occur if two prerequisites are met. First, the religiously oriented must believe that conversion is vital.[27] Second, the devout must believe they have some role in producing religious conversion in themselves and in others. Obviously, there will be few conversions in a thoroughly secularized society that does not take religious

23. McLoughlin, *Revivals, Awakenings, and Reform*, pp. 1–23, 98–140.
24. Paul E. Johnson, *A Shopkeeper's Millennium: Society and Revivals in Rochester, New York, 1815–1837* (New York, 1979), pp. 136–41; Wallace, *Rockdale*, pp. 296–98; Paul Faler, "Cultural Aspects of the Industrial Revolution: Lynn, Massachusetts, Shoemakers and Industrial Morality, 1826–1860," *Labor History* 15 (Summer 1974): 367–94.
25. Ryan, *Cradle of the Middle Class*, pp. 60–104; Nancy F. Cott, "Young Women in the Second Great Awakening in New England," *Feminist Studies* 3 (1975): 15–29.
26. John L. Hammond, "The Reality of Revivals," *SA Sociological Analysis* 44 (Summer 1983): 113; Terry Bilhartz, *Urban Religion and the Second Great Awakening: Church and Society in Early National Baltimore* (Rutherford, N.J., 1986), pp. 91–99.
27. To some degree, this idea is always present among evangelicals because they believe such an experience is necessary for eternal life.

ideas seriously. The existence of the first precondition alone will
not foster revivals. A traditional Calvinist, for instance, would
believe that salvation is solely dependent on the will of God and
that one must wait for conversion, not try to promote it. In such a
context, conversions tend to be sporadic and occur relatively late
in the life cycle. The second concept, that humans have a role in
producing conversions, is as necessary as the first. Among certain
groups, in specific times and places, both concepts become central
to the organization of human behavior and mass conversions will
occur.

In his interpretive essay *Revivals, Awakenings, and Reform*, William McLoughlin contends that by the early nineteenth century
Calvinist ideology was incongruent with the experience of most
Americans. The doctrine of election, held dear by Presbyterians,
Congregationalists, and Baptists, did not fit the image most citizens had of themselves. As revolutionaries, Americans had won
independence from Britain. Many had decided to move west and
carve communities out of the wilderness. In a free market economy, farmers and merchants daily made calculations that affected
their economic well-being. By the late 1820s universal white male
suffrage was a reality. Men could choose their leaders and,
through representative government, establish public policy. Why,
then, could they have no control over their own salvation? It was
not until Lyman Beecher and especially Charles Finney led the
movement to "Arminianize" or "Methodize" Calvinism that the
conflict between personal freedom and Calvinist doctrine was
resolved. The invitation to "vote for Jesus or vote for the Devil"
was readily received, and thousands joined the "Lord's Cause."
Thought and experience were once again brought together, and
religion was revitalized.[28] In short, the shift toward Arminian
theology can be seen as a "spiritual republicanism," applying
democratic values to religious issues.

Much in the above scenario fits the early religious history of
western New York. Even before Lyman Beecher reformulated
traditional Congregationalist thought in the early 1820s, orthodox Calvinism was fracturing on the New York frontier. Change
came first in the form of altered behavior. Despite the traditional

28. McLoughlin, *Revivals, Awakenings, and Reform*, pp. 98–140.

Calvinist view that humans could not promote their own salvation, women in Oneida County were seeking to promote the redemption of their kinsfolk. As early as 1813, some local Presbyterians rejected the Calvinist position of the total depravity of infants in favor of the view that children were moral agents whose character could be shaped by proper parenting. The county's first Female Missionary Society was formed a year later, and it began to raise funds for the salvation of local as well as distant sinners.[29] The attempt to induce conversion, either through proper parenting or missionary activity, was a step toward evangelical Arminianism—the concept that salvation was determined not by God but by each individual, who ultimately chose his or her own redemption or damnation. After all, it made no sense to persuade people to "yield to Christ" if the human will had no effect on the eternal outcome.

At approximately the same time, creeping Arminianism began to alter the behavior of Calvinists in Cortland County. The county's first major revival occurred in the winter of 1812–13. Not content simply to wait for the Almighty to act in the Homer community, a woman in the Jacob Hoar household organized regularly scheduled prayer meetings. When the number of supplicants outgrew the Hoar home, the sessions moved to a neighboring schoolhouse. Soon a revival burst into flame. By summer 1813, the Homer Congregationalists had added 160 converts and the local Baptists had added 80. The demographic composition of this initial revival resembled eighteenth-century New England awakenings in that 55 percent of the converts joining the Homer Congregational Church were married adults.[30]

The revivals of 1816–17 and 1820 demonstrate that Cortland Calvinists were not content to leave the redemption of their children solely up to the Almighty. Unlike the 1813 revival, the next two waves of enthusiasm centered on the offspring of the elect. Local records reveal that four out of every five converts entering the Homer Congregational Church in the 1816–17 and 1820 awakenings were single. The records of the Homer Baptist

29. Ryan, *Cradle of the Middle Class*, pp. 60–61, 69–70.

30. Fowler, *Historical Sketch of Presbyterianism*, p. 423; Davis, *History of the Methodist Episcopal Church*, pp. 43–45; Harvey, *Memoir of Bennett*, pp. 79–81; Cortland First Baptist Church, Record Book, 1812–13; Homer Congregational Church, Minutes, 1812–13.

Church are not complete enough to allow similar analysis, but the memoirs of the Reverend Alfred Bennett, the Homer Baptist minister at the time of the 1820 outbreak, portray an incredible amount of lay activity. Bennett noted that, in 1820, "There was very little secular labor performed for two or three months, and many devoted the whole of that time to meetings and visiting from house to house. Some went two by two . . . through different parts of the town, calling upon every family on their way."[31] The central message of the Homer Congregationalists and Baptists may have been Calvinist, but both groups spread that message in a very Arminian fashion.

Changed behavior did not automatically lead to revised theology. In spite of their activist evangelical techniques, local Calvinists continued to view revivals as sovereign acts of God, as is shown in accounts of the 1820 revival. Throughout 1819 the Homer Congregational Church was torn by factional strife after two prominent members openly declared their pastor "not qualified for a gospel minister and . . . not fit to preach." Representatives of eight churches were called in to settle the controversy. Instead of passing judgment, they sought to reconcile the offending parties. The January 4, 1820, congregational minutes describe an unexpected revival with repentance and forgiveness replacing acrimony. The "Spirit was placed down and sinners began to enquire what they should do to be saved. . . . Great and marvelous are thy works, Lord God Almighty."[32] County Baptists also attributed the 1820 awakening to supernatural origins. Hezekiah Harvey, a local Baptist minister, contended that in 1820 "the multitudes thronged the sanctuary, not drawn by the eccentricities of the preacher, but by solemn influences on high."[33] In short, Cortland County Calvinists, like those in Oneida County, began to behave like Arminians even as they professed allegiance to traditional Calvinist doctrine.

The gradual Arminianization of Calvinism in Cortland County

31. Homer Congregational Church, Minutes, 1816–17, 1820; Harvey, *Memoir of Bennett*, pp. 92–100.

32. Homer Congregational Church, Minutes, November 4, 18, December 2, 1819, January 4, 1820, and church membership roster. The revival in this church is also described in Fowler, *Historical Sketch of Presbyterianism*, pp. 423–24, and in Hotchkin, *History*, pp. 421–22.

33. Harvey, *Memoir of Bennett*, pp. 92–100.

is ironic because Congregationalists and Baptists were determined to contain Methodist influence. This non-Calvinist denomination had British origins, an "undemocratic" episcopal form of
government, and a relatively uneducated clergy, none of which
was as troublesome as its doctrine concerning human salvation.[34]
Unlike most evangelicals in Cortland County's early years, Methodists did not subscribe to the Calvinist doctrine of election.
Instead, they upheld the Arminian idea that humans could play a
role in their own salvation by choosing either God or the Devil.

Calvinist opposition to Methodism was virulent. Circuit riders
were described as "uneducated," "unauthorized" to minister in
sacred things, "Popish Jesuits," and "British spies." In 1817, for
example, the Madison Baptist Association decried "the great exertions which are made to spread the corrupt doctrines of Arminianism."[35] Not surprisingly, some local Baptist ministers saw
nothing wrong in proselytizing recent Methodist converts. Noting
that a circuit rider had not yet arrived to lead a Methodist service,
one Baptist preacher took over the meeting. Although he willingly went back to his seat when the Methodist preacher arrived,
the incident was long remembered as an example of Baptist
opportunism.[36] Congregationalists were not willing to accept
Methodists as full partners, as is indicated in the minutes of the
Freetown Congregational Church for July 4, 1816: "Voted that
no Minister be admitted by the Church to preach to them except
of the order of Presbyterian, Congregational, or Baptist."[37]
Clearly, Congregationalists thought Methodism theologically suspect. Attempts to contain Methodist doctrines regarding free will
appear to have been futile, however. Cortland County Calvinists
believed they were simply fighting the Arminian heresy when, in
reality, they were struggling against a general cultural move toward greater individual autonomy.

During the 1820s, political and religious controversies in Cortland County revolved primarily around the issue of free will: did
humans operate within a hierarchy in which certain vital ques-

34. Davis, *History of the Methodist Episcopal Church*, p. 47.

35. Ibid., pp. 45–46; *Minutes of the Madison Baptist Association*, 1817, pp. 15–16.

36. George Peck, *Life and Times of George Peck, D.D.* (New York, 1874), p. 88;
Davis, *History of the Methodist Episcopal Church*, pp. 92–93.

37. Cincinnatus First Congregational Church, Records, July 4, 1816, Accession
No. 6238, CUA.

tions were determined by those higher up, or were they free to determine all important matters for themselves? In the political sphere, the debate was between limited versus expanded suffrage. In the religious realm, it was between Calvinist and Methodist explanations of human salvation.

Cortlanders addressed the political question first. In 1821 the New York legislature drafted a new state constitution that extended suffrage to large numbers of previously disfranchised white males. In a statewide election, a majority of Cortland County's voters approved the new document, although support for the change was not uniform. The most commercial town, Homer, opposed the new constitution whereas the less developed remainder of the county overwhelmingly supported it.[38]

The voting reflected divergent worldviews. Homer's population was heavily Calvinist with 58 percent of the adult male population belonging to a Congregational or Baptist church or society.[39] The Calvinists operated in a hierarchical universe in which a higher authority (God) made important decisions (salvation) for lesser beings (humans). The idea that humans uppermost in human hierarchy (men with property) should make decisions for those of lower rank (men without property) fit nicely with the traditional view of election. As a result, Homer's Calvinists were reluctant to abandon the existing paternalistic political system. The outer towns, however, had been the focus of considerable circuit rider missionary activity and therefore had sizable numbers of Methodists. Arminian theology fit well with expanded suffrage for both subscribed to the notion that humans were responsible for their own destiny. Not surprisingly, the new state constitution received heavy support in areas where Methodism was strong. Politically, Methodists were in tune with the expansion of individual freedom, whereas Calvinists were out of touch with the political direction in which the county and the country were moving.

38. *Cortland Advocate,* August 21, 1834.
39. The male population (ten years old and over) of Homer can be calculated from the tables in U.S. Census Office, *Fourth Census, Book One, Census for 1820.* To yield 58 percent, the male membership of the First Religious Society of Homer, the Homer Baptist Society, the Homer Congregational Church, and the Homer Baptist Church was totaled (accounting for double listings and expected losses from attrition) and that figure was then divided by the adult male population of Homer.

Theological discussions also focused on the question of human freedom. Early in the century, a local Baptist contemporary observed that "religious discussions . . . turned mainly upon the points at issue between the Calvinistic and Arminian theology."[40] The conflict between the two evangelical camps intensified by the mid-1820s, and both tried to win over the unchurched. At Port Watson, a small hamlet a few miles east of Homer, a Calvinist lecturer launched into a tirade against Arminianism. The Methodists responded by bringing their own polemicist, Israel Reynolds, who argued against predestinarian theory in favor of "the principles of free and sufficient grace." Inasmuch as the larger culture was predisposed to the values of personal independence and self-determination, the results of this debate are not surprising. There was no revival among local Calvinists, but the Methodists had "the greatest revival that had yet been enjoyed by this people."[41]

By 1830 Cortland County's Congregationalists, Baptists, and Presbyterians found themselves in a difficult position. As orthodox Calvinists, they were committed to the sovereignty of God, the total depravity of mankind, and the doctrine of election, but these ideas had little appeal to the religiously unaffiliated in an era when the common man prided himself on his political, social, and economic independence. If human beings were responsible for a multitude of decisions, why could they not choose to be saved? For most, the conflict between daily experience and Calvinist doctrine was too great. They would become Methodists or join no church at all. The incongruence of ideas and experience even affected Calvinist church members. Since 1812 the local devout had promoted conversions in an Arminian manner, even as they verbally assented to the notion that God alone can save. By the mid-1820s, some Calvinist communicants, such as John Dyer of the Homer Baptist Church, were absenting themselves from worship because they could not reconcile themselves to the doctrine of election.[42]

A few Calvinist leaders looked outside the county for ideas on how to resolve these conflicts and infuse new life into their congregations. The Reverend John Keep, pastor of the Homer Congregational Church, was well aware of Charles Finney's emer-

40. Harvey, *Memoir of Bennett*, p. 72.
41. Davis, *History of the Methodist Episcopal Church*, pp. 88–92.
42. Cortland First Baptist Church, Record Book, February 17, 1827.

gence as a Presbyterian home missionary. Finney was successful partly because of his adoption of the Methodist doctrine of free will. By eliminating predestinarian theory, Finney resolved the conflict between Calvinist faith and republican political self-reliance. He also relied heavily on Arminian evangelistic techniques. Arguing that humans could not only choose their own salvation but that they could induce the experience of saving grace in others, Finney introduced a set of evangelistic techniques (which he called the "New Measures") long used by the Methodists but emotionally devastating to uninitiated Calvinist audiences.[43]

John Keep was so impressed with the number of Finney's converts that he introduced the New Measures into the Homer Congregational Church in 1831. Like Finney, he adopted an Arminian view of salvation, even as he claimed that the "doctrines inculcated in this revival . . . are the doctrines of grace, as they are received by the great mass of the Congregational and Presbyterian Churches in our land." In February 1831, Keep conducted his first "protracted meeting." The four-day series of religious services drew in a significant number of converts, and five more protracted meetings were held by mid-1833. During each, special sessions were held to encourage the conversion of children. At the close of the adult services, those seeking salvation were invited to come forward to sit on the "anxious seat" while others prayed for their souls. Private spiritual counsel was offered in special inquiry rooms. The propounding period, the traditional three-to-four-week waiting period between application and acceptance into membership, was dropped in favor of bringing new converts into the protective womb of the church as quickly as possible.[44] In the sixth and last revival, a professional evangelist, the Reverend Jedediah Burchard, was employed to save as many remaining recalcitrant souls as possible. The antiformal Methodists may have invented many of the methods, but once in the hands of the Congregationalists, salvation-inducing techniques were systematized as never before.

The 1831–33 revivals in the Homer Congregational Church signaled the collapse of local Calvinist resistance to Arminian

43. McLoughlin, *Modern Revivalism*, pp. 84–100.
44. John Keep, *A Narrative of the Origin and Progress of the Congregational Church in Homer, N.Y., with Remarks* (Homer, N.Y., 1833), pp. 1–17, quote on 13.

doctrine. When the largest and most prestigious Calvinist church in the county experimented with the New Measures and brought in 207 converts in less than three years, other Calvinist churches quickly followed the Homer example. In the spring of 1831 the Union Congregational Church of Cincinnatus and Solon adopted some of the New Measures. A year later the Freetown and Scott Baptist churches held successful protracted meetings. In 1833 the Cortlandville and Truxton Baptist churches employed Finney's techniques. Before the decade ended, the Freetown Congregational, McGrawville Baptist, and Preble Presbyterian fellowships joined the list of New Measures congregations.[45] By the 1840s, both Baptist and Methodist sources suggest that the New Measures had conquered and that the differences between Calvinist and Arminian were minimal. L. D. Davis, a local nineteenth-century historian, wrote that the "peculiar doctrines of free grace which lie at the foundation of Armenian theology, had by [the 1840s] secured a favorable hearing, and were commended by nearly all classes of community as in entire accordance with the principles of revealed truth."[46]

The New Measures and Arminianized doctrine brought large numbers of converts into Cortland County churches. Desiring to measure changes in the rate of conversion, I created an evangelism index, which shows a church or denomination's annual number of conversions per hundred members in a given time period.[47] By observing changes in the evangelism index, one can see

45. Cincinnatus and Solon, Union Congregational Church, Record Book, June 4, 1831, May 27, 1836, *Minutes of the Cortland Baptist Association,* 1832, pp. 5–6; 1833, p. 10; 1839, p. 5. Freetown Presbyterian Society, Book, November 1835, Accession No. 6238, CUA. The New Measures men gained control of the Preble Presbyterian Church in the late 1830s; see Chapter 10.

46. Davis, *History of the Methodist Episcopal Church,* p. 127.

47. The evangelism index was calculated in the following manner. For each year between 1815 and 1860 the number of converts was divided by the number of members the previous year and the product was multiplied by 100 to yield the number of converts per 100 members. This procedure was conducted for both congregations and denominations. Five-year indexes were created by dividing converts by members for five years and multiplying by 100. Years when revivals occurred produced unusually high indexes. In 1820, for example, the Homer Baptist Church accepted 122 recent converts as members. With the 276 members in 1819 as the prerevival base, the evangelism index for 1820 was 44.2 converts per 100 members. The same year, the Baptist and Congregational churches in Truxton had an index of 91.0 and 131.3 respectively. The highest index in the county was 341.7 in 1826 at the Cortland Presbyterian Church, which is a remarkable

the impact of free will ideology on conversion patterns. During the 1820s, Baptists typically had evangelism indexes around 7; Congregationalists and Presbyterians registered rates around 5. With the advent of the New Measures, however, Calvinist conversion rates skyrocketed. In each year between 1830 and 1834, local Baptists added ten converts for every one hundred members already in the fold. Congregationalists and Presbyterians did even better, absorbing thirteen converts per hundred current members annually (Table B.3). The influx of new members led to extraordinary growth among the county's Calvinist denominations. Between 1829 and 1835, Congregational membership grew 50 percent, Presbyterian numbers increased by 54 percent, and Baptist parishioners expanded their numbers by 41 percent.

The power of Arminian theology was most evident in Methodist membership. In 1829 the Methodists were the third largest evangelical group with about 400 members. Six years later, they assumed second place with 1,250 communicants, an increase of 213 percent. This phenomenal growth was not the result of the alleged efficiency of circuit riding in sparsely settled areas; it did not occur until after circuit riding had been abandoned in favor of permanently settled ministers. The reason for Methodist success was that Methodist doctrine fit American self-perceptions better than Calvinist theology. After 1830 Calvinists did their best to incorporate the free will doctrine on a predestinarian superstructure, but the addition never fit well. People tended to gravitate toward the genuine article, Methodism, which was Arminian throughout. After a brief decline in membership in the late 1830s, the Methodists resumed a rapid growth rate while the other evangelical groups languished. By 1860 the Methodists were the largest denomination in Cortland County.[48]

---

figure when one realizes that in one year seven persons were converted for every two who were in the church the year before. The evangelism index is also sensitive to periods when little revivalism was taking place. It sinks to levels near zero during "dry" times, and low index readings are highly correlated with ministerial laments over "spiritual wantonness" and "lack of light."

The use of an evangelism index is not new. H. C. Weber used a similar device by the same name. For an explanation of his technique, see *Evangelism*, pp. 38–42.

48. Denominational membership figures are based on the *Minutes of the Cortland, Madison, Chenango, Cayuga, Seneca,* and *Berkshire Baptist Associations,* ABHS; *The Minutes of the General Assembly of the Presbyterian Church in the U.S.A.,* both Old

William McLoughlin has argued that during the Second Great Awakening, American culture was transformed as the nation chose evangelical Arminianism over Calvinist theories of election and readily embraced "freedom of the will." Charles Finney and the Methodists were "New Lights" preaching human freedom in opposition to the traditional Calvinism refined the previous century.[49] The Cortland County experience fits well with this framework. Personal autonomy was heralded in the county's political and economic structures, and the Arminians (Finneyites and Methodists) won an astonishing victory over their Calvinist opponents. Yet is is possible that McLoughlin overemphasized the importance of evangelical Arminianism in the early nineteenth-century cultural transformation. In 1835, after Calvinism had been Arminianized and enormous revivals had taken place, only 27 percent of Cortland County's adult population had experienced saving grace and joined one of the four major evangelical denominations (Table B.1). It is hard to see evangelicalism at the heart of cultural transformation when only a quarter of the population was involved. It makes more sense to argue that in Cortland County the Calvinist churches were responding to broader cultural forces (individualism and self-determination) that were already present. Once they Arminianized, Calvinists reaped the numerical benefits of preaching in language their nineteenth-century audience understood. Most Cortlanders, however, celebrated their freedom by joining no church. Nearly half gave no financial support to any organized religion. Within Cortland County, the cultural transformation certainly focused on freedom of the will, but the popularity of Arminian ideas among Methodists and Calvinists was more a secondary consequence than a primary cause of new attitudes among the general population.

Earlier, I stated that there were two prerequisites for revivalism. The first was that people believe individual salvation to be vitally important. In Cortland County's early years, there was always a

---

School and New School, PHS; *The Minutes of the Annual Conference of the Methodist Episcopal Church,* vols. 1–3, SU; the records of individual churches; *Census of the State of New York for 1855;* and various county histories and documents.

49. McLoughlin, *Revivals, Awakenings, and Reform,* pp. 113, 122–38.

sizable minority who fulfilled that condition. The second prerequisite was that the devout believe they can have an impact on their own salvation and the salvation of others. Before 1815 only a handful of Methodists took that position. As the three Calvinist denominations absorbed Methodist ideas and practice (slowly between 1815 and 1830 and rapidly between 1830 and 1840), they no longer "waited on God" but actively promoted religious conversion. As the second precondition was met, the number and size of Cortland County religious revivals increased dramatically.

4

Women: Agents of the Gospel Message

The massive cultural shift from eighteenth-century tradition and deference to nineteenth-century experimentation, egalitarianism, and self-reliance was central to the Second Great Awakening. Evangelical thought had to adapt to the emerging republican mentality or lose its audience to Deism, rationalism, or indifference.

The Great Awakening hypothesis does not provide a comprehensive explanation for revivalism in the United States or in Cortland County. Revivalistic intensity varied greatly from group to group and from situation to situation. Women were more prone to evangelicalism than men, Baptists and Methodists were more given to revivalism than Presbyterians and Congregationalists, and churches varied greatly in their evangelical zeal, depending on their institutional circumstances. Arminianization influenced the perceived ability of humans to find salvation, but gender, denomination, and institutional circumstances affected the perceived importance of individual salvation.

Women were central to evangelical religion in Cortland County. Dorothy Hoar's dream led to the formation of the Homer Congregational Church in 1801. A woman organized the prayer meetings that precipitated the county's first major revivals. In the sixty years before the Civil War, 60 percent of those who joined Cortland County evangelical churches were women. Even though females were given few leadership opportunities in the official church hierarchy, they were the heart and soul of local congregational life.

Religious records from the early nineteenth century reveal that not only were women more numerous than men, they probably were more committed evangelicals. Considering the small amount of property at their disposal, Cortland County females gave extraordinary sums of money to denominational benevolent projects. The Cortland Baptist Association minutes list all contributions to projects such as foreign missions, domestic missions, and various Bible and tract societies. In 1828–29, 52 percent of giving for Cortland Baptist Association benevolent activities came from individual women or organized women's groups. Between 1830 and 1834, 30 percent of such giving came from female contributors (Table D.1). These percentages actually understate female contributions because some donations are listed by church, and it is impossible to estimate the female share of a congregational gift. A significant portion of female giving came from the production of domestic goods organized by women's societies, although in numerous cases, solitary women contributed "a ring," "a string of gold beads," or "25 cents," which suggests that the gifts were monetarily small but entailed significant personal sacrifice.[1] It was no accident that several women's groups were named "Mite Societies" in honor of the New Testament woman who gave her mite, which was all she had, to the Lord's service.

Why were Cortland County women so involved in evangelical activities? Answers that fit other locales do not work as well here. Nancy F. Cott revealed that the increasing unpredictability of young women's lives in early nineteenth-century New England led them to "seek security" in the church through religious conversion. Two of the primary "unsettling" elements were an absence of marriageable men and the need to leave the parental household to seek employment, often in a textile factory.[2] In Cortland County, men outnumbered women and there were few local industries until the 1850s, long after revivalism had peaked.

Mary Ryan argued that changing household structure encouraged middle-class Utica women to form female voluntary organizations, which promoted conversion among the young.[3] In Cortland County, agriculture dominated the local economy

---

1. *Minutes of the Cortland Baptist Association*, 1828–34.
2. Cott, "Young Women."
3. Ryan, *Cradle of the Middle Class*, esp. pp. 102–3.

throughout the revival period, and the household structure did not undergo great change for most people. The middle class was influential but very small by Utica standards, and the organization of females into benevolent associations was incomplete and haphazard.

Cortland County women were at the heart of local evangelical activity, but their involvement was in response to ideological, not social, change. The growth in republicanism, individualism, and self-reliance was central to American self-definition in the early nineteenth century, but the experience of personal independence varied greatly by gender. As a result, male and female attitudes toward the corporate church differed in significant ways.

Men sought to embody the new republican ideal. In the early 1800s, large numbers of young men tossed off traditional constraints and sought their fortunes on their own terms. Young apprentices ran away from their masters in republican defiance. Schoolboy rowdiness reached shocking proportions. Drinking large amounts of whiskey was a statement of political independence, as well as a social pastime, and American males consumed enormous amounts of alcohol.[4] Men sought to make their fortunes in all manner of speculative businesses. By the 1820s, white American males wanted unlimited political opportunity to go with their alleged boundless economic freedom. Soon after demanding and receiving universal white manhood suffrage, these untamed men elected Andrew Jackson, the prophet of moral, economic, and political laissez-faire, to the presidency. To most American men, republicanism meant the freedom *not to defer* to traditional hierarchical authority, whether in the form of king, community scion, or church.

The corporate church as it existed in early nineteenth-century Cortland County directly contradicted this male republican ideal. Instead of promoting personal independence, the church demanded submission to the authority of the group. The church maintained the right to monitor nearly every aspect of a member's behavior, including commercial endeavors, political activities, use of leisure time, and choice of friends and acquaintances. During the 1820s and 1830s, 40 percent of charges levied against church members involved indiscretions in everyday life rather than

4. Rorabaugh, *Alcoholic Republic,* pp. 90–92, 131–33, 138–40.

wrongdoing in the ecclesiastical domain (Table C.1). Even men who submitted to church membership chafed against congregational authority. Between 1801 and 1839, men constituted 64 percent of all Baptist, Congregational, and Presbyterian excommunications even though they were only 40 percent of all Calvinist members.

Men probably found the congregation's jurisdiction over the commercial activities of its members the most threatening of the church's powers. Evangelical denominations were disturbed by the growing wealth and materialism after 1815 and steadfastly maintained their right to discipline members whose acquisitive instincts overwhelmed their commitment to Christian piety. Theft, fraud, intentional property damage, bad debts, broken contracts, and any other form of commercial dishonesty fell under the jurisdiction of the corporate church. Furthermore, congregations demanded that business differences between members be settled by the congregation, not by a court of law.

Sanctions against commercial dishonesty were not ecclesiastical paper tigers: they were enforced. In 1816 the Homer Congregationalists excluded Luther Rice, in part for "taking usury." Four years later, Isaac Chafee was excommunicated for fraud in a land deal.[5] The Cincinnatus Congregationalists disfellowshipped Thomas French for passing an allegedly counterfeit bank bill and prosecuted Joshua Sanders for having obtained $30 in goods under false pretenses.[6] In 1822 the Truxton Congregational Church expelled Betsy Lansing for "Fraud in deal with a Pedler."[7] The Homer Baptists had numerous cases of commercial wrongdoing. Elisha Salsbury was accused of altering a receipt, Sylvanus Hopkins of "forfeiting his word in a matter of material consequence," John Cleveland of deception involving a bond and a mortgage, Miriam Foster of cheating in "counting yam," and James Monrose of absconding "for the purpose of defrauding his creditors."[8] All were found guilty and were excluded. Between

5. Homer Congregational Minutes, January 21, March 10, 1817, June 24, 1819, June 11, 1820, lists of excommunicants.
6. Cincinnatus First Congregational Church, Records, May 13, 1815, November 12, 1816, February 11, 1832.
7. Truxton First Presbyterian Church, Record Book, December 17, 1821, October 15, 1822.
8. Cortland First Baptist Church, Record Books, April 20, 1816, April 14, May 16, December 19, 1818, August 14, April 17, 1819, February 16, 1822, December 20, 1828.

1801 and 1849 Cortland County's evangelical churches investigated sixty-eight charges of commercial misbehavior, which accounted for about 7 percent of all charges leveled against church members (Table C.2).

In the Jacksonian era, men were expected to be this-worldly in thought, crafty in business, and wise in politics. Yet church membership demanded that males be otherworldly, totally honest in business, and submissive to congregational authority. For most men, the contradictions were too great. In addition, many believed that pondering the state of their souls was a poor use of time when fields needed to be cleared of trees, barns needed building, and wheat needed to be transported to the local mill. Not surprisingly, no more than a fifth of all adult males belonged to an evangelical church during the 1820s.

Some Cortland men found religious societies a convenient alternative to formal church membership. A majority of those who joined a religious society never joined a church. From a secular perspective, society membership was superior to church membership. The religious societies promoted the moral life of the community, controlled the use of the church building, helped set church budgets and salaries, and voted on prospective clergy. Society members who did not belong to a church were exempt from all religious sanctions, thus preserving a noncommittal religiosity as well as personal independence.

The county's religious societies fostered a minimalist religious orientation, and many of their members rejected all religious sanctions over their private and public lives. Nevertheless, minimalists expected the church to endorse their values—social respectability, orderly and outwardly moral behavior, and the maintenance of the political and economic status quo. Men in the religious societies were generally wealthier than those in the churches they supported so such social conservatism is not surprising.[9] Even though they were not church members, some

9. The conclusion that men in the religious societies were generally wealthier than male church members was based on a comparison of Union Congregational and Cortland Baptist Society subscription lists for new church buildings (1832), a First Religious Society of Homer list of pew holders (1855), a Union Congregational Society building repairs subscription list (1859), a list of Scott Methodist Society members (1860), and a Cortland Baptist Society remodeling subscription list (1861) with lists of men belonging to the corresponding churches during the same period. The sharpest differences occurred among the Methodists; Scott society members were much wealthier than church members. The smallest differ-

wealthy society members went to great lengths to demonstrate their financial and social power over a local congregation. For instance, in the Cortland Presbyterian Church, a wealthy society member, who attended worship regularly but never joined, maintained an ostentatious display of personal wealth and influence. His personal box pew "was fitted up as a drawing room and contained sofas, rocking chairs, foot stools and foot stoves." When the Presbyterian minister gave his sermon Sunday morning, he could not help but see which listener had the greatest influence over his salary.[10]

Women had a very different experience in republican America. Although they were as nationalistic as their male counterparts, women were not allowed to reenact the revolution in their own lives through independent commercial and political action. Instead, custom dictated that they be submissive, deferential to traditional authority, and dependent in all affairs economic and political.

Cortland County women suffered the same contradictions between republican ideology and restrictive social conditions as women elsewhere in the United States. In rural areas, male and female spheres were not as tightly defined as in urban centers, where home and workplace had already been separated.[11] Nevertheless, men were arbiters between the household and the outside world whereas women were expected to be concerned only with domestic matters. Decisions as to which crop would bring the best market price, which miller, artisan, or general store owner

---

ences occurred between the Congregationalists and their society members. Between 1832 and 1859–61, the wealth differences between the Union Congregational and Cortland Baptist congregations and their societies shrank significantly.

The various lists are found in First Religious Society of Homer, Minutes, 1855; Homer First Baptist Society Minutes, 1832, 1861; Cincinnatus and Solon, Union Congregational Society, Records, 1832, 1859, Accession No. 6235, CUA; Scott Methodist Episcopal Society, Minutes, CCHS.

10. *First Presbyterian Church, One Hundredth Anniversary, Cortland, N.Y., April 16–19, 1925*, p. 12, Accession No. 1151M, CUA. The name of the individual in question does not appear on the Cortland Presbyterian Church membership rosters before 1860, which implies that he was a member of the Cortland Presbyterian Society only.

11. Gerda Lerner, "The Lady and the Mill Girl: Changes in the Status of Women in the Age of Jackson," in Jean E. Friedman, William G. Shade, and Mary Jane Capozzoli, eds., *Our American Sisters: Women in American Life and Thought* (Lexington, Mass., 1987), pp. 125–38.

charged the most reasonable rates, and which local citizen would be the best constable or road overseer all fell within the male domain. Lacking significant economic or political decision-making power, farm women had little to focus on but domestic production, household management, and religion.

Evangelical religion provided the only arena where many women could play out the republican vision. In an era when opportunities for female voluntarism were limited, evangelical women could improve the community by promoting the salvation of neighbors and kin. They naturally gravitated toward Arminianized evangelicalism rather than traditional Calvinism because the former gave a much larger role for humans (i.e., women) in the conversion process. Kept from making political choices, women concentrated on making the correct religious choice (vote for Jesus, not the Devil) and encouraged others to do the same. From 1812 on, Cortland County's evangelical women promoted revivals and pushed Calvinism in an Arminian direction. When local Calvinism collapsed in the early 1830s, women were at the Reverend John Keep's side (even as many men muttered about pastoral excesses), testifying to their faith and running children's inquiry sessions.[12] Women's preference for Arminian theology is substantiated by church transfers recorded in congregational minutes. Of forty people who migrated from local Calvinist to Methodist fellowships before the Civil War, 75 percent were women. Ideologically, women were attracted to Methodism because its Arminian theology gave female spiritual republicanism its freest reign.

There were also powerful social reasons why early nineteenth-century farm women saw evangelical religion as a liberating, not a constricting, influence. Because women had been socialized since birth to be submissive, corporate church requirements that members yield significant autonomy to congregational authority did not alarm them. Membership enlarged women's social sphere as they were able to pray, plan, and work with their "sisters in Christ" on church projects.

Even though men held a monopoly on official congregational positions, Baptist women had considerable influence over day-to-day church functions. They could speak to the covenant, relate

12. Keep, *Narrative*, p. 7.

their religious experiences, and initiate church discipline proceedings. In 1810 Scott Baptist women offered their opinions as to whether one of the male members had the gift of preaching.[13] Women could block a prospective member's acceptance into the church. In 1815 two Solon Baptist women were not satisfied with a recent convert's experience, and as a result, his admittance was postponed upon further investigation.[14] Females occasionally served on church discipline committees. In 1820 one of the young women in the Homer church gave birth out of wedlock. The visitation committee sent to investigate included both husbands and wives.[15]

Opportunities for women were even greater among Congregationalists. At one point, the Union Church of Cincinnatus and Solon chose nine women "to solicit donations for benevolent objects for the ensuing year." Occasionally, women's freedom extended to church suffrage. In 1813 Homer Congregational females were allowed to vote on an excommunication case. In 1835 women in the Truxton church voted along with the men on whether to continue with the current pastor. Six years later, the Homer women were asked to vote on the retention of the minister, although this time their votes were counted separately and were probably no more than advisory.[16] Even though women were denied access to ongoing institutional power within the evangelical denominations, they did have opportunities to break out of the women's sphere.

Evangelical women discovered that the corporate church also had a beneficial effect on gender relations. Once men became church members, they were no longer autonomous but were subject to the higher authority of the congregation and the Bible. Men who abused weaker relatives were not tolerated. In 1819 the Scott Baptists withdrew the hand of fellowship from Ambrose Salsbury for whipping his wife.[17] Three years later, Jacob Gray

13. Scott Baptist Church, Record Book, March 27, 1830, February 24, 1810; Truxton Baptist Church, Record Book, August 24, 1833.

14. Solon First Baptist Church, Minutes, July 22, 1815.

15. Cortland First Baptist Church, Record Book, December 16, 1820.

16. Cincinnatus and Solon, Union Congregational Church, Records, March 29, 1844, Accession No. 6235 (pt. 2), CUA; Homer Congregational Church, Minutes, August 18, 1813, July 31, 1841; Truxton First Presbyterian Church, Record Book, June 24, 1835.

17. Scott Baptist Church, Record Book, June 19, September 25, November 13, 1819.

was forced out of the Homer Baptist Church in part "for neglect-ing to provide for his family."[18] The Freetown Congregational Church accused Ansel Tobey of "indecent speaches and un-becoming Conduct towards his Aged parants while they Lived."[19] In 1848 a member of the Cortland Presbyterian Church was brought before the session for quarreling with his wife and ver-bally "wishing [her] dead." Unlike Tobey, the Cortland church member did not repent and was eventually excluded.[20] In an era when few community institutions had the will or the ability to intervene in domestic life, Cortland County's corporate churches offered women some recourse against irresponsible or ill-tem-pered spouses.

As in Oneida County, evangelical renewal in Cortland County was spearheaded by women. In revivals involving forty or more converts between 1812 and 1843, females constituted 61.4 per-cent of recently redeemed Baptists, 60.5 percent of newly confess-ing Congregationalists, and 56.4 percent of Presbyterian con-verts. Not only did women dominate numerically, they tended to be the first within any family group to be converted and formally join an evangelical church. Most converts appear to have entered county churches in the presence of relatives. Between 1825 and 1843, 72 percent of Cortland Baptist converts, 62 percent of new Union Congregational confessors, and 49 percent of newly pro-fessing Cortland Presbyterians were preceded into the church by someone with the same surname. In each of the three churches, women were more than twice as likely as men to be the first member with a given surname to join. In Cortland County, as in Oneida County, "women cajoled, manipulated, or simply led their children into the evangelical sects."[21]

The focus of the female-led revivals changed over time. Super-ficially, Cortland County revivals appear to replicate those in Oneida County. In both counties, revivals passed through two distinct stages. Initially, in what I call "stage one revivals," groups of converts had fairly balanced sex ratios and a high percentage of

18. Cortland First Baptist Church, Record Book, December 14, 28, 1822.
19. Cincinnatus First Congregational Church, Records, February 13, 1826.
20. Members of the Cortland Presbyterian Church must be kept anonymous because of restrictions placed on the documents at the request of the church. See Cortland Presbyterian Church, Records, August 7, 1848–September 21, 1850, Accession No. 6260, CUA.
21. Ryan, *Cradle of the Middle Class*, p. 81.

married individuals. Eventually the demography of conversion changed. During "stage two revivals," many more women than men were converted. A high percentage of the new confessors were not married with the single largest group being teenaged girls.

Mary Ryan has argued that the shift in Oneida County's revival demography is related to fundamental changes in family structure. In the 1810s the adult conversions fit the traditional patterns of patriarchal authority. By the late 1810s and 1820s, traditional household patterns changed as the workplace became separate from the household. Middle-class women, freed from production responsibilities, used female benevolent organizations to encourage the salvation of their children. A large percentage of adolescents converted in the stage two revivals can be linked to mothers converted in stage one and active in missionary and maternal societies. Oneida County's great revivals during the 1820s and 1830s can be attributed to the high birth rate of the 1800s and 1810s, which led to large numbers of adolescents in later decades, and the changing household structure, which allowed middle-class women to evangelize the young.[22]

Ryan's explanation may fit the revival pattern in Utica, but it does not work particularly well in Cortland County, where the timing of stage one and stage two revivals was haphazard. Homer Congregational Church moved from stage one to stage two between the 1812–13 and the 1816–17 awakenings. In nearby Cortland, roughly the same size as Homer, the Presbyterian Church had a stage one revival in 1826. The Freetown Congregational Church had a stage one revival in 1816–17 and another in 1831. Cortland County revivals usually moved from stage one to stage two but in an irregular pattern that does not fit a tight chronology. Even more important, stage two revivals occurred in a predominantly rural county where most people lived on farms, where home and workplace were generally the same, where there was a minuscule urban middle class, and where female benevolent societies were comparatively few in number. Apparently, stage two revivals occurred in Cortland County without many of the ingredients that supposedly caused them in Oneida County.

The shift from stage one to stage two revivals in Cortland

22. Ibid., pp. 83–86, 93, 102–4.

County churches was closely linked to congregational needs. Since churches were vital to the lives of evangelical women, it is not surprising that female evangelistic efforts changed to meet a church's changing needs. In the first years in a congregation's life cycle, the primary need was to bring adult membership up to a level at which the congregation's survival was no longer in question. It was very important to have a large number of men who could contribute financially, and so it is not surprising that there were a large number of adult male converts in any church's early years. Once a congregation had absorbed enough adult males to ensure viability, women could shift their attention to converting their children, thus bringing on a second phase of revivalism.

With this perspective in mind, the erratic revivalistic patterns in Cortland County can be explained. Homer Congregational Church had an enormous revival in 1812–13, which brought in 161 converts. As a result, membership jumped 131 percent to a total of 305 communicants by 1813. The church's survival was certain, members could concentrate on converting their offspring, and a series of stage two revivals ensued from 1816 to the 1850s. The Cortland Presbyterian Church had a stage one revival in 1826. The church had been formed only a year earlier and had a mere 24 adult members. Although it was located in one of the most urbanized parts of the county, the Presbyterian church desperately needed more adult members and held a stage one revival. By 1827 the Cortland congregation had 131 adult members, and all future revivals were of the stage two variety. In contrast, the Congregational Church in rural Freetown never became truly viable. Though it was one of the county's oldest Congregational churches, the Freetown fellowship could never draw enough adult members to build a meetinghouse before the Civil War. As a result, the Freetown Congregational revivals in 1816–17 and in 1831 were both of the stage one variety. On the other hand, the Preble Presbyterians, located in an equally rural area, had a stage two revival as early as 1826, when they had a worship house plus 76 adult members.

The targets of female-led revivalism ranged from adult males to adolescent children, and the methods used by the women varied. Some Cortland County women organized benevolent societies to further the gospel at home and abroad. Nineteenth-century documents indicate that there were a number of female associations in Cortland County, but, unfortunately, the minutes of the Female Branch Bible Society are the only such records extant.[23]

The Branch Bible Society was organized in Homer in 1822 and continued to raise money for publishing Bibles until after the Civil War. As in other communities, such voluntarism provided a haven for middle-class women. Only 4 percent of Homer men were merchants or professionals in 1840, but 16 percent of Branch Bible Society members between 1835 and 1840 were married to such men of influence. Farm women dominated the organization with 57 percent of the total membership. All women, irrespective of class, benefited from the organization's gradual expansion of female opportunities beyond the domestic sphere. The Branch Bible Society not only facilitated the spread of the gospel, it gave women opportunities to conduct meetings, plan long-term projects, raise funds, and generally exert leadership in an environment devoid of men. Minutes covering the period from 1822 to 1871 indicate that the women did their jobs very well. The society's record book is better organized for a longer period of time than that of any of the male-dominated religious societies.

The Branch Bible Society also appears to have had an impact on local revivals. Between 1822 and 1825, 54 percent of its members were church members. This percentage is lower than one might expect, partly because of incomplete records but also because Christian matrons used the society's meetings to evangelize their daughters. Sometimes mothers and other female kin would pay the membership dues for youngsters to remove any barriers between adolescents and the evangelical fellowship. Many of the society's younger members were converted in the revivals of 1826 and 1831–33.

Female benevolent societies in Cortland County promoted the salvation of adolescents but were relatively less important than similar organizations in urban places such as Rochester and Utica. Before the massive awakenings of 1831–33, female voluntary associations were restricted to village churches or unusually large rural churches. The Branch Bible Society was located in Homer

23. Female Branch Bible Society, (Homer) New York, Records 1822–71, Accession No. 6240, CUA.

village and drew its membership primarily from nearby Congregational and Baptist churches. The *Minutes of the Cortland Baptist Association* contain lists of money and goods donated and raised by Baptist female missionary, mite, and benevolent societies. Only three of ten county Baptist churches had any female society in 1830. The Baptist churches in Homer and Cortlandville were essentially village churches. The Truxton Baptist Church had a rural congregation with the county's largest Baptist membership (353 members in 1830). By 1843 64 percent of the county's Baptist churches had female societies, but this growth occurred after the peak of revivalism.[24] Apparently in most churches, women promoted the conversion of youths through traditional means—exerting personal influence within the family.

Demographic data for the county provide a clue as to why informal female pressure for conversion peaked in the early 1830s. Cortland County was reaching economic maturity, and inexpensive productive land was rapidly disappearing. Many newly independent adults who lacked financial support from their parents found it was necessary to relocate somewhere with more opportunity. As in Oneida County, some migrated to the nearest urban place in search of employment in the crafts or service industries. Between 1830 and 1860, the populations of the urbanized towns of Homer and Cortland grew 31 percent; the rest of the county expanded a mere 2 percent.[25] Compared to Utica, however, the transportation-poor villages of Cortland and Homer offered few opportunities; most young adults in search of opportunity had to look west. Young people began to leave the county in large numbers between 1831 and 1835.

Evangelical women were probably the most distressed over the changing economic circumstances. Now more than ever the Calvinist formula of waiting for God to save one's children seemed inadequate. Perhaps a mother could patiently wait for God to intervene in her child's life when the child lived within reach of

24. *Minutes of the Cortland Baptist Association*, 1828–43. The following Baptist churches had female benevolent societies: First Homer (Cortland) and Truxton, 1828; Homer village, 1829; McGrawville, 1835; Marathon, 1838; Freetown, 1839; and Scott, 1843. There is no evidence that the First Solon, Second Solon, Virgil Village, and South Virgil Baptist churches had female societies in 1843.
25. *Census of the State of New York for 1855*, p. xxxiii.

her spiritual influence. But in the 1830s, children left home for the West, where parental influence was nonexistent and worldly influence rife. Therefore, in the early 1830s, saving grace had to be produced before the child reached maturity and left home. Salvation would come in Cortland County or not at all. Thus it makes perfect sense that the New Measures, which produced instant salvation, were quickly adopted by the county's Calvinist churches. It also comes as no surprise that during the 1830s, children's inquiry sessions held during revivals and Sunday Schools were religious innovations that had explosive growth during the decade.[26]

Evangelical women were the primary agents of the gospel message because they were convinced of the vital importance of personal salvation. Unlike men, who sought to implement republican ideals in the outside economic and political realm, married women confined their attempts at self-determination to the domestic and spiritual realms. Naturally, Cortland County females gravitated toward Arminian thought and practice because that theological system legitimized human efforts to encourage saving grace in others. In comparison to Oneida County females, who lived in a more economically developed region with a significant middle class, Cortland County women were less reliant on benevolent associations as a means of evangelism and more prone to work through traditional means such as church and family. Revivals peaked in Cortland County in the early 1830s partly because young people were leaving in record numbers and their mothers believed their salvation was critically important. Evangelical women endorsed the New Measures as a way to promote the immediate salvation of their children, bringing them into the Kingdom of Heaven before they migrated west in search of economic opportunity.

---

26. Keep, *Narrative*, p. 7; *Minutes of the Cortland Baptist Association*, 1828–39; records of individual congregations. Sunday Schools are known to have been formed in the Homer village and Truxton (1830), Cortland (1831), McGrawville (1832), Freetown (1834), First Solon, Second Solon, and Virgil (1835) Baptist churches in the 1830s. There is no evidence that the Scott or Marathon congregations formed a Sunday School during the decade.

5

Denomination, Institutional Circumstance, and Rural Revivalism

The shift in Calvinist theology toward Arminianism and the pervasive influence of evangelical women do much to explain the gradual increase of revivalism in the 1810s and 1820s and the evangelistic crest of the early 1830s, but they do not capture the full story of local enthusiasm. The success of evangelical efforts varied from church to church and was influenced by the denomination and institutional circumstances of each church.

There were vast differences among the various evangelical groups. Early in the nineteenth century, Cortland County Methodists and Calvinists battled each other over the issue of free will. Local evangelicals were also divided, although with less acrimony, over the best use for congregations' resources and energy. Two groups emerged: the formal evangelicals and the antiformal evangelicals.[1]

Ideological divisions among the county's evangelicals reflected national religious patterns of the early 1800s. Large, powerful denominations that once had the advantage of government endorsement generally fell in the formalist camp. Some formalists were evangelical (Presbyterians and Congregationalists); others were not (the majority of Episcopalians). Formalist evangelicals

1. The basic differences between formal and antiformal orientations are explained in Rowe, *Thunder and Trumpets*, pp. 71–93. Rowe differentiates between formal and antiformal "pietists." I prefer to use the more familiar terms *evangelicals* and *nonevangelicals*.

and nonevangelicals shared the conviction that the Christian mission went beyond individual salvation and involved religious endeavors that would benefit the larger community. Years of formal theological training prepared ministers of all three denominations not only to be shepherds of the flock but to assume the role of community leader. Whether directing their efforts toward saving souls or toward community betterment, formalists were committed to transforming society.[2]

In contrast, antiformalists doubted whether humans could change society. They believed that only direct divine intervention could bring social improvement. Antiformal evangelicals (principally Methodists and Baptists) believed that the primary function of the church was to save souls. Because they valued spiritual fervor more than biblical scholarship, their clergy tended to be relatively uneducated and noted more for passion than for erudition. In the early 1800s, Methodist circuit riders and Baptist lay preachers ignored social questions and focused on personal salvation. This was a natural outgrowth of the antiformalist view that society could be saved only if God changed individuals through the redemptive process. They considered the formalists' efforts to improve society by organized social activity futile at best and heretical at worst.[3]

Not all antiformalists were evangelicals. Universalism was one antiformal response to the withered orthodox Calvinism of the 1780s. Although Universalists saw no need to save souls from perdition, they agreed with their antiformalist evangelical brethren on the importance of a direct relationship with God and the futility of human efforts to redeem society.[4] Churches of the Christian Connection also rejected the traditional Calvinist creeds. Initially pietistic, they were increasingly influenced by Unitarianism as they migrated across western New York.[5] Despite some doctrinal change, these "Christians" continued to oppose formal and mechanical techniques promoting personal and social redemption.

2. Ibid., pp. 71.
3. Ibid., pp. 71, 74.
4. Rowe makes it clear that the Universalists and the antiformal pietists did not get along (ibid., pp. 78, 80, 96). They disagreed over doctrine, not organizational orientation. Universalism was shaped by eighteenth-century "radical evangelicalism" (p. 49) and kept that movement's antiformal orientation but not its orthodoxy. Universalists and the evangelical Millerites attacked the restriction against women preaching (pp. 126–29).
5. Ahlstrom, *Religious History,* 1:485, 581.

The frontier experience and New York's disestablishment shifted all of Cortland County's evangelical groups toward anti-formalism. With educated clergy scarce, churches struggling for money and members, and evangelicals making up a minute fraction of the population, the antiformalist strategy—emphasizing church needs over societal improvement and implementing lay leadership—suited most congregations. Even so, from the very beginning, the county's evangelical churches retained many of the formalist and antiformalist tendencies exhibited on the national level. The differences between competing evangelical types can be seen by comparing the Homer Congregational and Baptist churches.

From its founding in 1801, the Congregational Church fit the description of formal evangelicalism. When confronted with a problem, the church members' first impulse was to form a committee. They also thought in terms of the larger community and saw the church's influence extending beyond the doors of the sanctuary. In 1803 many members were concerned about the religious education of the town's children. A seven-point proposal was quickly developed and implemented. In 1808 a committee was formed with one representative from every school district to supervise the educational program. A year later, a committee was formed to evaluate the children's progress. In 1813 the church "voted that twenty persons belonging to this church, be appointed Catechists, to visit families of professors, to confer with them on the religious education of their households, to catechise and instruct the children." The catechist program was conducted for several years, only to be replaced by two more popular innovations—the singing school and the Sabbath School—around 1820. Education was not the only part of church life to be run by committee. In 1810 the church decided that prospective members should be examined by a committee, not by the congregation as a whole. Other church functions such as collecting funds for the poor appear to have been highly organized.[6] Clearly, the Homer church was willing to apply organizational techniques to religious and community problems.

Minutes of the Homer Baptist Church show a sharp contrast

6. Homer Congregational Church, Minutes, March 29, 1803, May 26, 1808, July 6, 1809, March 25, 1813, September 17, 1818, January 19, March 25, April 8, 1819, June 9, 1814, June 1, 1815, May 10, 1810, June 8, 1815.

with the Congregationalists in that problems were not solved by standing committees but were dealt with on an ad hoc basis. The church's organizational structure was simple, and problems were addressed by temporary committees that would act on their assigned task and then disband. A remarkable amount of space in the minutes is devoted to commentary on the spiritual life of the church. The relative fervor of every covenant meeting was recorded. Gatherings are frequently characterized as a "low time," a "comfortable time" or a "dark time." More detailed passages dwelt on the spiritual state of the church. The minutes for May 17, 1806, state, "Asked the minds of those present. There seem to be a mind to try to go forward and tho in trouble yet some gleam of light (or hope) of an increase of light and Love." The minutes for March 18, 1815, comment on "some trials and complaints of coldness and wicked hearts, yet on the whole a comfortable Season, Some minds Stirred up and in general mind to go forward."[7] Only in the revival year of 1813 were comments more positive than negative. The general mood was to complain of lack of fervor but to manifest a will to continue on in the cause.

In sum, Congregationalists and, later, Presbyterians sought organizational solutions to church problems. It was not that they devalued personal piety. Instead, they prayed about problems and then quickly sought an organizational solution. Baptists and Methodists put little stock in human solutions, believing change was to be implemented by the Holy Spirit working in the hearts of mankind. To Baptists and Methodists the church's responsibilities rarely went beyond saving souls and inducing personal piety.

The philosophical differences between formal and antiformal evangelicals affected their relative evangelistic success. Baptists generally converted and absorbed more new members than did Congregationalists and Presbyterians. Except for the period 1830–34, when evangelist Jedediah Burchard rocked the Homer Congregational Church with impassioned "Finneyite" oratory, the Baptists had a higher evangelism index than the Presbyterians and Congregationalists in every five-year period from 1816 to 1859 (Table B.3). That result is hardly surprising. As antiformalists, the Baptists were pietistic, introspective, and greatly con-

7. Cortland First Baptist Church, Record Book, May 17, 1806, March 18, 1815.

cerned over the state of every soul under their "watch and care." They doubted the appropriateness of the church mixing into community affairs and employed the time, money, and talent of their parishioners almost exclusively for saving souls. The evangelism indexes indicate that the Baptists' single-mindedness led to their winning numerous converts.

Presbyterians and Congregationalists divided their attention between individual salvation and community betterment. Only in the Keep-Burchard era of 1831–33 did formal Calvinists focus nearly all of their organizational skill on evangelism. This concentrated effort reaped spectacular results in the early 1830s, but eventually formalists broadened their approach, and their evangelism index once again fell below that of the Baptists.

Some historians contend that institutional factors were central in promoting religious enthusiasm. John Hammond, for instance, has argued that revivals are "best explained not by any imputed anomie, anxiety, or discontent arising from large-scale social and cultural forces, but rather by the internal life of the churches themselves. Revivals serve institutional purposes and are promoted for institutional ends." Terry Bilhartz expressed a similar position: in early nineteenth-century Baltimore, Bilhartz wrote, "Revival erupted among those who wanted it, and who labored diligently to promote it. It was one strategy for church survival in a competitive and increasingly materialistic era."[8] Both scholars agree that revivals originated inside the church, not from the larger culture, and were promoted to further the institutional goals of evangelical congregations.

Cortland County's religious history indicates that although institutional factors were important, they had less impact than religious ideology or gender relations in fostering revivalism. Whether one is speaking of the Arminianization of Calvinism or the antiformal evangelicals' single-minded focus on personal conversion, the driving force behind revivals was the powerful perception that it was both possible and necessary for humans to achieve immediate salvation. Indeed, a central argument of this book is that, by 1860, changes in religious ideas destroyed corporate congregational structure, replacing it with modern institu-

8. Hammond, "Reality of Revivals," p. 113; Bilhartz, *Urban Religion,* p. 99.

tions. In contrast, the institutional impact on religious ideas was ever-present but relatively mild. Nor do institutional factors such as congregational needs for more members and money explain why in church after church, women were at the center of the revivals, both as promoters and as converts. Nevertheless, internal factors such as the financial and organizational status of a congregation explain why some churches were revivalistic and others were not. Furthermore, at least in Cortland County, the internal affairs of local churches reinforced the chronological pattern of revivalism described earlier.

The institutional circumstances of various congregations were expressed primarily in the importance churches placed on recruiting new members. All evangelical church members had to profess the importance of personal salvation, but they were much more likely to act on this belief when the survival of their congregation depended on bringing in new converts. Thus the congregations that experienced the greatest revivals were usually the ones in the greatest need of new members. The link between adverse institutional circumstances and revivals can be demonstrated in two ways. First, comparing changing circumstances in churches with the ebb and flow of revivalism, one sees that evangelism peaked when churches were in greatest institutional need. Second, examining the churches with the greatest evangelism indexes during the explosive 1830s indicates what factors led congregations to be highly evangelistic.

Cortland County churches had a high level of evangelism in the late 1810s, lower rates in the 1820s, huge numbers of converts in the early 1830s, and gradually declining evangelism indexes thereafter. This chronological pattern generally follows the level of institutional need in each period.

Between 1816 and 1819, county churches were struggling against all of the adversities that faced frontier religion. Churches were small, had meager financial resources, found it difficult to find suitable clergy, and rarely had permanent places of worship. This subsistence-level condition could be reversed by increasing church membership. If a congregation could obtain about sixty to seventy adult members, it usually could build a worship house.[9] State law required that a religious society be organized about the

9. See Chapter 2, note 17 and Table B.2.

time construction began. This was a crucial step because the new organization would include a large number of minimalists as well as evangelical church members, thus vastly increasing the funds available for hiring clergy. Once a religious society was formed and a worship house was built, the congregation usually had enough financial contributors to remain viable.

From 1816 to 1819, only three county churches had worship houses and supporting religious societies. The remainder had to draw in large numbers of new members to ensure their survival. In-migration was large enough that most fellowships could maintain current membership levels without evangelism (Table B.3). But if congregations were to grow, converts were needed. For a church to grow 50 percent in five years, it needed one convert for every ten current members every year.[10] Not surprisingly, efforts at conversion were great, and evangelism indexes high in this era.

The 1820s brought material prosperity to Cortland County churches. In-migration remained high, and transfers continued to join county churches. The exact number of churches that had permanent houses of worship is hard to determine. Of fifteen Calvinist fellowships for which information is available, nine had erected church buildings by 1829. Most churches were reaching viability. Some grew so large that they subdivided. In 1825–26, a number of Homer Congregationalists broke off from the main body to support the new Presbyterian fellowship in Cortland village. In 1827 the Homer Baptists split into three fellowships located in the villages of Homer, Cortland, and McGrawville.[11] Compared to the previous decade, the 1820s were materially prosperous. The need for new converts declined, and evangelism indexes were only about 50 to 60 percent of what they had been in the late 1810s.

Evangelism rates soared during the early 1830s. A major por-

10. The relationship between church growth and evangelism indexes was determined by bivariate regression. The percentage gain or loss in membership (church growth) and the index was calculated for each county church in each five-year period for which data were available. In each equation the evangelism index was the independent variable, the growth rate the dependent variable. Once the intercept and slope were determined for county churches in each five-year period, it was possible to determine the rate of conversion necessary to yield no membership increase, a 50 percent increase, or a 100 percent increase in any given half-decade. The regression equation also made it possible to determine average membership losses if no or few converts were gained.

11. *First Presbyterian Church: One Hundredth Anniversary*, pp. 7–8.

tion of the increase was attributable to the Arminianization of Calvinism, which resolved the conflict between faith and experience. Women, seeking the salvation of their offspring before they moved west, encouraged large numbers of conversions. There were also institutional reasons for the peak of evangelism in the 1830s. Growing out-migration affected more than parents' concern about their children's salvation: it also influenced the viability of each congregation. The changing ratio of in-migrants to out-migrants made it harder for churches to maintain membership levels than at any other time before the Civil War. In the early 1830s, 7.5 converts per 100 current members were needed every year to maintain the existing membership (Table B.3). Failure to gain these converts could be fatal. If a congregation had an evangelism index of 3.2 between 1830 and 1834, it could well lose half its membership by 1834. If a congregation could muster an evangelism index of only 1.1, three-fourths of its membership, on average, would be gone by 1834.

Nineteenth-century evangelicals understood the relationship between aggressive evangelism and church growth. "God builds up his church upon the earth by the revivals of religion," wrote the Baptist Association, "[so] let us, dear brethren, as churches and individuals, labor and pray for their promotion." Some churches realized that the failure to gain converts could lead to serious difficulty. In 1841 the Marathon Baptist Church's letter to the association reported that it had "no cheering intelligence of souls converted to God the past year, and [its members] fear they will not be able to sustain their Pastor without aid from the Convention."[12] Although Cortland County's religious leaders were probably not aware of the statistical connections between revivalism and church growth, they had a sense that successful churches evangelized and that struggling churches failed to convert sinners. Therefore, during the 1830s, when the demographic need for new church members was the greatest, evangelicals employed greater energy to draw in new members.

From 1835 into the early 1850s, there was a decline in the number of converts each church had to gain each year simply to maintain its current membership. Not surprisingly, church evangelism indexes dropped as well. One reason for this decline was

12. *Minutes of the Cortland Baptist Association,* 1840, p. 14; 1841, p. 12.

that the novelty of the New Measures was falling off. The Cort-land Baptist Association reported in 1840 that many Christians were crying for "an old fashion revival. Our faith is lost in these protracted meetings." It is also possible that failure to conduct revivals with the same urgency as before contributed to the failure of the New Measures. The association pointed out that by 1840 many churches had a mechanical faith in New Measure tech-niques, which suggests that much of the prayerful urgency of the early 1830s had evaporated.[13]

The chronology outlined above demonstrates that the peaks and valleys of county revivalism closely parallel patterns of rising and falling church need. One more step needs to be taken before a link can be established between institutional circumstances and high rates of evangelism.

To determine how churches with high evangelism rates dif-fered from those with a less revivalistic bent, data were col-lected on seventy-eight Baptist, Congregational, and Presbyterian churches in and near Cortland County for the period 1829–41. Correlation analysis of these churches reveals several important patterns. The highest levels of evangelism occurred in relatively new congregations with no worship house. The age of a church (number of years since its founding) had a strong negative rela-tionship with evangelism indexes (−.35) as did congregational ownership of a worship house (−.32). Smaller congregations were more likely to have higher rates of evangelism, although the relationship is not particularly strong. The average size of each church between 1829 and 1841 was negatively correlated (−.12) with its evangelism index during the same period. The only institutional factor absolutely necessary for successful evangelism was clerical leadership. The correlation between evangelism in-dexes and the percentage of the time churches had a minister was .27.

The correlation analysis suggests that the churches that con-verted the most new members per capita were relatively new, small, and struggling, large enough to have a minister in regular attendance but still lacking an established place of worship. In short, the congregations that drew in the most new converts dur-ing the 1830s were institutionally similar to most county churches

13. Ibid., 1840, pp. 13–14.

from 1816 to 1819. In both periods, the churches that had the most successful revivals had not yet solidified as viable institutions. Members of such fellowships believed that personal salvation was vitally important, not only because of their commitment to a particular religious ideology but because recruiting new members was essential to the survival of their religious community.

Overall, denominational and institutional factors were important in promoting revivals. Antiformal evangelicals were more likely to have large numbers of converts because they channeled all of their efforts into evangelism, whereas formal evangelicals divided their energies between saving souls and social improvement. Institutionally, churches that were most in need of new members worked the hardest to promote revivals and generally had high evangelism indexes. It is difficult to demonstrate exactly to what degree institutional factors, as opposed to ideology and gender relations, were responsible for revivals. Most of the time there was an interplay among these various forces, with ideology and gender relations setting the stage for the important role of institutional circumstances. Whether one looks at gender, ideology, or institutional need, one lesson is clear. Cortland County churches that considered revivals vitally important and had identifiable reasons for focusing their efforts on procuring converts were the same ones that had the highest evangelism indexes during the Second Great Awakening.

6

The Failure of Economic Explanations
of Rural Revivalism

In recent years, a number of historians, including Paul Johnson, Anthony F. C. Wallace, and Paul Faler, have argued that early nineteenth-century revivals were attempts by the rising industrial bourgeoisie to discipline the unruly laboring classes. This theory posits that even though the industrialists' efforts were shaped more by subconscious psychological needs than by overt plots, they essentially used revivalism as a means to an economic end. This interpretation does not hold true for Cortland County, where class and wealth had little positive effect on religious revivals. In fact, in Cortland County the well-to-do tended to dampen, rather than fan, the flames of religious enthusiasm.

Economic explanations of religious enthusiasm generally take three forms, all of which fail to explain revivalism in Cortland County. The first interpretive framework is the Marxian formula that those who control the means of production use religion to manipulate those without access to productive means. The second is a modified Marxist view that holds that society's wealthier members seek to control those with fewer resources. The third version presents a struggle between market-oriented and subsistence agriculturalists with access to the market shaping the economic and religious worldviews of a region's farmers.

The Marxian formula, the purest form of class-conflict argumentation, pits the religious bourgeoisie against the irreligious proletariat. Following this motif, Johnson, Wallace and Faler contend that the men who controlled the means of production sought the religious conversion of propertyless workers who were likely to challenge bourgeois control. Once converted, the proletariat succumbed to evangelical precepts—respect for private property, obedience to superiors—and industrialists could rest easy, knowing that their power monopoly would not be challenged.[1] This model fails to provide an adequate general interpretation of antebellum revivalism. At the time of the Second Great Awakening most American communities had no landless proletariat. During the 1830s, the vast majority lived in places that were agricultural, preindustrial, and rural. The Marxian formula works only for industrial villages and cities such as Rochester, Lynn, and Rockdale, but even in some of these places, there are significant reasons to challenge its validity.[2]

1. See Johnson, *Shopkeeper's Millennium*, pp. 136–41; Wallace, *Rockdale*, pp. 296–98; Faler, "Cultural Aspects," pp. 367–394.
2. Much social control argumentation is based on data for the formal denominations (Presbyterian, Episcopalian, and Congregationalist). In any given community, formalist records are likely to be the most complete because formalists were generally the best educated and their organizational orientation predisposed them to careful recording and preservation of church documents. By comparison, antiformalist church documents are often incomplete and, in the case of the antebellum Methodists, very difficult to find. The distinction between formal and antiformal denominations is important because Presbyterians, Congregationalists, and Episcopalians were generally wealthier than antiformalists. Unless data are weighted by denomination, as I have done in this study, the greater availability of formalist church rosters biases estimates of wealth in an upward direction, thus giving evangelical membership and activities a much stronger middle- to upper-class tinge than it actually had.
    Johnson's central argument in *Shopkeeper's Millennium* is that there was a two-stage revival. In the first stage (1830–31), the revival was confined to middle- and upper-class elements (p. 103). In the second stage (1832–38), the newly converted sought to extend the "benefits" of their faith to the working class (p. 116). Thus evangelicalism is seen to progress from the bourgeoisie to the proletariat.
    Unfortunately, Johnson's book suffers from the upper-class formalist bias described earlier. The only complete church records for Rochester between 1815 and 1838 belong to two Presbyterian churches and two Episcopal churches (p. 157). Johnson's history of evangelicalism in Rochester, then, is actually the history of these two denominations. If there were more records of antiformalist groups, a much different picture of the Rochester awakening might emerge.
    If the revivals of 1830–31 extended beyond the Presbyterians and Episcopalians to include Baptists and Methodists (both blue-collar churches according to Johnson, p. 155), it is likely that Johnson's claim that "in the revival of 1830–31, new church members came disproportionately from businessmen, professionals, and master workmen" (p. 103) is correct only for formalist churches—not for Rochester churches generally.
    There is evidence that a strong working-class element participated in the 1830–

In Cortland County, typical of the rural North, the vast majority of residents gained their living from the soil. As late as 1840, 80 percent of all county household heads were farmers. Most were self-employed and owned their own land. The 1835 census reveals that 77 percent of all household heads owned at least one acre of land. Many of those without land were either older men who had granted land to their children or young men still waiting to receive their inheritance. The few who were not farmers were primarily professionals, storekeepers, and craftsmen who owned their own shops and businesses. Marxian theories of social control are not valid for those who owned the means of production and were members of the landed class. In such a relatively classless society, conflict over property rights was minimal.

The second economic interpretation of religious enthusiasm considers "upper class" as including men with large amounts of real property and "lower class" those with little or no land. Class conflict could occur if wealthy persons joined the evangelical churches and then used religious authority to curtail the personal liberties of society's less wealthy and unchurched members. This interpretation, too, breaks down when applied to Cortland County. There were no significant differences in wealth and occupation between local evangelicals and other residents during the revivalistic 1830s. In 1835 evangelical church members owned slightly more land than the typical county resident; 21 percent of evangelicals, compared to 18 percent of all residents, owned more than fifty acres. After weighting to compensate for the differences in age distributions, 19 percent of evangelicals owned more than fifty acres of land compared to 18 percent of all county household heads. Church members, however, were slightly overrepresented among the propertyless. After weighting for age, 25 percent of

31 revival, despite the weakness of local church documents. *The Minutes of the Annual Conferences of the Methodist Episcopal Church* report in 1829 that there were 374 Methodists in Rochester: by 1831 this number had grown to 725. Between 1830 and 1832, the Rochester Baptist population leaped from 161 to 385 (*Monroe Baptist Association Minutes*, 1830–32). The combined Methodist-Baptist membership was only slightly below that of the Presbyterians, both immediately before and after the Finney revival. (See *The Minutes of the General Assembly of the Presbyterian Church in the U.S.A.* for 1830 and 1832.) With the working class involved in the 1830–31 revival, the progression of evangelicalism from bourgeoisie to proletariat is no longer evident, and Johnson's "social control through religion" argument can no longer be seen as central to revivalism in Rochester.

church members had no property compared to 23 percent countywide (Table B.4). Evangelical church members had virtually the same occupational profile as the remainder of the county (Table B.6). Wealth and status-oriented social control thus was not a factor in the revivals of the 1830s because the differences between evangelicals and their neighbors were minimal.

Wealth did influence religion in the county during the 1830s but in the opposite direction suggested by social control theorists. Instead of trying to increase evangelical churches' control over members' lives and the local community, wealthy citizens frequently sought to undermine the power of local congregations.

The local religious societies, not the evangelical churches, were the power base of Cortland County's upper echelon. Joining a society involved no religious confession and posed no threat to personal autonomy. Religious societies served as refuges for minimalists, who resented the corporate church's authority over the private and public lives of its members. In the early 1830s, joining a religious society was a genuine alternative to church membership. By this time, the majority of county churches had built worship houses and were legally required to be supported by religious societies that owned all church property.

The well-to-do found religious societies eminently attractive, and as a result, these organizations were invariably wealthier than the churches they supervised. In 1832 the Cortland Baptist Society gathered pledges for building a new meetinghouse from eighty-five men. Only 38 percent of the society's contributors were members of any church. Forty percent of the society's members owned more than fifty acres of land in 1835 compared to 23 percent of the male church members who were household heads. The same year, the Union Congregational Society circulated a similar subscription list. Less than half of the signers were church members. As in Cortland, the signers were wealthier than the church members, although by smaller margins; 25 percent of society members owned fifty or more acres compared to 17 percent of church members. No society member was landless whereas 7 percent of male church members were. Examinations of subscription lists from four different religious societies between 1832 and 1861 revealed that all were slightly to vastly wealthier than the churches they supported.[3]

3. For a complete list of the four societies, see Chapter 4, note 9.

The wealthy minimalists within the religious societies tried to curtail the enthusiasm of the revivals of the 1820s and 1830s. A Methodist contemporary, L. D. Davis, argued that the decade of the 1820s, when the Cortland Methodists had "a good church, a large congregation, and an excellent minister," was "one of the most perilous periods in the history of this people." The reason for this gloomy assessment was that the Cortland Church was "so feeble, that deprived of the aid of friends without [the Cortland Methodist Society], it could not sustain the interests of a station." This situation was deemed dangerous because ministers and congregations "not unfrequently conform to the wishes of irreligious persons, who kindly consent to relieve them of their precuniary burdens and consequently become, in a great measure, conformed to the world around them." Minimalist pressure from the society to water down Methodist preaching was averted because "God . . . preserved them from the threatened danger."[4]

In the early 1830s, minimalists led a successful coup in the Homer Congregational Church. After assuming the pulpit in 1822, the Reverend John Keep often offended minimalist sensitivities by advocating religious positions on private and public moral issues. Keep alienated wealthy conservatives by attacking alcohol (a major local consumable in the 1820s) and by denouncing slaveholders (important trading partners in Baltimore).[5] Keep's use of Finney's revivalistic New Measures brought such opposition that he wrote a book-length apologetic in response to the criticism.[6] In 1833 wealthy merchant Jedediah Barber and his cronies decided that they had had enough of John Keep. The dissidents met at Barber's Great Western Store and planned the minister's resignation. Their efforts succeeded even though a majority of the congregation wanted Keep to continue. How did Barber, who was not a church member, have so much clout? As one of the richest and most influential men in the Religious Society of Homer, Barber, along with his friends, threatened to withdraw financial support from the Homer Congregational Church. Rather than lose that funding, the church acquiesced. Barber and his fellow minimalists won a further victory when the

---

4. Davis, *History of the Methodist Episcopal Church*, pp. 84–87.
5. Herbert Barber Howe, *Paris Lived in Homer* (Cortland, 1968), pp. 18–19.
6. Keep's defense, *A Narrative of the Origin and Progress of the Congregational Church in Homer, N.Y., with Remarks*, was published in 1833 by the Homer printing firm of Kinney and Aikin.

next two Homer Congregational ministers were forbidden to speak on controversial social issues, thus restricting the church's ability to influence public and private morality.[7] Keep's successors were allowed to preach "personal salvation," but they presumably did so in a comparatively restrained manner.

The locus of Cortland County's wealth was not in the evangelical churches but in the religious societies, which wealthy minimalists could use as a base to restrict the power of the county's corporate churches. They were not seeking to expand the power of local congregations so as to discipline the lower classes. Rather, the elite sought to hamstring evangelical fellowships for fear that they might judge the values and behavior of the wealthy and find them wanting. Far from promoting revivals and the evangelical ethos, wealthy minimalists sought to restrict the impact of the corporate church both in social action and in the realm of personal salvation.

The third class-oriented argument contends that market orientation shaped attitudes toward religion and politics. According to this theory, there were two classes of agriculturalists—subsistence farmers and commercial farmers. Subsistence farmers were forced by lack of access to markets to value self-reliance and independence. These farmers would naturally gravitate toward denominations and political organizations that shared subsistence values. The Democratic party, eulogizer of the common man, and Methodism, with its Arminian theology, both emphasized the right of ordinary people to choose. Thus these groups were particularly popular among noncommercial farmers. Farmers who were integrated into local and regional markets, on the other hand, benefited from their position in the economic hierarchy. They also saw the value of improved transportation and the advantages of cooperative, organized solutions to common problems. The commercial farmers' worldview endorsed hierarchy, order, and organization, values that fit nicely with Calvinism (particularly the formal variety of the Congregationalists and the Presbyterians) and with the Whig party platform.

Part of the market orientation argument works very well in Cortland County. One of the best indicators of market penetra-

7. Howe, *Paris Lived in Homer*, pp. 18–19; Minutes of the Cortland Presbytery, September 10, 1833.

tion within a community is the amount of homemade cloth produced per capita. As the market became more efficient, farm women made less cloth at home, preferring to channel their energy into cash-producing activities and buy cloth at local stores. A general rule is that the lower the per capita production of homemade cloth, the greater the community's market integration. If the market orientation argument is correct, one would expect a positive correlation in Cortland County's towns between per capita cloth production (a subsistence economic function) and Democratic vote. Such a relationship does exist: the 1836 Democratic vote has a .51 correlation with per capita cloth production in 1835. One would also expect Methodists to vote more heavily Democratic than Calvinists. From 1832 to 1834, in the town of Cortlandville, 47 to 61 percent of Methodist voters cast Democratic ballots compared to 19 to 30 percent of the Baptists, 20 to 21 percent of the Presbyterians, and 8 to 23 percent of the Congregationalists.[8]

8. Evangelicals in the town of Cortlandville, like Cortlandville residents generally, gave only a small share of their votes to the Democratic party in the early 1830s. In the elections of 1832 and 1834, the Jacksonians received 36 percent of the town's vote. Formal evangelicals were least likely to vote Democratic. Congregationalists gave 8 to 23 percent and Presbyterians 20 to 21 percent of their votes to the Democrats. Baptists were slightly under the county average with 19 to 30 percent. Universalists (36 to 44 percent) and those with no or unknown church background (39 to 41 percent) were slightly more Jacksonian than the county at large. The Methodists had the strongest Democratic orientation, casting 47 to 61 percent of their votes in the Jacksonian column. Overall, antiformalists were consistently more Democratic than formalists.

The data for the above calculations come from a list of Democratic partisans in an 1832 issue of the *Cortland Advocate* and from Cortlandville residents who answered the Whig call to protest Jackson's bank policies in an August 1834 issue of the *Cortland Republican*. The names in these lists were then matched with lists of male church members in the years 1832–35. The political lists often gave only first initials and surnames so two lists of politically involved churchmen were created: a "minimum" one giving links between religious and political rosters that could be made with certainty and a "maximum" one including possible matches as well as certain identifications.

The above percentages were arrived at by first dividing the minimum and maximum number of church members in each denomination by the proportion of each party's vote represented on each list. Thus the number of church members on the 1832 Democratic roster was divided by .590 and the number on the 1834 Whig list was divided by .532. If the lists are representative of the town's voters, dividing by .590 and .532 will yield the approximate number of church members voting for each party. The number of Whig and Democratic church members in each denomination was then totaled. The Democratic percentage was derived by dividing the number of Democrats by the total number of Whigs and Democrats in

The market explanation breaks down when one tries to link an underdeveloped market with Methodism. If the market hypothesis is correct, one would expect significant homemade cloth production (a sure sign of underdevelopment) in areas of Methodist strength and little cloth production in places where Methodism was weak. In short, one would expect a positive relationship between cloth production and Methodism when data from the county's towns are correlated. Unfortunately for the market explanation, the relationship between Methodism and homemade cloth production is negative. The correlation between the number of Methodist churches per capita in 1845 and cloth production per capita in 1835 is −.09. When the same church data are compared to cloth production in 1845, the result is −.37. For 1855, the percentage of Methodists in each town correlates negatively (−.28) with per capita cloth production. The consistently negative relationship between homemade cloth production and Methodist popularity suggests that underdeveloped markets did not predispose local residents toward Methodism.

The most damaging argument against the market explanation is that it runs counter to the county's religious history. Between its founding and the Civil War, Cortland County gradually moved from a subsistence to a market economy. If the market orientation hypothesis is correct, one would expect Methodism to wither and Calvinism to flourish as more and more individuals adopted a commercial perspective. In actuality, the opposite happened. Methodism grew in strength as the market penetrated the county's farthest reaches. By 1860 the Methodists had become the largest single denomination, and Arminian theology with its emphasis on individual free choice had conquered the Calvinist doctrine of election.

None of the three class or wealth-oriented arguments fits Cort-

---

that denomination. Each denomination's percentage was calculated twice, once using the maximum list and again using the minimum list. A range is given because the two calculations yielded slightly different figures.

Because of the lack of membership lists for the Cortland Methodist Church, a list of society members was used to determine Methodist voting behavior. Before these records were used, tests were run to see if society and church members voted similarly despite differing spiritual orientations. A comparison of the voting preferences of Homer Baptist and Homer Congregational society and church members showed no significant political differences. Thus it seemed reasonable to interpret the Cortland Methodist Society records in the same manner.

land County particularly well. The pure Marxian framework is not appropriate in this preindustrial rural setting because the vast majority of household heads controlled their own means of production. The contention that well-to-do evangelicals used revivals to control those of lesser means does not accurately describe the county for church members were not much different from their fellow citizens in wealth and occupation. When the wealthy had an impact, they sought to impose a minimalist perspective that limited evangelical influence. The market orientation hypothesis also fails in that no clear link can be established between subsistence agriculture and local preferences for Methodism. Furthermore, Methodism grew in influence and popularity as the market expanded within the county, a relationship that runs directly counter to market orientation theory.

In his recent study of Baltimore religion, Terry Bilhartz maintains that there are essentially two explanations for antebellum revivalism. "Demand-side" interpretations contend that the emotional religious upheavals of the early nineteenth century were created by changing economic and cultural conditions. William McLoughlin's argument about shifting cultural paradigms and Paul Johnson's theories about class conflict in Rochester are examples of the demand-side school. According to that theory, factors outside the church created a demand for religious renewal, causing revivals to grow in size and intensity during the 1820s and early 1830s. Bilhartz offers a "supply-side" interpretation. He contends that revivalism grew because churches became more committed to aggressive evangelism. The supply of protracted meetings and tent gatherings grew because evangelicals increased their efforts to produce such religious events.[9]

Just as economic studies become skewed if they focus only on supply or demand interpretations, investigations into antebellum religion become equally shaky if one side of the equation is emphasized to the exclusion of the other. Persuasive cases can be made for both approaches in Cortland County. On the demand side, the growth in republican values of independence and self-reliance created a predisposition for Methodist doctrine. Large revivals occurred in response to the Arminianization of Calvinism

---

9. Bilhartz, *Urban Religion*, pp. 91–99.

between 1815 and 1840. Women, barred from broad political and economic participation because of traditional cultural constraints, sought to discover independence and leadership in the religious sphere. As a result, they became the driving force within the county's corporate churches. Their efforts to win souls redoubled in the early 1830s, when their children began leaving the community in unprecedented numbers. On the supply side, the churches that were most successful in evangelism were also those in greatest need of converts. Once churches became viable and financially secure, they no longer had a great need for converts and their evangelism indexes declined. Unusually intense revivalism occurred in 1816–19 because churches were desperately seeking institutional viability and in 1830–34 because congregations struggled against heavy out-migration to maintain membership levels.

Cortland County's religious revivalism reached a crescendo in the early 1830s largely because two prerequisites for evangelism were fulfilled to an unusual degree. The first, that salvation be deemed vitally important, was met by several groups. Women, fearful for their soon-to-depart offspring, ardently sought the salvation of their children. Churches, fighting the draining effects of out-migration, had to convert large numbers to survive. Small, struggling congregations, which were at the greatest risk, fought hardest of all. But the second precondition, that people believe they can have an impact on the salvation of themselves and others, was also fulfilled in unprecedented proportions. John Keep and Jedediah Burchard sought to destroy years of Calvinist complacency. As startled churchgoers came to believe they could choose to be saved, several hundred responded. The New Measures provided numerous outlets for those who sought to encourage the salvation of kinfolk and neighbors. As Arminian doctrine and New Measures spread to nearby Calvinist churches, the second precondition was met throughout Cortland County.

PART III

DIVIDED CHURCHES,

1826–1846

7

Discipline and the Island Mentality

Between 1826 and 1846, Cortland County's evangelical churches were split by the evangelicals' new emphasis on freedom of the will, which triggered a wide-ranging assault on the religious authority of the county's congregations. Before the mid-1820s, local evangelical churches maintained their position as islands of holiness in a world they perceived as sinful. County fellowships were corporate churches in that each religious body demanded that members yield significant autonomy to the congregation. Religious beliefs and everyday behavior were largely governed by the local religious fellowship, not by individual conscience. Strict regulation of thought and action was considered necessary if the corporate church was to maintain its purity as a "city upon a hill."

Vigorous discipline was central to the functioning of the corporate church. The "island mentality," the sense of evangelical alienation from the larger community, drew its strength from the discipline process. Essentially, churches were subcommunities within the larger society of the county. As a community, each church needed to define itself, and the clearest way to do so was by delineating acceptable and unacceptable behavior. Church members knew they were separate from the world because they did not participate in worldly behavior. Sociologist Kai Erikson explains: "People who live together in communities cannot relate to one another in any coherent way or even acquire a sense of their own stature as group members unless they learn something about the boundaries of the territory they occupy in social space, if only because they need to sense what lies beyond the margins of the group before they can appreciate the special quality of the experience which takes place within it." Boundaries are defined and maintained essentially through the punishment of deviance. Erikson argues that "on the whole, members of a community inform one another about the placement of their boundaries by participating in the confrontations which occur when persons who venture out to the edges of the group are met by policing agents whose special interest it is to guard the cultural integrity of the community."[1] In Cortland County's corporate churches, discipline established the boundaries between local evangelicals and nearby worldly folk by punishing evangelical flirtations with worldly activity. In addition, church governance provided sanctions against members who dared to challenge congregational edicts regarding proper Christian behavior. As long as these procedures remained strong, the line dividing the "godly" from the "damned" remained clear and county churches successfully maintained the island mentality.

Discipline proceedings varied little among denominations. Upon notice of alleged misconduct, visitation committees were formed to investigate the charges. If there was substantial reason to believe the accusations were true, the committee urged the offender to repent. If the accused refused to listen to the visitation committee, the matter went before the entire church (or in the case of Presbyterians, before the session or board of elders) and the case was tried. If the accused was found guilty and he or she refused to admit and cease wrongdoing, the individual was excommunicated from the congregation.

Recognizing the importance of effective discipline in evangelical church life, local ministers urged uncompromising enforcement of Christian standards from the beginning of the nineteenth century. Corporate church leaders knew that many prospective members were hesitant to yield personal autonomy over their lives, so the evangelical leadership made submission to the authority of the church a membership requirement. The Madison Baptist Association stated in 1817 that "great care is necessary, not only to learn that a candidate for the church of Christ, professes to

1. Kai Erikson, *Wayward Puritans: A Study in the Sociology of Deviance* (New York, 1966), pp. 10–11.

have experienced a change of heart; but that he is sound in faith, and willing to conform to the discipline of Christ's house."[2] Other precautions were used in addition to screening members for potentially rebellious attitudes. Some churches made the right of the congregation to correct its members a part of the Articles of Faith and Practice.[3] Thus when new members accepted the articles, they agreed to bend to church authority.

Although it is clear that all local evangelical churches were ideologically committed to maintaining group norms, statistical measures are necessary to compare the use of discipline across denominational lines and over time. One very helpful measure is the excommunication index, which indicates the number of exclusions a church had annually per one hundred members. The conviction rate is another useful statistic. This percentage is obtained by dividing the number of exclusions by the number of cases in any given time period.

In spite of ideological agreement on the importance of church discipline, the four denominations varied significantly in enforcement. Antiformalists, who stressed personal piety over organizational activity, placed enormous importance on maintaining behavioral guidelines. The conduct of both male and female members was observed carefully. Between 1801 and 1819, eighty men and forty-six women were charged with wrongdoing by the Homer and Truxton Baptist churches.[4] Overall, the Baptist excommunication index for 1801 to 1819 was about five times greater than the Congregationalist index (Table C.3). The scant information available on the Methodists indicates that they followed discipline procedures with nearly the same intensity as the Baptists. From 1825 to 1827, the Cincinnatus Methodists had an excommunication index of 1.13, which was far above the Congregational and Presbyterian rates for the same period.[5]

Congregationalists, the county's dominant formalist group between 1801 and 1819, were far too busy developing church proj-

2. *Minutes of the Madison Baptist Association,* 1817, p. 11.
3. For example, see Homer Congregational Church, Minutes, Articles of Faith and Practice, Articles 11–17, and Scott Baptist Church, Record Book, Covenant and Articles of Faith and Practice, Article 15.
4. Cortland First Baptist Church, Record Books, 1801–19; Solon First Baptist Church, Minutes, 1807–19.
5. Calculated from membership roster in Cincinnatus Methodist Class Book, 1825–27, Cincinnatus Town Collection, 1825–65, CCHS.

ects, providing community education, introducing religious innovations, and encouraging evangelism to expend much effort on
discipline. Because inculcating personal piety was only one of
their concerns, Congregationalists were reluctant to devote much
energy to correcting petty problems. Only the worst and most
obvious misdeeds were punished. As a result, the Truxton, Freetown, and Homer Congregationalists, with a larger combined
membership than the Homer and Truxton Baptist churches,
charged only twenty-three persons with wrongdoing between
1801 and 1819. Unlike the pietistic antiformal Baptists and Methodists, Congregationalists sought to discourage, not totally eradicate, sin within the local fellowship.

Despite the differences between formalists and antiformalists,
the discipline policies of the corporate churches between 1801
and 1819 were effective because of a widespread acceptance of
the congregation's right to rule. The small number of new cases
arising each year suggest that few evangelicals challenged group
norms. During the first decade and a half of the nineteenth
century, Cortland County churches averaged only one new case
per year (Table C.5).

Transcripts and descriptions of church trials provide further
evidence that evangelicals generally accepted the right of the
corporate church to govern their everyday lives. Between 1801
and 1819, church members accused of violating a religious ordi-
nance rarely used the occasion to challenge ecclesiastical authority. Defendants usually meekly bowed to the judgment of the local
congregation. When a Homer Baptist committee questioned
Brother Babcock in 1804 on his failure to attend church, Babcock
pledged to "attend more steady" in the future. Ten years later, a
similar committee questioned Brother Crandall and reported that
it "found him comfortable wishing to keep his place in the
church."[6] During the century's first two decades, no member of
the five congregations studied challenged the right of a local
fellowship to rule on his or her alleged misbehavior. Occasionally,
a defendant might ask for an outside church council to ensure
impartiality, but this action was equivalent to appealing to a
higher court, not rejecting the rule of law. Generally, people

6. Cortland First Baptist Church, Record Books, July 14, 1804, January 5,
1814.

who were eventually excommunicated "had no ears to hear the church" and failed to appear for their trial. Such members who were eventually excluded did not confront the religious fellowships; they simply walked away.

Failure to redeem the fallen brother or sister was the exception rather than the rule between 1801 and 1819. The offending member usually repented of his or her misdeeds, and few discipline cases ended in exclusion. Of the twenty-three individuals investigated in the Homer, Freetown, and Truxton Congregational churches, only 6 (26 percent) were eventually excommunicated. Only 23 percent (29 of 126) of the Homer and Truxton Baptist members brought under discipline were eventually excluded.

The corporate church was based on the effective discipline of its members. Only the conscientious enforcement of behavioral standards could maintain internal purity, a sense of group identity, and an attitude of separation from the world. The system worked exceptionally well in Cortland County between 1801 and 1819. No one challenged the churches' right to shape their members' lives. Cases were few in number. On those rare occasions when church norms were violated, most members accepted the verdict of their peers, asked for forgiveness, and meekly returned to their place within the congregation. Before 1820 church discipline was a sturdy barrier against worldliness and was instrumental in maintaining the integrity of the corporate church.

8

Competition Disrupts
the Evangelical Order

Before 1820 four evangelical denominations dominated the religious life of Cortland County. Congregationalists and Presbyterians cooperated under the Plan of Union. Baptists received grudging respect from their fellow Calvinists despite different theories regarding the sacraments. All three Calvinist groups had doubts about the Methodists in spite of the latter's protestations of Christian orthodoxy. Despite interdenominational debates over pedobaptism versus adult baptism, formalism versus antiformalism, and Calvinism versus Arminianism, the four Protestant denominations shared an evangelical orthodoxy. As long as religious discussion was restricted to the beliefs of these evangelical groups, only the peripheral aspects of faith could be disputed— not its essentials. With debate limited and evangelical hegemony secure, the corporate church remained essentially unchallenged.

During the 1820s, the heavy influx of migrants from outside Cortland County undermined the corporate church's position within society. During the county's early years, religious fellowships were the first and, in many areas, the only social institutions. One reason why so many nonevangelicals joined religious societies was that the church performed a social function that relieved the tedium of frontier life. The rapid in-migration of the 1820s undercut the churches' social monopoly. As the population density increased, it became easier to find alternative social outlets. Between 1820 and 1825, the number of distilleries within the

94

county grew by more than 50 percent.[1] One may assume that taverns and other "watering holes" proliferated as well. Balls and dances were organized in the county's villages and larger hamlets. Horse racing was another local pastime. By 1830 those who wanted to find God went to church; those who simply wanted social interaction and amusement went elsewhere.

The evangelical establishment was hardly immune to the onslaught of reinvigorated worldliness. Churchgoing parents were apparently satisfied with the somewhat staid religious traditions, but their offspring sought to dabble in the newly available frivolities. Predictably, discipline proceedings were initiated against those engaging in temptations. In May 1819 Joseph Simson was excluded from the Homer Congregational Church for cardplaying and attending balls.[2] The Truxton Congregationalists tried Miles Dunbar for having "spent his time improperly at Taverns and grogshops."[3] The Homer Baptists fought the tide of worldliness with the most vigor. In the 1820s, Charlotte Collins was excluded because she "had been in young company with the world and had joined with them in their vain amusements."[4] Other serious charges included gambling, intemperance, joining "in vain amusements such as plays and dancing," having "joined loose company," and the ubiquitous catch-all of having "joined in affinity with the world." All evangelical churches struggled with increasing external temptations. Charges of worldliness more than doubled between the 1810s and 1820s, and accusations of worldly behavior grew from 13 percent of all charges in the 1810s to 17 percent in the 1820s (Table C.1).

Religious competition was even more threatening than secular amusements. The four-denomination monopoly dissolved in the 1820s in the face of massive and religiously diverse in-migration. Each of the major evangelical groups would be challenged by a traditional adversary in the next decade and a half. Sometimes the opponent would differ theologically in only the smallest details. Other times the incoming group would be the reverse image of

1. Spafford, *Gazetteer* (1824), p. 134; *Census of the State of New York for 1825*, Senate Journal, 49th sess., 1826, Appendix A.

2. Homer Congregational Church, Minutes, March 11, May 16, 1819.

3. Truxton First Presbyterian Church, Record Book, February 11, March 3, 1825.

4. Cortland First Baptist Church, Record Books, April 16, August 27, 1825.

the evangelical group already present. In these cases, the old and the new had only a mutual denominational ancestry in common. During the 1820s and 1830s, Cortland County's religious portrait would fracture into a kaleidoscopic array of diverse theologies.

Cortland County's Baptists received the first challenge. In the late 1810s, a few Seventh Day Baptists filtered into the northern part of the county, and in 1820 they established a fellowship in the town of Scott. This new group shared much with the Regular Baptists long present in the county. The chief dispute was over whether the Sabbath was the first or seventh day. The same year the Open Communion Baptists, also called Free Will Baptists, organized a church in the town of Virgil. This variation differed from the Regulars in that its theology was Arminian and it had no qualms about sharing the communion table with believers who had been baptized as children, not as adults.[5]

The presence of two new Baptist groups undercut the authority of the Regular Baptists, and doctrinal controversy quickly invaded existing Baptist congregations. Slowly, the Open Communion Baptists began to draw off members from the Regulars. In 1821 Billy Trowbridge was excluded from the Truxton fellowship for wanting to join a church with different views on communion. A few years later, John Dyer was excluded by the Homer Baptists for questioning the doctrine of election. In 1827 the same fellowship investigated Ruhannah Phelps and Clarissa Smith for opposing the church's closed communion stance.[6]

If the Open Communion Baptists posed a chronic problem, the Seventh Day Baptists produced an acute crisis for Regular Baptists in Scott. For years, the Scott fellowship had struggled to survive against small numbers, weak finances, and internal division. In 1818 a council of outside churches met and restored order among most parishioners and excommunicated the rest. But many still in the church wanted to leave. The organization of the rival Seventh Day Baptist Church in 1820 intensified problems within the older congregation. From 1821 to 1831, at least eleven people were expelled from the Regular Baptist Church for their

---

5. Goodwin, *Pioneer History*, p. 190.
6. Solon First Baptist Church, Minutes, July 29, 1820, March 15, 1821; Cortland First Baptist Church, Record Books, December 16, 1826, February 16, 1828, December 15, 1827, June 14, 1828, February 17, 1827, June 16, 1827.

Sabbatarian views.[7] The Seventh Day controversy may have triggered other forms of rebellion because the Scott Baptist excommunication rate soared to 6.9 exclusions per 100 members annually between 1820 and 1824.

Increased resistance to church authority was hardly unique to the Scott Baptist Church. As the two Baptist variations undercut the doctrinal authority of the Regulars, the frequency of exclusions in local churches doubled. Countywide, Baptist excommunication rates rose sharply from 1.05 in 1815–19, to 1.68 in 1820–24, to 2.11 in 1825–29 (Table C.3).

Theological liberalism had struck fear in the hearts of the county's Congregationalists and Presbyterians since the first decade of the nineteenth century. The pedobaptist Calvinists who were early settlers were well aware of the theological wars in New England, where liberals had battled conservatives for control of the pulpit and ownership of the worship house. The Unitarians were the primary opponents in New England, but Universalists came to be held in equal suspicion by the orthodox as the two liberal theological systems grew closer in doctrine.[8]

From the very beginning, orthodox Calvinists entering Cortland County raised bulwarks against heterodoxy, condemning the distinctive doctrines of both Unitarianism and Universalism. In 1805 the Virgil Congregational Church placed denial "of the divinity of Christ" and "the future and endless punishment of . . . all that die impenitent" on its list of "heresies."[9] Adherence to any doctrine on the list would disqualify prospective members and lead to the excommunication of any liberal who had earlier been accepted into membership. Other Congregational and Presbyterian churches resisted Unitarian and Universalist doctrine with equal ferocity. Until the 1830s, orthodox Congregationalists and Presbyterians had few tangible reasons for concern. Around 1808, a Universalist fellowship met in the southern part of the town of Homer, but the group never really established itself, struggled for a few years, and then disappeared from public view.[10]

7. French, *Gazetteer*, p. 254; Scott Baptist Church, Record Book, June 23, 1821, July 6, 1822, May 3, 1829, August 21, 1830.
   8. Ahlstrom, *Religious History*, 1:477–88, 582–84.
   9. Virgil Presbyterian Church, Church Book of Virgil, Articles of Practice.
   10. Local sources are not clear whether the first group of Universalists dis-

The liberal challenge was far more formidable in the 1830s, when Universalist churches were founded in Virgil (1831), Cortland village (1835), and Homer (1839).[11] But Universalism did not remain isolated within the county's liberal fellowships. Before 1830 no local Congregationalist or Presbyterian had been dismissed for heterodox beliefs, but now a steady stream of disputants began to question traditional doctrine. In 1831 the Preble Presbyterians excluded Lawrence Van Valkenburg, in part for "disbelief of certain parts of the Bible."[12] The same year, the Truxton Congregationalists charged Melancton Burhans with "having embraced the Doctrine of Universal Salvation." Three years later, the same charge was leveled at Leurtus Burhans. Both were eventually expelled.[13] In 1834 James Bennet was ousted from the Freetown Congregational Church for "indirectly Supporting the Doctrin of Universal Salvation of All mankind."[14] Even worse than lay heresy, in the presbytery's view, was the spread of liberal ideas among the clergy. In 1834 the Cortland Presbytery excommunicated the Reverend Joshua Leonard, pastor of the Scott Congregational Church, for denying the Trinity and the authority of the presbytery.[15] Like the Baptists, Congregationalists and Presbyterians watched as new religious alternatives undercut their influence. No longer did those interested in religion have to choose one of the four major denominations.

The burst of Universalist activity in the 1830s was a male-oriented minimalist response to changes in Calvinist theology. As long as Congregationalists and Presbyterians believed that "God chose whom He will," minimalists—who wanted no congrega-

---

banded. Smith suggests an early demise (*History of Cortland County*, p. 272). However, *History: All Souls' First Universalist Church* indicates that circuit riders occasionally addressed local Universalists between 1815 and 1831 (pp. 28–29). In either case, Universalists were without congregational organization, a worship house, regular preaching, and visibility among the public until the 1830s. Also see Blodgett, *Stories of Cortland County*, pp. 222–23.

11. Goodwin, *Pioneer History*, pp. 174, 190; *History: All Souls' First Universalist Church*, p. 29.

12. Preble First Presbyterian Church, Book of Discipline, March 1, April 25, 1831, Accession No. 6256, CUA.

13. Truxton First Presbyterian Church, Record Book, February 15, 1831, September 22, 1832, January 15, July 16, 1834, membership list.

14. Cincinnatus First Congregational Church, Records, February 1, April 26, June 15, 1834.

15. Minutes of the Cortland Presbytery, June 18, September 9, 1834.

tional influence over their private and public lives—could reign over the religious societies, reap the social benefits from such philanthropy, and comfortably wait for some future religious experience. Since such an event could only come through divine instigation, there was no disgrace in not being among the "hopefully converted." The introduction of the New Measures and Arminian theology into Calvinist churches destroyed the old formula. Failure to be redeemed was no longer the fault of God—only stubborn willfulness kept one from being saved. Minimalists were now on the defensive. Yielding to God meant accepting the church's authority over one's personal life—a move no minimalist took lightly. Refusing to be redeemed, according to revised Calvinism, was an admission that one was a hardened, unrepentant sinner—hardly a position of great social prestige.

Minimalism maintained at best an uneasy coexistence with recently Arminianized Calvinism. Some men repudiated the new development and disappeared from the religious society rosters while others remained in the societies and steadfastly resisted family pressure to convert. Many capitulated to the new doctrine and became full evangelicals. Some men, however, chose to join a church that was free from fervent evangelicalism. They chose Universalism, which, like traditional Calvinism, did not stress the need to seek immediate salvation. This complacency regarding redemption, however, was due to the Universalist rejection of ultimate damnation, not to a lack of belief in free will.

Unlike evangelicalism, Universalism had much more support among men than women. All nine local Calvinists excluded between 1830 and 1860 for theological liberalism were men. In 1835, when the First Universalist Church was formally organized in Cortland, 66 of the 101 founding members were men. The governing documents of the new church fit the minimalist perspective. As was the case with the Religious Society of Homer, a major function of the Universalist Church and Society was "the promotion of religion, morality and good order in society." Discipline procedures were very different from those of evangelical fellowships. The covenant promised that "we will not disfellowship or reject any brother or sister, merely on account of a difference of faith on particular points of doctrine." The Universalists investigated only cases of "immoral or unchristian conduct." The emphasis was on love and acceptance, not congregational purity.

In the worst case, when all efforts at reconciliation had failed, the Universalists promised to "pass no other sentence or judgment against any irreclaimable member than barely withdrawing the hand of fellowship."[16] Among the Universalists, an independent-minded man could be free of church interference in his private affairs and worship his God in peace.

The presence of theologically liberal churches, which shared the Congregationalists' and Presbyterians' historic ties to New England rationalism, clearly threatened local fellowships. As late as 1859, the Cortland Presbyterian Church excommunicated Stephen Brewer for attending lectures at the "Stone Church." Brewer argued that his doctrine was totally orthodox. He had simply gone to hear Wendell Phillips, Ralph Waldo Emerson, William Lloyd Garrison, and other prominent lecturers. The session did not consider such a defense sufficient, believing that if Brewer continued to visit the Universalist Church on the Sabbath, Presbyterian young people might do the same, being "led astray" by his example.[17] Prosecuting Stephen Brewer was a last-ditch effort to retain ecclesiastical authority in the face of liberal religion. The real battle had occurred between 1825 and 1844, however, when Congregational and Presbyterian excommunication rates were high, partly because of the Universalist challenge.

In 1831 the Calvary Episcopal Church was organized in Homer. Just as the Universalists provided an antiformalist nonevangelical reverse image of formal evangelical Calvinism, the Episcopalians offered a formal nonevangelical alternative to antiformal evangelical Methodism. Just as Universalism and Congregationalism had a shared background, the Methodists had once been a pietistic subgroup within the Episcopal church, then broke away in 1784.[18] Local records do not reveal the Methodist response to the Episcopalian presence in Cortland County, but the early cross-denominational support for the fledgling Calvary fellowship came from fellow formalists, not from Methodist sources.[19]

16. *History: All Souls' First Universalist Church*, pp. 29, 31–33.
17. *Proceedings of the Trial of Stephen Brewer before the Presbyterian Church of Cortland Village* (Cortland, 1859).
18. Ahlstrom, *Religious History*, 1:449–52.
19. For example, in 1823 and in 1828, the Reverend John Keep invited the Reverend Reuben Hubbard, rector of St. James Episcopal Church in Danbury, Connecticut, to speak at the Homer Congregational Church. Hubbard's visit to Homer may have encouraged the formation of the county's first Episcopal church in that village three years later. See Smith, *History of Cortland County*, p. 230.

The Christian Connection entered the county in the late 1820s and established congregations in Virgil and LaPeer in 1827–28.[20] The two small fellowships appear to have merged into the Harford Christian Church by 1839.[21] A second Christian church was organized in Cortlandville the same year.[22]

The Christian sect was originally formed in an attempt to unite all Christians in one large body. The attempt at unity failed and the Christians became just another denomination.[23] Of all the religious groups, the Christians were the most antiformal as no member is known to have participated in any local nonreligious community organization.[24]

Chart 1. The ideological configuration of Cortland County churches in 1840

	Formal	Antiformal
Evangelical	Congregationalists Presbyterians	Baptists (Regular, Seventh Day, Open Communion) Methodists
Nonevangelical	Episcopalians	Universalists Christians

By 1840 each of the major denominations had an opponent with which it shared a common background and important theological differences. The Regular Baptists fought Open Communion and Seventh Day Baptists, the Presbyterians and Congregationalists contended with Universalists, and the Methodists saw the arrival of their parent denomination, the Episcopalians. In the first two cases the newcomers directly challenged doctrinal views of the original and dominant denominations. In the latter two, recent arrivals undercut evangelical authority by providing reverse-image nonevangelical alternatives.

From the days of the Homer Religious Society, Cortland Coun-

20. Goodwin, *Pioneer History*, pp. 190, 258.
21. Harford Christian Church of Christ, Minutes, 1839–61, Accession No. 6243, CUA.
22. Smith, *History of Cortland County*, p. 318.
23. Ahlstrom, *Religious History*, 1:485, 541.
24. This lack of voluntarist involvement fits the extreme antiauthoritarian, antigovernment stance of Christians elsewhere in New York. See Rowe, *Thunder and Trumpets*, pp. 28–29, 74, 77, 85–86.

ty residents defended their religious viewpoints through reason, experience, and Scripture. Despite some major differences, members of the four major denominations had formed an evangelical consensus that grew stronger as the Calvinists gradually Arminianized. The coming of five more denominational groups disrupted evangelical hegemony by introducing a host of new answers to residents' spiritual questions. Diversity undercut authority. How dare any religious group claim "truth" when one could find several different answers to religious questions by sampling the diverse denominational opinions on Church Street? Between 1801 and 1819, when evangelicals asked themselves, "Who is the enemy?" the answer was predictable. It was the world. By the 1830s, despite the growth in the number of worldly attractions, the answer was not so clear. To many church members, the threat most to be feared was not distant worldly pleasures but the church down the street.

9

Individualism and the Embattled Corporate Church

The growth in republican individualism from the 1820s through the early 1840s created increasing difficulties for Cortland County's corporate churches. With the freedom to choose among the growing number of secular and religious alternatives, the changing cultural climate had a devastating effect on evangelical religious organizations.

Traditionally, local Protestant churches maintained their corporate structure by screening out applicants who would not subject themselves to ecclesiastical authority. Obedience to the "gathered brethren" was a part of the covenant, and admission meant submission. Church demography was skewed toward women and the young, social segments conditioned to submit to authority. Men of the minimalist perspective did not apply for admission because the threat to personal autonomy was too great.

Until the late 1820s, church members generally accepted the church's all-encompassing governing role over their lives. It is true that members occasionally criticized ministers, but these were personal objections and not an attack on the church itself. Before 1824, the only time individuals attacked the church as a body was in a major dispute among Scott Baptists.[1] People sometimes failed to follow church directives. For instance, in 1815 John and Abigail Holmes were excommunicated for "refusing to hear

---

1. Scott Baptist Church, Record Book, December 19, 1818.

the church" on the subject of their nonattendance.[2] More typical was the attitude of Thaddeus Palmer before the Homer Baptist Church. On January 8, 1825, Palmer stated that "he thought the church had done their duty but he had not done his. He had many doubts and fears as to his adoption yet he thought sometimes he did take comfort in trying to pray. He confessed he had been out of the way and had neglected his travel with his brethren, that he now felt sorry and asked forgiveness."[3] Individuals might occasionally disobey church rules, but challenges to the church's authority to establish guidelines were rare.

The authority of the corporate church began to be questioned in the late 1820s and early 1830s, when some parishioners demonstrated significant resistance. Some of the earliest indicators of this defiance occurred in the Scott Baptist Church. In 1826 the Scott fellowship indicted "Brother Crumull Anthony for falswood and raling against the church." A year later, the same church "Voted to withdraw the hand of fellowship from Brother Assahel Thomas for Rayling against the Church and imbraicing false Doctrin." At about the same time, the Scott fellowship excluded Ansel Wilcox for "laughing in Meating" and Elisha Stevens for saying "hard words against the church."[4] Baptist authority was challenged in less direct ways as well. Ephraim Griswold and Isaac Kinney, Jr., chose to take their complaints to court rather than let the Truxton Baptist Church resolve a dispute between members.[5]

Resistance to ecclesiastical authority cut across denominational lines as Congregational and Presbyterian fellowships experienced unprecedented verbal assaults from their members. In 1824 Tappan Wilkinson accused the Union Congregational Church of "popery" because the church's articles "would hold its members whether they were witting or not."[6] Eight years later, the Freetown Congregationalists accused Sister Sanders of "laying unreasonable Charges and unchristian like sensure against the

2. Solon First Baptist Church, Minutes, May 3, September 2, 1815.
3. Cortland First Baptist Church, Record Book, January 8, 1825.
4. Scott Baptist Church, Record Book, May 27, 1826, May 5, 26, 1827, October 5, 1826, March 3, 1827.
5. Truxton Baptist Church, Record Book, February 25–July 1831, July 25, October 23, 1830.
6. Cincinnatus and Solon, Union Congregational Church, Records, February 3, 1824.

church."[7] The harshest attacks, however, were reserved for the elders who conducted church trials in the Presbyterian sessions. In 1828 Eli Morey stormed out of the Preble Presbyterian session which was investigating rumors regarding his drinking behavior. Later he informed the elders that he "did not wish to be hammered at any longer" and that "he would not live longer in this way continually harrassed by the Session on the Subject [of drinking] and wished to be rid of them." Three years after Morey was disfellowshipped, Lawrence Van Valkenburg was brought before the same body on a host of accusations. The session's messenger later reported that when Van Valkenburg was informed that he had been found guilty, he "appeared to be much enraged . . . and said, 'they [the Session] . . . had lied like the Devil, he could prove it . . . that he supposed he was now excommunicated or freed from them and that he was glad of it. I thank God,' said [Van Valkenburg] 'yes, glory to God, I am rid of them.'"[8]

Challenges to church authority in the late 1820s were not isolated, random events. In all three Calvinist denominations, complaints that members "refused to submit themselves to discipline," "had no regard for the discipline of the church," and "refused to hear the church" became increasingly common. As the rebellion grew, congregations sought to maintain the traditional power structure, which, in the face of widespread resistance, led to growing church caseloads. In the frontier era, the typical Baptist church could expect a new case once every six months. Between 1825 and 1834, the same church could expect to initiate new proceedings once every five to six weeks. Likewise, Congregationalists saw a nearly sixfold increase in the frequency of discipline cases between 1801–14 and 1825–34 (Table C.5). As the caseloads grew larger, so did excommunication rates. Between 1825 and 1829, Baptists annually excluded 2.1 communicants per 100 members, a rate double that of the first two decades. Congregationalist excommunication rates more than tripled those of earlier periods (Table C.3).

The massive revivals of the early 1830s brought a temporary lull in intracongregational controversy. Church resources were

7. Cincinnatus First Congregational Church, Records, February 25, 1832.
8. Preble First Presbyterian Church, Book of Discipline, February 18, March 31, May 19, 1828, April 25, 1831.

poured into converting friends, neighbors, and kinfolk, not into supervising the redeemed. Revivals were times of drawing in, not casting out. Often long-excluded former members would return to the fold amid tears of repentance. Restorations to full fellowship were more frequent during revivals than at any other time.[9] The respite did not last. Revival fires inevitably ebb, and by 1835 the county's corporate churches returned to the task of maintaining rather than expanding their "island" domains. Rising excommunication rates accompanied the shift in attention. Formalist exclusion rates rose in the late 1830s. By the early 1840s, Congregational and Baptist excommunication indexes were at near record levels and Presbyterian exclusion rates were higher than ever before (Table C.3).

A number of contemporary ministers and lay leaders, as well as a few twentieth-century historians, blamed relaxed procedures during the revivals of the early 1830s for the increasing numbers of excommunicants. At first glance, the argument appears to fit conditions in Cortland County. During protracted meetings, John Keep and other local New Measure men suspended the traditional propounding period, a time when the "hopefully converted" could demonstrate by their actions whether their conversion experience was genuine. Instead of requiring three to four weeks for propounding, Keep went against the advice of many of his parishioners and allowed all those confessing Christ to join the church immediately because "the design of a church is to form a nursery for spiritual children—or young converts." Once the revivals were over and church discipline cases began to monopolize business meetings, the New Measure men were blamed for letting so many new and untested converts into the fold.[10]

Closer analysis reveals that though the New Measures contributed significantly to increased exclusion rates, the relaxation of propounding rates had relatively little effect. If abandonment of traditional acceptance procedures was the key problem, one would expect most of those excluded to be young, financially

9. Between 1825 and 1845, on four occasions the Cortland Baptist Association had seven or more restorations in a year. In all four years (1830, 1831, 1838, and 1843), the association's evangelism index was above 10, which indicates that the restorations came in times of revival.

10. Keep, *Narrative*, p. 11. Keep responds to these accusations on pages 7–13. Also see Hotchkin, *History*, pp. 169–70.

insecure, and recent additions to the church. Most of those excluded from county churches between 1831 and 1844 do not fit this profile. First, most were not recent converts; the typical ex-communicant had been in the church for six years before being excluded. Although many recent converts were ejected (26 percent had been members for two years or less), they were more than balanced by seasoned church members (32 percent had been in the church for eleven or more years). Some of those excluded were long-standing patriarchs. Chester Kinney had been a member of the Cortland Baptist Church for thirty-five years, and twelve others had been members for twenty or more years. The list of those driven from the county's churches included deacons such as Orlanna Beebe of the Union Congregationalists and preachers such as Nathan Peck of the Cortland Baptists.[11] John Hooker of the Truxton Congregationalists and Etherel Brooks of the Cortland Baptists owned 250 and 150 acres of improved land, respectively, and were among the wealthiest 1 percent of Cortland County household heads.[12] Excluded household heads were about as wealthy as the typical county resident.[13] The surge in excommunications in the 1830s and 1840s involved members of widely varying ages, levels of wealth, and tenures as church members.

Clearly, rising excommunication rates involved much more than backsliding adolescents who, in the throes of religious excitement, had not counted the cost of joining an evangelical community. The growing exclusion rates can be tied in part to the continuing competition from secular and religious sources. Another factor was the drop in religious commitment that attended the inevitable decline in revivalistic ardor. The post-1834 disci-

11. Cincinnatus and Solon, Union Congregational Church, Records, November 21, 1834, October 28, 1836; Cortland First Baptist Church, Record Books, June 15, 1839.

12. Truxton First Presbyterian Church, Record Book, January 19, 1831; Cortland First Baptist Church, Record Books, August 15, 1835. The wealth figures are for 1835.

13. Sixty-six household heads excluded between 1825 and 1845 had virtually the same wealth profile as all evangelicals when the two groups were compared based on the 1835 census. Furthermore, the excommunicants' wealth profile was similar to that of household heads throughout Cortland County in 1835. Twenty-six percent of the excommunicants owned more than fifty acres compared to 18 percent countywide. Twenty-one percent of those excluded owned no land compared to 23 percent of all county household heads.

pline problems can also be linked to a fundamental shift in religious ideology. Critics and historians correctly relate rising exclusions to the introduction of the New Measures in the 1830s. They err, however, in assigning the entire problem to the change in propounding procedures.

The Finneyite message and methods changed attitudes toward the organized church in two ways. First, the introduction of Arminianized theology altered the ideological composition of entrants into the county's Calvinist churches. Before 1831 many residents declined to become members of Calvinist churches because the doctrine of election ran counter to American individualism. Once Finney's doctrines were proclaimed by John Keep, Jedediah Burchard, and others, many converted, convinced that salvation, like voting and commercial decisions, was a matter of free choice. In the 1830s, with the conflict between predestinarian theory and personal autonomy resolved, full-blown individualists comfortably joined local Calvinist churches. Once accepted into the church family, however, they were less willing than earlier converts to accept the guidance of the corporate church. Instead of following the guidelines of their religious community, many chose their own course of behavior and encouraged others to do the same. Thus the New Measure men undermined corporate church authority by removing the constraints that kept independent, less submissive Christians from seeking church membership.

Second, New Measures preaching undercut corporate church authority by undermining the theological consensus upon which the corporate church rested. Few local evangelicals realized that the Arminian doctrine that led to conversions would have a detrimental effect on church discipline. When local Finneyite enthusiasts such as John Keep stressed that each sinner, not God, was ultimately responsible for his or her eternal fate, they raised a disturbing question for the corporate church. If salvation was within the realm of individual free choice, why could not the individual Christian, guided by the Holy Spirit, be free to determine proper behavior? Finney's doctrine of perfectionism, which said that Christians could become "perfect," underscored this point.[14] If a Christian had attained a true state of Godlike holi-

14. McLoughlin, *Revivals, Awakenings, and Reform*, pp. 128–30; Ronald G. Walters, *American Reformers, 1815–1860* (New York, 1978), p. 28; Cross, *Burned-over District*, pp. 241–42.

ness, what right did any group have to pass judgment on his or her activities? In earlier decades, evangelicals were afraid to stand alone in a godless world and sought the help of their Christian brothers and sisters in withstanding temptation. Correction by the body of believers was recognized as necessary because the Devil might deceive individual believers and lead them astray. Because of these fears, "working out one's salvation" was a group activity. By the 1830s, when individual aspects of salvation were emphasized, the group was seen as less important. Armed with the Holy Spirit, evangelical perfectionists sought to obey their own consciences rather than follow the dictates of the gathered body. Sanctification was seen as a private affair; the spirit-filled Christian need not take corporate church directives very seriously. The New Measures men had taken American individualism, baptized it with Arminian and perfectionist doctrine, and set it loose to wreak havoc within the corporate church.

New Measure thinking regarding sanctification accompanied the revivals of the 1830s. The records of church discipline proceedings reveal a spirit of independence toward the corporate church. In 1844 Lucy Downs told the Preble Presbyterian session that it was wrong to punish her for nonattendance because she "did not believe in being bound to any one church."[15] In making this argument, Downs was contending that the individual, not the corporate church, reigned supreme and that people should be free to worship in the church of their choice on any given Sunday. Apparently, Downs preferred a spiritual smorgasbord to the limited menu offered by the Preble Presbyterians. A few years later, Hiram Bishop applied the individualistic ethic to church discipline. When accused by the Homer Congregational Church of selling alcoholic beverages, Bishop argued that the "church had no right to make bye-laws which should bind the conscience of any brother."[16] Bishop was contending that the individual, not the church, should be the ultimate judge of Christian behavior. In their separate testimonies, Downs and Bishop questioned the philosophical underpinnings of the corporate church.

Church finances suffered from the new independence of parishioners. Earlier in county history, when nearly everyone accepted the notion that membership involved yielding certain

15. Preble First Presbyterian Church, Book of Discipline, June 28, August 2, 1844.
16. Homer Congregational Church, Minutes, February 14, 1850.

rights to the corporate church, evangelicals did not challenge the congregation's right to extract money from its members. The most successful system, usually referred to as the "average" or "equality," based each household head's required contribution on the assessed value of his or her real estate and a mill levy, which was determined by a church committee. With these data the church could determine the appropriate tax to be charged to each property-owning member. Initially this brought little opposition. Between 1801 and 1829, only four county parishioners were brought to trial for failing to support their congregations financially. But after Arminianism had undermined the right of the corporate church to govern members' lives, rebellion against church taxing became widespread. Between 1830 and 1849, twenty-three evangelicals were accused of "failing to pay dues" or "refusing to support the gospel" (Table C.2). Amos Jones expressed this attitude best when he told the Cortland Baptist Church that "the 'taxing' as he termed it was wrong, and to him, appeared unscriptural."[17]

After 1835 the saints expressed their rebellion in escalating verbal attacks rather than calmly reasoned objections. For the first time, members voiced their criticism publicly. On December 22, 1835, John Thomas, a member of the Cortland Presbyterian Church, blasted the session in the *Cortland Republican*. In 1838 William Skiels, objecting to the Preble session's continuing his trial after he had confessed to all charges, "cast manny severe reflections on the Session, Said they wanted to disgrace him [and] Said he had no confidence in them."[18] In 1841 the Homer Congregationalists disciplined Jesse Harvey for "speaking lightly of his church relations and covenant obligations." A year later, the Homer church excluded Joshua Atwater because "he did not consider the preaching of the Pastor according to the Bible."[19] A few miles to the south, the Cortland Baptists struggled against rampant individualism. In 1844 they excluded Martin Kinney for "insubordination." A year later Parker Crosby condemned the Baptist church as "the offspring of the Mother of Harlots." Ira

17. Cortland First Baptist Church, Record Books, December 14, 1839, April 19, 1840.
18. Preble First Presbyterian Church, Book of Discipline, November 26, 1838.
19. Homer Congregational Church, Minutes, September 4, 1841, May 31, 1842.

Grant's attack on the congregation lacked Crosby's imagery but was more dangerous. Grant was "unyielding" in "denying the church as it exists being the Church of Christ." In making this argument, Grant assumed the position of judge, prosecuted the church for its doctrinal errors, and then condemned it as lacking Christian authority. It is hard to imagine a more direct assault on the corporate church; Grant reversed the traditional judge-defendant relationship between church and communicant. Not surprisingly, Grant was excommunicated.[20]

The revolt against ecclesiastical authority was not restricted to a few irate members but spread throughout the county's congregations. Traditional methods of discipline failed with increasing frequency. Originally, the purpose of church discipline was to maintain church purity and to reclaim the offending brother or sister. Before 1835 this strategy usually worked, as only 32 percent of cases ended in exclusion. After 1835 Baptist and Congregational conviction rates soared as churches found it much more difficult to induce repentance. Between 1835 and 1844, 53 percent of cases brought before Baptist congregations ended in exclusion and 61 percent of Congregational cases failed to reclaim the "wandering" member (Table C.4). Instead of producing repentance, church discipline brought increased resentment.

The clash between republican individualism and religious authority reached into the larger community. During the 1830s and 1840s, nonmembers were openly disrespectful in ways that earlier Cortlanders would have found shocking. Shortly before the end of his tenure at the Homer Congregational Church, the Reverend John Keep underwent the humiliation of having his horse sheared by anonymous town rowdies.[21] By 1841 the Reverend Dennis Platt had assumed the pastorate of the prestigious Homer church. On the night of July 5, Platt was perturbed when a group of drunken young men began firing weapons and caroused on the town green from midnight until near daylight. The sleep-starved minister "went out and attempted to reason with some of the young men on the impropriety of their course, but they resisted all his arguments and treated him with insult." The partying resumed the next evening. When Platt again tried to persuade the

---

20. Cortland First Baptist Church, Record Book, June 29, June 14, 1845.
21. *Cortland Republican*, October 15, 1833.

young men to retire, "his voice was soon drowned by yells of a portion of the company and he retired amidst execrations and insults." Many then went home, but the remainder resumed shooting rifles even closer to Platt's house and threw eggs at him while he observed from his doorway. At about one o'clock, the town's cannon was brought out and fired, accidentally blowing out the windows in the church meetinghouse.[22] Clearly, by the early 1840s the prestige of local evangelical churches was flagging badly, both in the eyes of local churchgoers and the county at large.

By the early 1840s the corporate church was an anachronism in an individualistic community. In an era when county residents sought to be masters of their own destiny, the evangelical churches mandated that believers be vassals to their chosen religious fellowships. For a time, the requirement of obedience kept many potential rebels out of the county's churches, but the revivals of the early 1830s broke down the bulwarks against individualism. Not only did more independent-minded people enter local churches, but Arminian theology and Finneyite perfectionism destroyed the intellectual basis for church discipline. Throughout the 1830s and early 1840s, evangelical church members rebelled in greater numbers and with greater intensity than ever before.

22. Homer Congregational Church, Minutes, September 11, 1841.

10

The Ultraist Revolt

By the early 1830s, Cortland County's evangelical churches were struggling against secular amusements, religious competition, and rampant individualism. The perfectionism implicit in the New Measures theology invigorated an already healthy independent streak among parishioners, but the impact of perfectionist thought went beyond demands for individual autonomy. Some evangelicals, including many who were converted in the revivals of the 1830s, believed that God demanded new standards of Christian conduct, an openness to personal and institutional innovation, and a total commitment to the eradication of individual, local, and national sin. Many contemporaries considered the demands of these enthusiasts extreme and uncompromising, and the perfectionists were commonly called "ultraists."[1] New Measure moderates, by contrast, had perfectionist goals but chose to keep their reformist impulses within the confines of traditional evangelical institutions and practice.

The New Measure men in Cortland County, whether ultraist or moderate, took their cues regarding sanctification, as in nearly everything else, from the Reverend Charles Finney. The doctrine of perfectionism was central to the new theology. In Finney's view, the spiritually reborn moved beyond personal selfishness to disinterested benevolence. Regeneration was "a change from selfishness to benevolence, from having a supreme regard to one's

1. Whitney Cross discusses ultraism at length in *The Burned-over District;* see esp. pp. 173, 198–208, and 268–84.

own interest to an absorbing and controlling choice of the happiness and glory of God's Kingdom." The true Christian would channel his or her energy into reforming the world, which in turn would hasten the millennium and the Second Coming of Jesus Christ.[2]

New Measures activism took two forms. The first was to expand organized efforts to spread the gospel. To many evangelicals, redeeming the masses, both abroad and in the United States, was the most direct way to perfect mankind and hasten the millennium.

Formal and antiformal evangelicals agreed on the importance of religious benevolence. Between 1830 and 1839, local Baptist churches increased their giving to the Cortland Baptist Association by 85 percent, and Presbyterian and Congregational churches increased giving to the Cortland Presbytery by 107 percent. Although the pedobaptists gave more money for denominational benevolence ($1,173 in 1838 compared to Baptist contributions of $373 in 1839), the Baptists appear to have exerted more effort organizing local evangelism.[3] Association records indicate that in 1830 only two county churches had Sunday Schools; five years later the number had grown to eight. Baptist female benevolent societies existed in two churches in 1829 and were present in six churches a decade later. By 1834 all ten of the county's Baptist churches had announced their support for the association's denominational tract, missionary, and Bible societies and general religious benevolence.[4] No similar surge can be detected in local Presbyterian and Congregational records. At most, only one new pedobaptist Sabbath School was formed.[5] Formalists supported religious benevolence monetarily, but they were more interested in other ways of spending their organizational energy.

Driving sin from American society was the second concern of New Measures activism. Many members of both formal and antiformal churches were interested in social reform. But the formalists' traditional concern with organization and social responsibility

2. McLoughlin, *Revivals, Awakenings, and Reform*, pp. 128–30.
3. *Minutes of the Cortland Baptist Association*, 1830, 1839; *Minutes of the General Assembly*, 1830, 1839. Presbyterian figures are from the previous year.
4. *Minutes of the Cortland Baptist Association*, 1829–34.
5. Cincinnatus First Congregational Church, Records, September 14, 1828.

meant that Christian perfectionists interested in improving society had much more success in Congregational and Presbyterian churches. Unlike the antiformal Baptists and Methodists, who were preoccupied with evangelism, formalist congregations saw redeeming sinners and attacking sin as twin priorities.

Intemperance was the first of two sins that galvanized the attention of Cortland County perfectionists. Liquor consumption was high for the same reasons it soared throughout most of the United States during the 1820s. Whiskey was cheap.[6] One local source lists the price in 1812 at "only fifteen cents a gallon with the jug thrown in."[7] Another source sets the price at fifty cents a gallon in 1821.[8] Residents who wished to imbibe clearly could do so with little concern for the financial cost. During the 1820s, the growing number of local distilleries kept farmers well stocked with whiskey. In 1820 the county had fourteen distilleries, by 1825 that number had risen to twenty-two.[9]

Because evangelicals constantly monitored member behavior through church discipline, they were more aware than most county residents of rising alcohol consumption. Before the 1830s there were no religious sanctions against the use of hard liquor; only its abuse was condemned. The corporate church assumed the responsibility of assuring that its members did not drink beyond acceptable levels. As whiskey consumption rose, the number of complaints registered by church members against their intoxicated brothers and sisters increased correspondingly. The minutes of ten Presbyterian, Congregational, and Baptist churches reveal ten charges of alcohol abuse between 1810 and 1819. The same records reveal twenty-seven charges of intemperance submitted to local churches for the 1820–29 period, an increase of 170 percent from the previous decade (Table C.2).

The flood of drinking cases in the 1820s brought significant embarrassment to the corporate church. Heavy drinking was often done in private, but parishioners were sometimes drunk in public. Stephen Hedges testified that he saw Captain Philemon

---

6. Rorabaugh, *Alcoholic Republic*, pp. 61–92.

7. Blodgett, *Stories of Cortland County*, p. 139.

8. Cortland First Methodist Society, Minutes, May 24, 1821, Accession No. 6250, CUA.

9. Spafford, *Gazetteer* (1824), p. 134; *Census of the State of New York for 1825*.

Andrews "twice, and I think three times, . . . when he was apparently intoxicated to such a degree that he fell down."[10] A church committee called on Hiram Wood only to find "he had been the worse for Liquor and other improper conduct to the dishonor of the cause of God." Even violators were conscious of how their behavior was viewed. In 1828 John Whitford confessed that "he had used to much ardent spirits so far as to wound the Cause of Christ Many Times and that in a public Manner."[11] By the late 1820s, many evangelicals were aware of the contradiction between church claims to be a "city on a hill" and the inebriated behavior of numerous members.

Traditional methods of church discipline had comparatively little effect on alcoholic members. During the 1820s, only about a third of all discipline proceedings ended in exclusion, but 70 percent of all cases involving intemperance ended in excommunication. Even when the offender begged for forgiveness and publicly repented before the church, he or she usually returned to the bottle and was eventually excluded.[12]

10. Truxton First Presbyterian Church, Record Book, October 2, 1824, December 12, 1825.

11. Cortland First Baptist Church, Record Book, April 17, 1824, February 16, 1828.

12. The case of Olive Vermilyear of the Homer Baptist Church reveals the difficulty churches had in reclaiming confirmed drinkers, even when such persons were receptive to help from their congregations. In late 1824 rumors were circulating that Olive Vermilyear had been imbibing to excess. The Homer church sought to regain her through visitation committees and written admonitions. On February 19, 1825, their efforts had apparently succeeded because the defendant came before the congregation and confessed that "she had drank too much several times for which she was sorry and wished to be forgiven and again to take up her travel." The church was satisfied and terminated discipline proceedings. A little more than a year later, similar complaints were heard. After the congregation had labored with her, Sister Vermilyear spoke with contrition before the assembled brethren. The June 17, 1826, minutes state that "she confessed she had taken too much stimulus some time ago for which she felt very sorry and hoped God had forgiven her and she wished the forgiveness of her brethren, that she had for three months past left it and that she enjoyed her mind very well and hoped God assisting her that she should be able so to live through life by refraining entirely from the use of it. Voted Satisfied with trembleing."

The congregation accepted her second confession but had doubts about Vermilyear's good intentions. Four months later, she was before the congregation again on new charges of intemperance. The minutes for October 14 report that Vermilyear "being present stated she did in July last drinke too much for which she was sorry and wished to be forgiven yet she did still use some and some times since July she had used too much. [It was] a case of repeated occurence and she could

Given the increased drinking problems of the 1820s and the perfectionist zeal in many evangelical churches, it is not surprising that church members were at the heart of the county's early temperance movement. Discipline had failed, and some evangelicals believed it was necessary to reach beyond the doors of the church and strike at the root cause—excessive drinking in the larger community. Cortland County's temperance movement operated on the assumption that urging moderation in alcohol use was doomed to failure. The only way to eliminate drunkenness from society (and consequently, the churches) was total abstinence. When voluntary methods failed, many, but not all, of the county's temperance enthusiasts sought legal means to ban the manufacture and sale of spirits.[13]

Although evangelicals were at the heart of the temperance crusade, levels of involvement varied sharply along formal-antiformal lines. From the very beginning, formal evangelicals led the drive to organize and legislate against iniquity. Mr. Hoisington, a licentiate who was temporarily serving the Union Congregational Church, organized the first local temperance society in the southeastern part of the county.[14] The Cortland County Temperance Society was dominated by the county's religious community.[15] Between 50 and 60 percent of the temperance society's members were also church members even though less than 21 percent of the county's adult male population belonged to a church. Formalists, with Congregationalists making up the single largest component, outnumbered their antiformalist brethren in the organization by more than two to one (Table D.2). Furthermore, any given

---

not be persuaded to agree not to use it at all of course—considerd it an hopeless case." The church did not normally require total abstinence, but in Vermilyear's case, it seemed to be the only option. Because she refused to give up liquor entirely, the congregation felt the situation was hopeless and excluded her.

13. By 1837 the Cortland County Temperance Society had abandoned voluntarism for a ban on local liquor sales licenses (*Cortland Republican and Eagle*, March 14, 1837). In 1845 the "friends of temperance" campaigned for "no local liquor licenses" (*Cortland Democrat*, December 3, 24, 1845). The county also had a strong Washingtonian movement in the early 1840s that did not waver from its voluntarist principles (*Cortland Democrat*, February 16, 1842).

14. Cincinnatus and Solon, Union Congregational Church. Records, 1830.

15. Cortland County Temperance Society, Records, 1829–40, CCHS. Membership lists were matched with lists of Cortland County church members for the years 1829–40. A range is given because of the difficulty of matching names across lists with absolute certainty.

formalist church member was four to five times as likely to join the society than a person belonging to an antiformal congregation (Table D.3).

Many temperance enthusiasts sought to enlist the support of their local congregations in the battle against grog. The formal evangelical churches, with the largest contingent of temperance society members, were pressured to abandon traditional tolerance for moderate drinking and make the temperance pledge mandatory for all church members.

The antiliquor reformers had some success among Congregationalists. In 1834 the Union Congregational Church of Cincinnatus and Solon resolved not to admit new members who did not totally abstain from ardent spirits.[16] Eight years later, the Homer Congregational Church voted "that we consider it the duty of every Church member to set an example of total abstinance from all intoxicating drinks as a beverage."[17] Although the Truxton Congregationalists never went so far as to ban the use of alcohol, they did ban church members from frequenting taverns and grog shops.[18] The Freetown Congregationalists, however, enacted no new regulations regarding alcohol usage.

The Presbyterians were ambivalent about adopting harsh sanctions against the use of alcohol. Local fellowships were generally unwilling to jump on the temperance bandwagon even though the Cortland Presbytery passed a resolution in 1837 that "any church member who continues in the manufacture, use, or traffic [of ardent spirits] . . . ought to be regarded as a proper subject of discipline."[19] Nevertheless, the Preble Presbyterian Church never forbade consumption of alcoholic beverages. The Cortland Presbyterian Church was not sure what to do. In 1834 the fellowship voted "that this church consider the manufacturing, vending, or using of ardent spirits, for a drink an immorality." Five years later the motion was rescinded. The reasons for the reversal were that "a diversity of opinion exists among the members of this church, as to [the] Constitutionality of [the] resolution" and that such proposals were not necessary for the "suppression of intem-

16. Cincinnatus and Solon, Union Congregational Church, Records, November 14, 1834.

17. Homer Congregational Church, Minutes, April 7, 1842.

18. Truxton First Presbyterian Church, Record Book, February 11, 1825.

19. Minutes of the Cortland Presbytery, February 14, 1837.

perance." In the 1840s, however, the Cortland fellowship partially reversed itself again when it began to exclude members who sold intoxicating beverages.[20] The formalists were clearly split between those who wished to encourage moderation or even voluntary abstinence and enthusiasts who wished to ban all alcohol consumption and thus eliminate the sin of intemperance altogether.

Unlike the formalist denominations, the antiformal Baptists were not sharply divided over legislating total abstinence for all church members. Many Baptists thought curtailing and even eliminating alcohol usage was a good idea. By 1834 six Baptist churches had identified themselves as favoring temperance. By 1840 the Cortland Baptist Association had passed two antialcohol resolutions.[21] Baptist temperance resolutions were much milder than those of the Congregationalists and Presbyterians. Neither the association nor any church was willing to do more than recommend abstinence on the part of its members. Baptist congregations would not tolerate drunkenness, but they believed that the decision to abstain totally was a matter of personal conscience.

Slavery was the second national sin that captured the attention of Cortland County perfectionists. As elsewhere in the United States, Cortlanders of the 1820s and 1830s were obsessed with freedom. Independence twice won from Great Britain, political liberty, and a free enterprise economy were all highly valued. Local residents held bake sales to raise money for Greeks fighting for independence from Turkey.[22] The most popular religious theme was mankind's freedom to choose between God and Satan. Temperance was touted as freedom from alcohol. Perfectionism took the form of freedom from sin.

In Cortland County it was relatively easy to convert general concern about human freedom into antislavery agitation. County residents had few economic ties to the South, a very small black population, and a deep commitment to personal liberty and republican principles. Some Homer residents castigated the "pecu-

20. Cortland Presbyterian Church, Records, March 20, 1834, January 24, 1839, October 31, 1846, January 1, 1848.
21. The churches that identified with the temperance movement by 1834 were the Freetown, First Solon, Truxton, Cortland, Scott, and Virgil Baptist churches (*Minutes of the Cortland Baptist Association*, 1831, 1832, 1834). For the resolutions see ibid., 1836, p. 8; 1840, p. 6.
22. "Ladies Fair," *Cortland Advocate*, December 12, 1833.

liar institution" as early as 1821. In response to the passage of the Missouri Compromise, one citizen referred to slavery as the "darkest spot on the American Escutcheon; rivers of water cannot wash it away." Another roasted the " 'Dough-faces' of the Northern States. . . . May they be rewarded by the poor man's scorn, and the proud man's contumely."[23] During the late 1820s the American Colonization Society received support from a number of sources including the Homer Baptist Church and the two major political parties.[24]

Once a strong dose of perfectionism was added to local emancipationist thought, the focus shifted from colonizationist benevolence to abolitionist agitation. In 1831 the Reverend John Keep—pastor of the Homer Congregational Church, initiator of local use of Finney's New Measures, and the most prominent perfectionist in Cortland County—invited Gerrit Smith to his church to crusade against alcohol. Influenced by Smith, Keep soon expanded his efforts to eradicate sin to include slavery. In 1832 the Homer pastor entered the pulpit with a copy of Garrison's *Liberator* in hand and proclaimed his opposition to human slavery.[25] The next year Keep was asked to resign so he had little opportunity to build on his abolitionist foray. His influence can be seen in the formation in 1835 of the county's first abolitionist society. Four of the society's seven directors had listened to Keep's preaching earlier in the decade.[26]

As was the temperance movement, local abolitionism was dominated by church members even though they were a small fraction of the county's population. The Cortland County Anti-Slavery Society was almost totally under the control of the devout.[27] Between 1837 and 1841, church members constituted 81 to 97 percent of the society's activists. Once again, formalists were far more involved than antiformalists. Congregationalists and Presbyterians made up over half of the organization (Table D.2).

23. Davis, *History of the Methodist Episcopal Church,* pp. 67–74.

24. Cortland First Baptist Church, Record Book, June 16, 1826; *Cortland Republican,* May 7, June 11, 1833; *Cortland Advocate,* June 29, 1832, July 11, 1833.

25. Howe, *Paris Lived in Homer,* pp. 18–19.

26. *Cortland Republican,* January 26, 1836.

27. Cortland County Anti-Slavery Society, Records, 1837–41, CCHS. Membership lists were matched with lists of county church members for the years 1837–41. A range is given because of the difficulty in matching names across lists with absolute certainty.

When the local abolitionist movement gravitated toward political action, church members again dominated. When a petition was circulated in 1841 in support of the Liberty party, 55 to 71 percent of the signatories were church members. Pedobaptist Calvinists made up 30 to 40 percent of all signers (Table D.2). Formalists were almost three times as likely to support the Liberty party as were antiformalists (Table D.4). Perfectionism, like the New Measures, penetrated nearly all of Cortland County's evangelical churches, but formal evangelicals—true to their prerevivalist heritage—were far more likely to try to perfect the world as well as the church. Antiformal evangelicals—maintaining a heavy emphasis on personal piety and significant doubts about the efficacy of secular action—tended to neglect temperance and abolitionism in favor of expanded religious benevolence.

In spite of the significant impact of perfectionism on local voluntarism, it is dangerous to overestimate its influence on county congregations. Not everyone in evangelical churches was pleased with the new doctrines or the implications stemming from perfectionist ideology. It is more accurate to say that the advent of perfectionist ideas set off an intense debate among minimalists, traditional Calvinists, New Measure moderates, and New Measure ultraists over the proper function of the church.

During the initial stage of theological warfare, the traditional Calvinists and minimalists fought New Measures advocates. The Old School Calvinists believed it was wrong to abandon predestination in favor of Arminian doctrine. Traditionalists believed that the church should preside over the private and public lives of its members, but to them organizing missionary, tract, and Bible societies was merely evangelical hubris. Saving souls was strictly God's domain. Traditionalists sought essentially to maintain the predestinarian, localized church they knew in the 1810s and early 1820s. Minimalists agreed with the doctrinal stance of Old School Calvinists but for different reasons. The doctrine of election fit minimalists well because it allowed them to focus on their commercial or agricultural endeavors and leave salvation up to God. The traditional church advocated public morality, yet except for ensuring the proper behavior of its members, it did not interfere much in the public arena. To the minimalists' discomfort, Arminianized Calvinism altered the terms of salvation. The lack of saving grace was not the fault of divine inertia but of the stubborn pride of those unwilling to submit to God's grace. Minimalists were no longer seen as waiting for grace but were considered unrepentant resisters. To make matters worse, the New Measures theology encouraged churches to depart from their "proper" functions. Instead of maintaining the moral status quo, Keep and his compatriots sought to change the social order, in the process challenging and interfering with long-established minimalist commercial practices.

The struggle began in the Homer Congregational Church. John Keep alienated a number of his parishioners with his Arminianized Calvinist message, his use of evangelist Jedediah Burchard, his support for temperance, and his abolitionist sentiments. The attack on slavery, in particular, brought comments that Keep was overstepping his ministerial prerogatives. After his fiery Garrisonian sermon of 1832, the vast majority of his listeners openly disagreed with the clergyman's acerbic rhetoric. One deacon articulated the minimalist-traditionalist perspective when he remarked, "These reforms have no place in the church for we meet here to worship God in peace and quiet."[28] Keep, however, would not yield, and he continued his perfectionist crusade against sin, intemperance, and slavery.

Before long, John Keep created some very powerful enemies. Jedediah Barber, a religious society member who sold alcohol at his Great Western Store and traded with slaveowners in Baltimore, was offended by Keep's preaching. In 1833 Barber and his minimalist cronies forced the minister's resignation. For a time, it looked as though Keep would survive the challenge because the church rejected the pastor's resignation by a vote of 74 to 20. Then twenty-four men sent Keep a letter stating they would no longer support him financially. Keep was torn between the majority that supported him and the small wealthy faction that sought his resignation. The case went to the Cortland Presbytery, which concluded, "From what is known of those men [who signed the anti-Keep letter] it is generally believed that their opposition will remain deep and strong. . . . In consideration of these circumstances, the presbytery are not prepared to say that the majority ought not yield to the minority."[29] The Homer congregation

28. Howe, *Paris Lived in Homer*, pp. 18–19.
29. Minutes of the Cortland Presbytery, September 10, 1833.

accepted the presbytery's cautiously worded advice and accepted Keep's resignation.[30] The minimalist-traditionalist coalition had cast a financial veto over Keep's ministry. The initial victory lay with the opponents of change.

The traditionalists and minimalists could not repeat this success in other churches. As in the Homer Congregational Church, the New Measures men generally had the support of the majority of church members. Almost half of some congregations had been converted during the revivals of the early 1830s. Unless the opposition in the religious society could form a well-organized coalition with the minority of traditional Calvinists, the chances of displacing a New Measures minister were slim.

As a result, the opponents of Arminianized Calvinism were generally limited to individual protests. In 1834 Orlanna Beebe, a charter member and deacon of the Union Congregational Church, stormed out of a protracted meeting, "bidding the church good by forever." During his trial, Beebe never recanted his opposition to the New Measures, stating that his departure that evening and his subsequent absence from the church were "for sufficient reasons."[31] The expanded benevolent activity that followed Baptist revivalism brought resistance from some members. In the 1830s Cortland Baptists excluded Harris Ellis and Desiter Barns for absenting themselves because of their anti-benevolent sentiments.[32] Henry Bell believed the relatively mild Baptist pronouncements against slavery to be too extreme and was excluded in the mid-1840s.[33]

The solitary opposition of scattered individuals did not deflect the Arminianized Calvinist churches from their benevolent activities. The churches had been revitalized by the New Measures in the early 1830s and were willing to test the perfectionist implications of their new doctrine within the confines of their formalist or antiformalist tradition. By 1834 all ten Baptist congregations in Cortland County had declared themselves in favor of benevolence. In 1837, when the national Presbyterian Synod

30. Howe, *Paris Lived in Homer*, pp. 18–19.
31. Cincinnatus and Solon, Union Congregational Church, Records, May 27, 1836.
32. Cortland First Baptist Church, Record Book, September 6, December 16, 1837, August 16, December 19, 1834.
33. Virgil Baptist Church, Minutes, March 1, 1845, February 13, 1847.

fractured into Old and New Schools, all of Cortland County's Congregational and Presbyterian churches joined the pro-revival New School.[34] By 1837 local Calvinist churches were firmly in the hands of the New Measures faction. For the time being, the traditionalist-minimalist coalition had lost.

With the conservatives out of the way, theological combat shifted to the struggle between moderate advocates of the New Measures and ultraists, who wanted the church to become totally committed to the perfectionist vision. The debate centered on the amount of attention the church should devote to eradicating sin in both the local fellowships and the general population. Moderates supported perfectionist goals but only in the context of a larger Christian mission. Before society could be rid of its evils, souls had to be saved, Sunday Schools had to be organized, and funds had to be raised for the minister and assorted benevolent projects. The ultraists contended that destroying social iniquity was part of the Christian mission. Personal salvation must lead to dedicating one's life to the eradication of sin. To the ultraists, the perfectionist vision was all-consuming; anything less was compromise with the world. To moderate New Lights, the single-minded focus was, at best, theologically imbalanced and, at worst, fanatical.

Ultraist success varied among denominations. Although all major evangelical groups were disrupted, antiformalists were best equipped to contain perfectionist enthusiasm. The Cortland Baptist Association endorsed temperance but never endorsed total abstinence as a membership requirement. Local Baptist churches followed the association's lead, apparently believing that a decision on total abstinence was a personal matter.

Baptist inclinations toward private piety and against organized mandates curtailed ultraist antislavery activism. The Cortland Baptist Association made a general declaration about the sinfulness of slavery in 1839 and urged "all christian measures for its removal." The vague resolution encompassed every view from voluntary emancipation to political abolition and thus typified Baptist ambivalence on the moral question. By 1847 Baptist fel-

---

34. *Minutes of the Cortland Baptist Association*, 1831, 1832, 1834. The Presbyterian split is described in Ahlstrom, *Religious History*, 1:559–68. All of the Cortland Presbytery's churches are mentioned in the *Minutes of the General Assembly* (New School) in 1839.

lowships in Scott and Virgil also spoke against slavery.[35] Other county Baptists exhibited extreme reluctance even to discuss the issue within congregational confines for fear of violating antiformalist traditions regarding freedom of conscience. In 1840 the Truxton Baptist Church declared, "We consider the subject of slavery as it now exists before the Publick to be a Political thing and not proper for us to act upon as a Religious body.... Not withstanding, each Brother is at liberty to act according to his own views on the Subject in an individual capasity."[36] Three years later, the Cortland Baptist Church passed a similar resolution. Although both resolutions were eventually rescinded, sentiment against discussing slavery remained strong. In 1846 Hiram Jones wanted to discuss the Cortland Baptist Church's connection with "slaveholding churches," but he was unable to garner much ultraist support and was denied a hearing. After Jones's departure from the church, the subject of slavery disappeared from the minutes.[37]

Local Methodist churches exhibited a similar reluctance to get involved in the growing abolitionist crusade. In 1838 a member of the Cortland Methodist Church apparently volunteered the use of the worship house for a meeting of the Cortland County Anti-Slavery Society. An unexpected furor arose from nonabolitionist members. A compromise was forged, and on March 20 the following announcement appeared in the *Cortland Republican and Eagle*: "That harmony and peace may exist in the Methodist Society at Cortlandville, we on both sides, agree that our meeting house doors may be opened on the 21st inst. for the use of the abolitionist, without opposition, calculating that the doors are not to be opened for such meeting again." Like the antiformalist Baptists, the Methodists managed to sabotage ultraist efforts almost as soon as they began.[38]

---

35. *Minutes of the Cortland Baptist Association,* 1839, p. 4; 1847, p. 9.

36. Truxton Baptist Church, Record Book, February 22, 1840.

37. Cortland First Baptist Church, Record Book, February 18, 1843, April 18, 1846.

38. Eventually, both the local Baptists and Methodists took a stronger stand against slavery. In 1851 the Cortland Baptist Association's circular letter noted the "controversy and division" of the past ten years and neatly sidestepped the slavery question, pointing out that "each disciple is entitled to form his own opinion." Four years later, the association finally adopted a free-soil position and requested that Congress repeal the Kansas-Nebraska Act by banning slavery in the territories north of 36° 30′. Local Methodists also unified in opposition to slavery in the

Because formal evangelicals traditionally combined evangelism and social action, it was far more difficult for Congregationalists and Presbyterians to curtail ultraist advances. Many thought of perfectionist doctrine as an energized extension of traditional Calvinist concern about the "good society." As a result, these denominations experienced more intense and disruptive ultraist-moderate disputes than did the Methodists and Baptists.

During the late 1830s, the Cortland Presbytery (which contained both Congregational and Presbyterian congregations) was split between moderates, who wished to encourage abstinence, and ultraists, who wanted to require church members to give up alcohol. Despite the presbytery's endorsement of the ultraist position regarding liquor, individual congregations took varying stances. The Cincinnatus and Solon congregation and the Homer fellowship tilted toward the ultraists. Moderates controlled the Truxton and Freetown congregations. The Cortland Presbyterian Church must have been fairly evenly divided between moderates and ultraists because it reversed its liquor policy several times. By 1840 Cortland County's formal evangelical churches had experienced significant disagreements over alcoholic beverages.

The temperance debate soon paled in comparison to other controversies in local Congregational and Presbyterian churches. By the early 1840s ultraists and moderates openly challenged each other, and several local fellowships fractured as a result. Preble Presbyterian Church was the first to be splintered. In 1837

1850s. In 1854 the Oneida Annual Conference (to which the Cortland County Methodist churches belonged) denounced the admission of slaveholders to fellowship in the Methodist church, the Fugitive Slave Bill, the repeal of the Missouri Compromise, and "the introduction of slavery into territory now free" (*Minutes of the Cortland Baptist Association,* 1851, pp. 8–9; 1855, p. 7; *Minutes of the Oneida Conference of the Methodist Episcopal Church,* 1854, p. 32).

Too much should not be made of these antiformal antislavery statements. By the time county Methodists and Baptists took a strong stand against slavery, Cortland County was fully in the antislavery camp. As early as 1846, all four local political parties (Whig, Regular Democrat, Free Soil Democrat, and Liberty) went on record favoring black suffrage. Two years later, each party sought to demonstrate its fervent opposition to the extension of slavery in the territories (Curtis D. Johnson, "Islands of Holiness: Rural Religion in Cortland County, New York, 1790–1860" [Ph.D. dissertation, University of Minnesota, 1985], pp. 403–6). The evidence indicates that the two major antiformal denominations did not take their antislavery positions until long after an antislavery consensus was emerging elsewhere in the county.

the congregation hired the Reverend Benjamin Fults, a New School revivalist with strong Oberlin tendencies. At about the same time, a major revival occurred and many of the seventy-one recent converts were entranced by the new minister. Before 1837 the Preble church was evenly balanced between moderates and ultraists, but Fults and the recent additions swung the balance in the ultraist direction. The Oberlin faction, with a majority of the male parishioners, was able to place four of its number on the five-man board of elders. By 1840 the ultraists controlled both the pastorate and the session and began to seek ways to drive sin out of the congregation.[39]

Church discipline appeared to be one of the most effective tools to achieve perfectionist ends, and the ultraists began to employ traditional methods with a new zeal. They did not have to wait long to exercise their power. On January 1, 1840, four young church members joined some friends who did not belong to any church and together went unchaperoned on a New Year's sleigh ride. In the course of their merrymaking, the group visited several local taverns. Not surprisingly, word of the escapade reached the Preble session. The board of elders was shocked by the group's behavior and placed the four young people under church discipline. Those who were from families that sympathized with the Oberlin faction meekly submitted to the ultraist-controlled session. But others were children of moderates. With significant adult support, several adolescents—the foremost being Elizabeth Trowbridge—defied the session by arguing that the elders had overstepped their authority, that the session had misconstrued the young people's confessions, and that going to taverns was sinful but that they had done no wrong in going on the sleigh ride. Trowbridge wisely brought in the Reverend Dennis Platt of the prestigious Homer Congregational Church to present her case before the session.[40]

Elizabeth Trowbridge's ploy did not lead to acquittal by the

39. The shift in power is outlined in the Preble First Presbyterian Church, Records, Book of Discipline, 1837–40. The analysis of who was on what side is based on who eventually left with the seceding Oberlin faction and who stayed behind with the New School moderates.

40. Preble First Presbyterian Church, Book of Discipline, January 15, February 22, March 4, April 3, 13, 1840; Van Hoesen, *History of the Presbyterian Church of Preble*, pp. 9–10.

Preble elders, but it did give her a powerful ally in Platt when the case was appealed to the Cortland Presbytery. The session, however, sought to derail any appeal by terminating all ties with the presbytery, thus denying the higher body any jurisdiction over the sleigh ride incident. The elders' decision to sever its connections with the presbytery terrified Austin Cravath, the sole moderate on the session, and the rest of the church's moderate minority. Joy-riding adolescents were not the only ones at risk. According to Cravath's letter, the elders' secession from the presbytery resulted in "denying us the privilege of appeal and subjecting us to the irresponsible control of a few individuals."[41] If the Preble session were to remain independent of the presbytery, all moderates, no matter how circumspect, were in danger of expulsion.

The presbytery took up the case of the Preble church in 1841. The issue was not the sleigh ride. Instead, the presbytery addressed the secession of the Preble leadership. John Thomas, who had publicly blasted the Cortland Presbyterian session in 1835, defended the Preble ultraists. He argued that the Cortland Presbytery had no official standing because it was not recognized by the Presbyterian General Assembly and, therefore, it had "no jurisdiction over the Session and church in Preble." George Duncan, an ultraist elder, claimed that he recognized only the authority of the Old School Presbyterian Assembly.[42] Duncan's argument was pure sophistry because Old School beliefs had little in common with the doctrines of Oberlin perfectionism. Duncan raised the argument solely to undercut the legitimacy of the New School Cortland Presbytery.

After hearing the arguments of Thomas and Duncan, the presbytery rejected the ultraist defense, deposed the entire elder board, and voted to reorganize the Preble congregation. The presbytery, with the help of the local religious society, kept all church property in the hands of the 90-member moderate minority. The disgruntled majority—110 strong—moved their worship services down the road to a local store, eventually joined the Unionist movement, and declared themselves the Free Church of Preble.[43]

---

41. Minutes of the Cortland Presbytery, March 2, 1841.
42. Ibid.
43. Ibid. The numbers in each faction can be determined by comparing the names on the church register before the split with the list of church members recorded immediately after reorganization.

The fracturing of the Preble Presbyterian Church marked the beginning of five years of intense controversy within the Cortland Presbytery. The Preble ultraists had many friends throughout the county, especially in the antislavery movement. All fifteen Liberty party activists in the Preble Presbyterian Church joined the "schismatics" at the store. The Unionists generally portrayed New Light moderates as imposters who did not truly believe in New Measure doctrine. The Unionists were ardent revivalists who regarded abolitionism as the truest sign of sanctification and complete separation from sinners (especially slaveowners) the most important religious practice. Once he had created a "pure church" in Preble, the Reverend Benjamin Fults turned his attention to the Scott Congregational Church. After a visit from Fults, the Scott Congregationalists also considered separation from the Cortland Presbytery.[44]

In 1842 the trouble spread southward to the Homer Congregational Church. Zelotis Hannum, a member of the Homer church, occasionally worshiped with the Preble seceders. Even worse from the moderate viewpoint, Hannum launched a personal vendetta against Dennis Platt, the moderate Homer minister who had defended the sleigh-riding Elizabeth Trowbridge in 1840. Hannum accused Platt of "misaprihend[ing] the doctrin of Oberlin." Furthermore, Hannum disliked Platt's lack of physical exertion when preaching; he "wanted a Minister who did not carry so stiff elbows [during sermons]" and accordingly he cooperated with the Preble perfectionists in preventing Platt from preaching in a protracted meeting at Little York. Although Hannum later confessed to wrongdoing, four other members, including Joshua Atwater, who claimed Platt's preaching to be unbiblical, refused to recant their perfectionist preferences and were excluded.[45]

The four excommunications did not bring peace to the Homer Congregational Church. In 1843 the issue of slavery emerged anew, and the Homer church passed several insipid resolutions against human bondage. The Congregational Church declared slavery "a great moral and political evil" but urged against "unlawful measures for its removal," which would only "increase the evil by . . . hardening the hearts of slaveholders, and thereby riveting the chains of the slave more firmly." The church also urged that

44. Homer Congregational Church, Minutes, May 31, 1842.
45. Ibid., May 26, May 31, 1842.

concerned Christians rely on "truth spoken in love" and that those opposed to slavery "meet the erring Master in the spirit of the gospel." Ultraists within the church were not satisfied. Oren Cravath, in particular, argued that antislavery platitudes were insufficient and urged the Homer fellowship to break all ecclesiastical ties with slaveholding churches. Cravath's pleas fell on deaf ears. In 1845 he reprimanded the Homer congregation for failing to follow up abolitionist professions with separatist action and formally withdrew his membership.[46] Soon thereafter, Cravath publicized his attack on the Homer church when a local printing firm published and circulated his sixteen-page position paper *A Case of Withdrawal from the Presbyterian Church with the Reasons for So Doing.*[47]

Abolitionist controversy reached the Cortland Presbyterian Church in 1846. Like Oren Cravath, ultraist leader John Thomas was frustrated by his unsuccessful attempts to radicalize his local fellowship into a total separation from Presbyterian synods and churches that permitted slaveholding.[48] When all efforts to get local Presbyterians to move past mere abolitionist professions had failed, twenty-seven men and women severed their ties with the Cortland church.[49] These "comeouters" then organized the Free Congregational Church in Cortland village and called the Reverend Samuel Ringgold Ward to be their minister. The call was remarkable in that Ward was one of New York's most prominent black abolitionist leaders and an important figure in the Liberty party.[50]

By 1846 at least three rabidly abolitionist churches existed in the county. The Seventh Day Baptist Church in Scott, the Free Church in Preble, and the Free Congregational Church in Cortland all sought the immediate eradication of slavery and the

46. Ibid., September 7, 1843, June 26, 1845.

47. Oren Cravath, *A Case of Withdrawal from the Presbyterian Church with the Reasons for So Doing* (Cortland, 1845).

48. John Thomas's role in the controversy is explained in the *Cortland Democrat,* June 16, 1847.

49. The twenty-seven "seceders" are listed in Cortland Presbyterian Church, Records, March 26, April 5, 1846.

50. *Cortland Democrat,* June 16, 1847, January 25, 1849. See also Samuel Ringgold Ward, *Autobiography of a Fugitive Negro* (1855; rpt. New York, 1968). For additional information on Ward, see Benjamin Quarles, *Black Abolitionists* (New York, 1969) and Gerald Sorin, *The New York Abolitionists: A Case Study of Political Radicalism* (Westport, Conn., 1971).

severing of all ties to religious institutions that in any way tolerated the "peculiar institution." In wealth and occupation, these
comeouters fit the county's profile almost perfectly, although they
were less financially secure than the moderate members of other
evangelical churches and far less wealthy than minimalists in the
religious societies (Tables D.5 and D.6). The ultraists compen-
sated for having fewer of the world's goods by zealously seeking to
eradicate sin, end slavery, and bring on the millennium. Unable to
attain social prominence through accumulated wealth, ultraists
could distinguish themselves in the political realm as the most
fervent enemies of slavery. They were far more likely to join the
Liberty party, the political version of comeouterism, than were
formalist Presbyterians, Congregationalists, and Episcopalians
(Table D.4). Characteristically, the county's religious abolitionists
refused to yield in 1848 when most Liberty party activists sought
to join the Free Soilers in an antislavery coalition. Refusing to
succumb to political expedience, a rump contingent of local Liberty men rejected the coalition ticket, preferring to lose with
"pure" candidates than to compromise. Foremost among the
"rump" leaders were the Reverend Samuel Ward, John Thomas,
and other religious comeouters who refused to trade their perfectionist birthright for the lukewarm porridge of political success.[51]

In 1846 the Cortland Presbytery, which oversaw all the county's
regular Congregational and Presbyterian churches, surveyed the
damage caused by the moderate-ultraist warfare. In February the
presbytery urged the General Assembly "to give a plain and
explicit condemnation of the [slave] system and recommend to
the churches under your care to regard the buying and selling and
holding of slaves for gain a disciplinable offense." No doubt, the
Cortland leaders hoped that more aggressive national leadership
regarding slavery would stop the fracturing of local churches over
abolitionism. The Cortland Presbytery stressed the importance of
a stronger position, noting that the "chief sources of division
among us at the present time are questions relating to the best
means of removing slavery." Later in the year, the presbytery
commented on the negative effect of the controversies on church

51. Ward's refusal to join other Liberty men in supporting the Free Soil ticket is
described in the *Cortland Democrat*, July 26, August 2, 1848. Supporters of the
"rump" Liberty party are listed in ibid., September 9, 16, 1848.

life: "There has been an estrangement of feeling among the brethren, exciting and distracting discussions." The controversy led to "a disposition to withdraw confidence in our long tried and heaven blessed Missionary Societies and a diversion of the prayers . . . and efforts of our churches from the great end of their existence, the promotion of the Redeemer's cause. Hence there are but few conversions."[52]

The formal evangelicals were exhausted. Armed with New Measures theology and a desire to eradicate social evil, formalists had entered into moral debates over alcohol and slavery. In so doing, they lowered the walls separating them from the outside world. The complexities of this political world came pouring into local congregations. Members could not agree to what extent temperance should be voluntary. Antislavery contention absorbed much attention, created bitter debate within the churches, and eventually split the Preble and Cortland Presbyterian congregations. Now, in 1846, the discouraged presbytery sought an escape from the debilitating controversy.

Antiformal fellowships had suffered less controversy, largely because their pietistic and antiorganizational tradition prevented moral issues from receiving much attention. The vast majority of antiformalists were not willing to venture beyond general statements regarding the sinfulness of intemperance and slavery to the more difficult question of how to bring an end to these evils. By keeping such political issues out of their churches, antiformalists maintained the walls of separation between themselves and the world. Internal peace had a price, however. Instead of helping to eradicate significant social problems, antiformalists were, for the most part, passive observers of the great moral crusades of their generation.

The best way to visualize what happened to Cortland County's corporate churches is to return to the island analogy. Initially, local evangelical churches served as islands of holiness in a less than righteous frontier environment. To protect themselves from worldly encroachments, Cortland's religious communities erected a disciplinary wall around themselves. This barrier was designed to keep the ungodly out and maintain purity within.

52. Minutes of the Cortland Presbytery, February 11, September 9, 1846.

Beginning in the 1820s, however, three successive waves hammered at the protective wall and the island communities it protected.

The first wave—competition—broke in the 1820s as new secular amusements attracted many away from the tame social opportunities available at church. Competition also came from religious sources. In the 1820s, the Seventh Day and Open Communion Baptists disrupted Regular Baptist hegemony. A decade later, Universalists and Episcopalians offered nonevangelical alternatives to those disinterested in Calvinist and Methodist evangelicalism.

The second wave—individualism—began to swell in the 1820s but did not threaten the church's disciplinary defenses until the early 1830s. When local Calvinism was Arminianized, large numbers of individualists entered the churches. Simultaneously, perfectionism undermined the notion that the corporate church was necessary to further sanctification. Throughout the late 1830s and early 1840s, the battle between local church members and the institutions that sought to govern their behavior became increasingly intense.

The third wave—ultraism—was perhaps the most devastating. Perfectionists, driven by an intense desire to purify the world, were not satisfied with the moderate attempts of Congregational and Presbyterian churches to eradicate the sins of intemperance and slavery. Instead of simply accepting church judgments or facing a series of exclusions, the ultraists fought back by seceding from established congregations and forming their own fellowships. Although only a few churches were so divided, the point was clear to the rest of the county's congregations. The reward of rigorous discipline was not purity but acrimony, rebellion, and division. As midcentury approached, the county's evangelical leaders, exhausted from the battles of the two previous decades, were seeking ways to restore peace and tranquillity to their battered island kingdoms.

PART IV

"MODERN" CHURCHES,

1846–1860

11

Evangelical Churches Search for Unity

In contrast to the tumult in Cortland County between 1815 and 1845, the period from 1846 to 1860 was remarkably tranquil. Socially, this mature agricultural community was more disposed to historical reflection than to frenetic change. Economically, prosperity reigned as improved transportation and modest urbanization opened the way for new enterprises, increased land values, and brought a higher standard of living. The county's evangelical churches sought to heal old wounds and to restore love and harmony. Above all, local Protestants desired unity within their assembled gatherings.

At midcentury, the term *frontier* had little personal meaning to most Cortland County residents. By 1855 over half of the county's population had been born after the last town had left the frontier stage of development in 1830.[1] Local young people knew little of the rapid settlement and boom times of the 1820s except what their parents told them. The deprivation and struggle of turn-of-the-century settlement was still another generation removed. Pioneers told their grandchildren tales of clearing the forests, killing off the wolves, and eating raw roots. Thoughtful community leaders sought to record the exploits of the original county residents before that generation died and their reminiscences were lost to posterity. In 1853 a "festal gathering" was held to honor the original settlers of Virgil. The stories shared by the elderly guests were duly recorded. Even more important was the printing of the

1. *Census of the State of New York for 1855.*

county's first history by H. C. Goodwin. The publication of the *Pioneer History of Cortland County* coincided with the county's fiftieth anniversary.[2] The volume paid homage to the survivors of the early settlements and described in great detail the events before the War of 1812. Cortland residents of the last antebellum decade realized that the founding generation was passing away.

The young people of the 1850s grew up in an economically mature environment. The era of explosive population growth was over, and population was growing by barely noticeable levels. Early in the century, the population grew rapidly because new family farms could be carved out of the abundant forests, but at midcentury improvable land was a rapidly diminishing resource. In 1850 71 percent of land capable of improvement had been cleared. Ten years later that figure had risen to 85 percent.[3]

By adapting to changing conditions, county families could maintain their economic position. Consequently, fertility rates dropped dramatically. By 1855 the number of children per thousand women of childbearing age (fifteen to forty-four) was less than half what it had been in 1820.[4] A large number of children were more of a hindrance than a help in an era of limited land resources. There was no longer a need for extra hands to help clear acreage of trees, and the days when one could bequeath inexpensive land to one's offspring had long since disappeared. Parents could no longer expect their children to live nearby and provide care and comfort in the parents' declining years. Instead, the second generation was likely to move west in search of better economic opportunities. Because large families brought more expense and fewer benefits than in earlier decades most young couples chose to have a small number of children.

For a growing minority, the farm experience was also receding into the past. People were moving to Cortland County villages in

2. See Nathan Bouton, *Festal Gathering of the Early Settlers and Present Inhabitants of the Town of Virgil, Cortland County, New York, Held at Virgil Village on Thursday, the 25th of August, 1853* (Dryden, N.Y., 1878); Goodwin, *Pioneer History.*
3. The maximum amount of improved land was recorded in 1900 (U.S. Census Bureau, *Twelfth Census*). "Improvable" land means the amount of land recorded as improved in 1900. The 1850 and 1860 data on improved land come from U.S. Census Office, *Seventh Census of the United States, 1850* (Washington, D.C., 1853), and *Eighth Census, 1860.*
4. See the *Census of the State of New York* for 1825 and 1855 and the federal census for 1850 and 1860 for the data on which fertility rates were calculated.

ever larger numbers. By 1855 Homer and Cortland each numbered around sixteen hundred residents. McGrawville and Marathon were becoming important secondary villages of about five hundred persons each. In addition, there were more than a score of smaller villages and hamlets. The urban population had risen rapidly since the days of Jackson. In 1835 13 percent of the county's citizens lived in a village or hamlet. Twenty years later, 29 percent of the county's population was urban.[5] In 1840 81 percent of the county's household heads were employed in farming. By 1860 only 59 percent were farmers.[6] Urban occupations picked up the slack. All nonagricultural pursuits expanded during the 1850s, but the fastest-growing category of urban employment was unskilled and semiskilled factory labor. As local companies absorbed many farmers' sons displaced from family homesteads, the percentage employed as factory laborers grew from 1.6 percent of household heads in 1850 to 9.4 percent in 1860.[7]

The growing number of villages and factories was prompted by more than the evolution of the county's economy. For years, transportation links to outside markets and sources of supply had been inadequate. Before 1825 western New York counties generally suffered isolation and high transport costs. The Erie Canal alleviated the problem for the northern tier of counties in the western part of the state, and soon feeder canals reached other areas of the state. Cortland County, however, never benefited from these internal improvements. As in the pioneer days, county residents were forced to rely on expensive land transportation northward and eastward or to use the Tioughnioga River when traveling south. County farmers and merchants were well aware of their economic disadvantage, and as early as 1835 they sought a railroad.[8] Their efforts were not rewarded until 1854. When the iron horse connected the villages of Homer, Cortland, and Marathon with the cities of Syracuse and Binghamton, the economic

5. See *Census of the State of New York for 1855* and French, *Gazetteer*, pp. 150–256.

6. U.S. Census Office, *Sixth Census, 1840;* Leonard Ralston's computerized censuses for 1860.

7. Leonard Ralston's computerized censuses for 1850 and 1860.

8. See *Cortland Republican*, November 24, 1835.

impact of the lowered transport costs was immediate.[9] The rail-road also raised county land values. In 1850 Cortland County's improved land was worth less per acre than land in all but one of the seven adjacent counties. Between 1850 and 1860 land values rose 46 percent, more than in any bordering county.[10] The heightened value of land boosted per capita personal wealth, which was only $95.69 in 1835 and by 1858 had more than doubled to $228.86 per person.[11]

Perhaps the most dramatic economic effect of improved trans-portation occurred in the domain of homemade cloth production. In 1845 Cortland County still produced 4.65 yards of homespun per person annually. Rail transport made available reasonably priced and more comfortable factory goods. As a result, the pro-duction of household cloth dropped by more than 80 percent between 1845 and 1855. By the mid-1850s, the more urbanized towns of Homer and Cortlandville respectively produced only .24 and .31 yards of homespun per capita. Only in relatively inaccessi-ble outlying towns did homemade cloth production continue to any significant degree.[12] A strong regional market meant that most Cortlanders chose to buy, rather than make, cloth and many other items used in everyday life.

The railroad had clearly changed Cortland County. The steam locomotive ended the county's comparative isolation and made new commercial opportunities available. In time, carriage build-ing and wire production would develop as local industries.[13] By the mid-1850s, Cortland County had reached economic maturity and its residents enjoyed unprecedented prosperity.

Protestant churches, exhausted by two decades of strife, faced declining prospects in the late 1840s. The attempt to maintain corporate church structure had met strong resistance as church members demonstrated unwillingness to be taxed and reluctance to accept congregational authority over their personal behavior.

9. Blodgett, *Stories of Cortland County*, p. 241.
10. The calculations of land value were made by dividing the total land value in the county by the number of improved acres. The data come from the 1850 and 1860 federal censuses.
11. Data on personal wealth come from Gordon, *Gazetteer*, pp. 416–17, and French, *Gazetteer*, p. 256.
12. Measures were calculated from data in the *Census of the State of New York* for 1845 and 1855.
13. Blodgett, *Stories of Cortland County*, p. 240.

Resistance to church discipline had stiffened with an increasing number of cases ending in exclusion. By the early 1840s excommunication rates were at record levels. The tendency of churches to split over controversial issues alarmed local officials, especially those who led the formal evangelical fellowships. The Preble Presbyterian Church fractured in 1841; the Cortland Presbyterians split five years later. The county's evangelical churches were discouraged, disrupted, and divided. The New Measures, revivalism, and perfectionism had led to upheaval. The time was ripe for doctrines that stressed love, forgiveness, and brotherhood. Local evangelical leaders realized that internal harmony had to be restored before other aspects of the Lord's work could be resumed.

The Cortland Baptist Association led that denomination's efforts to bring unity to local congregations. During the late 1840s and early 1850s, association documents were preoccupied with establishing a proper "Christian spirit" within constituent congregations. In 1848 the association's circular letter spoke of "the duties of Church Members to each other," stating that Christians "should love one another" for this responsibility was "fundamental to every religious duty." Faithfulness and unity were the other two mutual obligations of church members. Three years later, in a letter addressing "the unity of the spirit," the association admonished its churches "to respect sacredly the right of private judgment [and] to avoid the spirit of contention." According to the circular, "It is the discordance of spirit among Christians, not the differences of judgment, which proves so disastrous to the interests of vital religion." The next year's topic was "the exercise of a right spirit," which was deemed necessary for the "union and harmony of the Church."[14]

Formal evangelicals were also interested in promoting the ideals of peace and cooperation. The records of the Homer Congregational Church, for example, reveal sensitivity toward the subject of unity. Beginning in 1843, the church secretary frequently commented on the attitudes of those involved in church discussions. The March 25, 1852, minutes read, "The meeting throughout was one of great harmony and interest, and was closed with a devout acknowledgement of God's goodness to the

14. *Minutes of the Cortland Baptist Association*, 1848, pp. 9–11; 1851, pp. 8–10; 1852, pp. 8–9.

church—especially in imparting such a spirit of brotherly love as had been exhibited."[15] The comments on unity and brotherly love suggest that such conditions were not always present. Praising the occasions when the congregation behaved amicably kept the "unity ideal" before the fellowship as a goal for which all should strive.

Pleas for unity alone were not enough to restore peace to Cortland County churches. The central problem was general resistance to corporate church authority. By the late 1840s many church members viewed church discipline not as benign guidance but as a vaguely sinister force. The change in attitude is closely related to the evolution of local religious life. Originally the practice of church discipline had been based on the covenanted community, a small, intimate fellowship in which members watched over each other to protect themselves from the snares of "the world, the flesh, and the devil." Over the past thirty years, this sense of "holy separation" had been weakened. The church was now only one organization to which people belonged. Congregations were larger and surveillance of behavior seemed more like bureaucratic imposition than a labor of love. By the late 1840s rigorous church discipline appeared to be a meddlesome, anachronistic holdover from an earlier, less individualistic age.

The decline in church authority is also evident in members' responses to discipline. Unlike the 1810s, when over three-fourths of the cases resulted in compliance, roughly half of the proceedings in the 1840s and 1850s ended in exclusion. Across all three Calvinist denominations, the pattern was one of resistance, not repentance. Between 1845 and 1859, conviction rates were highest among Baptists and Congregationalists with 51 percent of Baptist defendants and 58 percent of the accused Congregationalists refusing to repent and being excluded. Overall, 46 percent of all defendants were eventually excommunicated, a rate only slightly lower than the 51 percent of the tumultuous 1835–44 period (Table C.4).

Instead of creating continued controversy, congregations chose to curtail their discipline efforts. Baptists, for instance, changed

15. Homer Congregational Church, Minutes, March 25, 1852. For other examples, see the church minutes for September 7, 1843, March 25, 1847, April 12, December 25, 1849, and March 27, 1851.

their approach to members who had broken their covenant vows by joining a church of a different denomination. Traditionally, the "hand of fellowship was withdrawn," and the offending member was formally excluded. In the 1850s, however, Baptist churches often dropped denomination-switchers from membership rosters, thus avoiding the unpleasantness of formal excommunication.[16] Local churches apparently ignored other offenses that once would have led to exclusion. Church caseloads plummeted from 3.5 new cases per year in the 1835–44 period to only 1.9 new cases annually between 1845 and 1859 (Table C.5). Church discipline was generally reserved for the most extreme cases. For the sake of unity, local fellowships now overlooked minor misdeeds that would have aroused church leaders a few decades earlier.

Fewer cases meant fewer exclusions. After 1844 the percentage of the evangelical population that was excommunicated each year dropped sharply. The decline took place because, although the conviction rates remained high, the number of cases dropped sharply. Annual exclusions for Baptists fell from 2.03 in 1840–44 to 0.72 in 1855–59. In the same periods, Congregational excommunications dropped from 0.57 to 0.21 annually and Presbyterian removals declined from 0.42 to 0.06. Overall, excommunication rates in the Calvinist churches fell 66 percent between 1840–44 and 1855–59 to their lowest level since the frontier era (Table C.3). The disgraced excommunicant was becoming rarer in Cortland County's religious scene.

By the 1850s Cortland County's churches had finally accepted the ultimate conclusion of Arminianized Calvinism. If humans could determine their eternal fate by choosing God or Satan, seeking a new life of godliness under the guidance of the Holy Spirit, and (according to some) achieving perfect sanctification, why was it necessary for the church to govern members' behavior? The sanctified individual, not the corporate church, was best qualified to determine Christian behavior. In this context, church discipline was an unnecessary encumbrance.

16. Electa Darling, Sarah B. Phillips, Ursula Gregory, and Esther Van Hosen all left the Cortland Baptist Church for the local Methodist church during the 1850s. Van Hosen and Gregory were excommunicated; Darling and Phillips were merely dropped (Cortland First Baptist Church, Record Books, October 14, 1854, June 18, 1852, June 18, 1859).

Initially, the county's congregations had not been willing to accept the new paradigm, but after a decade of bitter strife, they acquiesced. Members were allowed to govern their lives in most areas and discipline was reserved for only the most serious offenses. Caseloads were reduced and the scope of church guidance was minimized. The individual, not the congregation, was dominant. With the protective wall of church discipline seriously eroded and congregational authority over the lives of its members sharply reduced, corporate church structure faced a bleak and uncertain future.

12

The Decline of the Island Mentality

While Cortland County's evangelical churches struggled with ineffective discipline and a loss of unity, more serious problems confronted local congregations during the 1850s. Internal squabbling and failure to get members to adhere to church rules were symptomatic of a larger question: what was the church's place in the larger community? The traditional answer, that congregations serve as islands of holiness within a larger worldly society, seemed less relevant than in previous decades. The island mentality was disappearing as the corporate churches' unique interpretation of reality, separate identity, and remnants of religious authority were severely battered by secularizing forces.

In comparison to earlier decades, evangelical churches were less able to inculcate an overtly religious worldview among their members. Early in the county's history, the local church was second only to the family as an interpreter of reality, at least for those who chose to abide by its precepts. From 1800 to 1825, the faithful were a distinct subcommunity within the county. They did not identify with "worldly" people and struggled to maintain their separateness. Social historians have sometimes described the church as a mirror of larger social trends. In the county's early years, however, the church functioned more as a prism that would refract cultural ideas and precepts through its unique doctrinal and social belief systems.

By the last pre–Civil War decade, evangelical churches tended to mirror society rather than offer a unique interpretation of reality. Where once the local minister had little competition for the attention of his flock, now voices from numerous quarters offered their explanations for how the world operated. Since the 1820s, mass political parties had risen. Sometimes churches were divided along political lines as partisanship had a greater impact on evangelical behavior than pleas for Christian unity.[1] Once the church or companion religious organizations had monopolized voluntary activity. Now temperance, medical, agricultural, educational, mechanic, abolitionist, and numerous other organizations competed with the church for members' attention, money, and energy. As the voice of the church became lost amid the voluntarist din, attitudes of evangelical activists were shaped largely by secular forces. In time, evangelical congregations absorbed the ideas of their more secularized members and eventually came to reflect, rather than alter, the larger community's worldview.

Voluntarism not only undercut the possibility of a unique evangelical cultural perspective, it also blurred the distinctions between church members and the world. How different could a church member be from a nonmember when both contributed to the same charities, served with the same fire department, and supported the same political candidates? The line dividing the "saved" from the "world" made sense when the two groups moved in separate circles. In the 1850s, when saints and sinners inhabited the same voluntarist universe (except for church), the notion that evangelicals were set apart had little social meaning.

An analysis of religious trials reveals the weakened sense of separateness of the 1850s. From the founding of the county's first church, evangelical fellowships struggled to curtail activities that were not specifically condemned by the Bible but were still deemed non-Christian. Particular "sins" such as dancing, card-playing, tavern haunting, and drunkenness, as well as "general wrongdoing," "wandering," and "affinity with the world," could be classified as "worldliness." During the 1820s, county churches reinforced "separation from the world" in the minds of their members by vigorously prosecuting worldliness. In the 1820s such

1. The Cortland Presbyterian Church provides a classic example of how politics could disrupt a local congregation. The controversy is described and perpetuated in the *Cortland Republican*, May 5, December 22, 1835. The reaction of the Cortland Presbyterian session can be followed in Cortland Presbyterian Church, Records, December 25, 1835, January 22, February 29, June 6, 26, July 6, 1836.

offenses accounted for 17 percent of all charges leveled at church members, but by the 1850s charges of worldliness rarely appeared in discipline cases (5 percent of all accusations) (Table C.1). Considering the widespread revolt against religious authority on other fronts, it is unlikely that church members unilaterally stopped participating in prohibited activities. It is more plausible that the church and its members had changed their concept of being set apart from society and now thought of themselves as functioning within society. As a result, sanctions emphasizing separation were less relevant and were less rigidly enforced.

Numerous forces undercut religious authority as the flood of challenges that began in the 1820s and 1830s swamped evangelicalism by the 1850s. Churches faced more competition for people's attention. The coming of the railroad destroyed the last vestiges of the county's "island" status, bringing books, newspapers, and pamphlets from distant places into Cortland homes. Finally, the victory of political egalitarianism and Arminian theology put the autonomous individual in competition with the church as an interpreter of reality.

The enfeebled state of evangelical authority was most evident among Cortland County young people. In the 1820s the youth of Homer treated the leadership of "Father" Keep with deference, if not obedience. By 1860 some Cortland Academy students created an elaborate parody of the once sacrosanct church and academy, referring to the latter as "God's Old Barn." Local historian Herbert Barber Howe commented that, in Keep's day, "there would have been public censure for such levity, and the rebuke would have been taken to heart by young and old."[2] In 1860 the Cortland Academy satirists went unpunished. In forty years, adolescent attitudes toward the county's churches had turned 180 degrees. In the 1820s young people quietly deferred to religious authority; in the 1840s they rebelled against it; in 1860 they ridiculed the church for its loss of authority.

Cortland County's changing social environment had done much to erode the evangelical island mentality by 1860. Overlapping voluntary memberships, religious competition, rising prosperity, and rampant individualism all undercut evangelical influence and helped erase the line separating the church from the

2. Howe, *Barber*, pp. 107–8.

world. Changes within the churches themselves, however, played an even more critical role in the secularization process.

The growing percentage of wealthy, prestigious men as members of Cortland County's evangelical churches was the primary internal force promoting secularization. County residents prospered in the 1850s, but those who had joined evangelical church fellowships advanced more than most. Between 1850 and 1860, the percentage of male household heads in the county with at least $2,100 in property grew from 21 to 35 percent. In the same time period, the portion of evangelical male household heads who had property worth at least $2,100 expanded from 30 to 48 percent. By 1860 only 12 percent of the evangelical heads of household were without land compared to 21 percent in the county at large (Table B.5). The divergence of evangelical church members from county wealth norms had grown steadily from 1825 to the Civil War. In 1825 wealth differences between evangelicals and other county residents were only marginal (Eta = .09). By 1860, after adjusting for age, Eta had increased to .15 (Tables B.4 and B.5).[3]

The divergence between male church members and the remainder of the county went beyond wealth—occupational differences emerged as well. In 1840 and 1850 the difference in occupational pursuits between the evangelicals and the rest of the county population was negligible. By 1860 the churches had almost double the county percentage of merchants, bankers, manufacturers, professionals, storeowners, and white-collar workers. The opposite was true for unskilled labor and factory employees. County residents were four times as likely to belong to these low-status occupations as were evangelicals (Table B.6). When comparing occupational differences between evangelicals and the rest of the county, Eta rose from .01 in 1840 to .17 in 1860 (Table B.6). For the first time in county history, genuine class differences between evangelicals and the nonchurched emerged during the 1850s as

3. Eta measures the differences in distribution patterns between two groups. In order to use Eta, the data must be placed in categories, whereupon the distributional pattern of the first group is compared to the distributional pattern of the second group. If the two groups have their data distributed among the categories in identical proportions, Eta equals .oo. When the percentage of cases falling into each category is sharply different for the two groups, Eta will be relatively large. For further explanation of this statistic, see Charles M. Dollar and Richard Jensen, *Historian's Guide to Statistics* (Huntington, N.Y., 1971), pp. 73–78.

the two groups developed markedly different wealth and occupational profiles.

The reasons why wealthier and higher-status individuals gravitated toward the county's churches are twofold. First, the religious societies appear to have lost much of their appeal. During the century's first two decades, many citizens viewed supporting a local congregation as their civic responsibility, even if they were not church members. The simplest way to offer such moral and financial support was through membership in a religious society. Up to 1820, the Homer Baptist Society and the Religious Society of Homer kept extensive membership lists of everyone who joined. These records reveal that about half the adult male population of Homer had joined one of the two societies by 1820. After this date, the organization of county societies became ill-defined and amorphous. Membership lists were not maintained by any of these religious support groups, which suggests that membership was not deemed particularly important even by the organizations themselves. Society activists can be identified only by annual election results, lists of those renting pews, and subscription lists for construction of or improvements to the worship house. By 1855 roughly 15 percent of the male population participated in religious society activities. This was an astounding membership loss. The religious societies lost their appeal because of the widespread adoption of Arminian theology, which undercut the social prestige of society membership; the larger size of most congregations, which guaranteed sufficient funds for all essential functions without outside community support; and the proliferation of other worthy voluntary organizations that competed with the societies for the public's attention and dollars. With societies declining in power and prestige, affluent minimalists reconsidered the prospect of church membership.

The second reason why congregations grew increasingly wealthy, in absolute terms and relative to the larger county population, is that wealthy members no longer had to fear the power of the corporate church. Church discipline had been curtailed for the sake of unity. With congregational control weakened, men who professed personal faith but who held a minimalist view of proper church authority dared join local evangelical fellowships.

Once in, wealthy males furthered the erosion of church influence by seeking to limit the scope of church discipline. These efforts went beyond reducing the number of cases; the charges against church members had to change. From 1801 to 1849, 42 percent of all charges against church members involved behavior outside of church and were thus in the public domain. Wealthy males resented this control because it gave the corporate church the right to regulate everyday social and commercial behavior. From the minimalist perspective, the church had the right to rule on religious matters and should leave other aspects of members' lives alone.

In the 1850s, as wealthy men entered the county's churches in ever-increasing numbers, the scope of church discipline shrank dramatically. Charges in the public domain dropped precipitously from 128 in 1840–49 to only 29 in 1850–59. A breakdown of this disciplinary collapse reveals that between 1840–49 and 1850–59, charges of breaking the commandments fell from 75 to 15, investigations of interpersonal conflict dropped from 22 to 6, and accusations of worldliness declined from 31 to 8. During the 1850s, charges in the ecclesiastical domain declined but by much smaller margins. As a result, the scope of the public domain was reduced from 43 percent of all charges in the 1840s to only 19 percent of all accusations in the 1850s (Table C.1). Corporate control of members' nonchurch behavior was now broken; the minimalist view of church discipline had triumphed.

Wealthy church members generally sought to reduce the church's authority in the public domain, but their greatest impact came in the realm of church regulation of business behavior. As late as the 1840s, wealthy church members who cut corners in their commercial dealings had reason to fear the church's authority. Between 1840 and 1849, at least twenty-five charges of commercial wrongdoing were leveled at church members. As wealthy men assumed control, secular business matters were removed from the congregational agenda. Between 1850 and 1860, only three such charges appeared in the county's ecclesiastical records (Table C.2). By midcentury, the merchant, lawyer, or large landowner could quietly occupy his Sunday pew without worrying whether a church committee would investigate his weekday behavior. Wealthy minimalists once had to hide out in the religious societies to be free from the searching eyes of the church discipline committee. In the 1850s, with the corporate church emasculated, the same men could enter the church on profession of faith and never worry about the congregation meddling in their personal financial affairs.

Not surprisingly, the memberships of churches and their affiliated religious societies gradually merged. As some society members abandoned the religious financial support groups, others asked why they should remain second-class religionists when church membership no longer threatened personal autonomy. In 1810 about 20 percent of society members also belonged to a church. Ten years later, this figure increased to 30 percent. By 1832, 34 percent of society members had joined a local congregation. The biggest surge of society members toward church membership came in the following two decades. By 1855–61, 58 percent of all society members had joined a local evangelical fellowship.[4]

The relative and absolute increase in congregational wealth affected numerous areas of church life. Two of the most important changes involved the nature of congregational activity and the role of women.

When the county's first congregations were formed, evangelical religion was homemade, heartfelt, and intensely personal. Church members had to be intellectually and existentially involved with their faith because religious sources were meager. Confessions of faith and practice were developed by a local committee. Music, if present at all, was sung a cappella. Perhaps only a handful of parishioners had hymnals. Covenant meetings tied people together in close-knit fellowships that shared personal religious experiences. When the congregation had no minister, these expressions were the primary means of expounding on the faith. The early churches struggled merely to survive, but out of their exertions came the intense personal piety that paved the way for the first large wave of revivals. Early evangelicals may have been poor, but their poverty was not of the spirit.

The churches of the 1850s lacked the intense piety of earlier generations. Congregational records reveal that a subtle, businesslike secularization had crept into local fellowships. Organization was emphasized over enthusiasm. Personal piety was ne-

4. The percentages were calculated by matching lists of society members against lists of church members. The First Religious Society of Homer and the Homer Baptist Society records were used for 1810 and 1820. The records which were used for 1832 and 1855–61 are described in chapter 4, note 9.

glected in favor of taking care of church business. The changes did not happen overnight but had been coming subtly over the past several decades. By the 1850s the concerns and practices of churches and their members were markedly different from those of decades before. Raising money, maintaining the church building, and dealing with petty monetary matters were now a major concern and consumed considerable space in the church minutes.

The best example of this shift is found in the records of the Cortland (formerly Homer) Baptist Church. Early in its history, this church's minutes were almost obsessively concerned with the spiritual health of the congregation. Hardly a covenant meeting went by without a notation in the minutes concerning the "state of feeling" of the gathered "brethren and sisters." By contrast, from 1851 through 1860, the degree of fervor within the congregation was commented on only once. The church's fiftieth anniversary, subscriptions for a singing school, blinds for the meetinghouse, offering a cleaning contract to the lowest bidder, paying the sexton for minor repairs, building a railing and sidewalk around the church, selecting a committee to repair the roof and clean the church, and repairing the church steps occupied the Cortland church's attention. Not surprisingly, the one time the congregation requested the pastor to speak on a specific subject, the matter to be addressed was "the duty of church members to sustain the interests of the church."[5] In an earlier era, congregational minutes primarily discussed personal and group spirituality; now they focused on organizational details.

The shift from personal piety to congregational prosperity can be traced to the rising influence of increasingly wealthy male members. Congregations had more money at their disposal than ever before, but the additional funds had a negative effect on personal faith. At one time, congregational articles of faith and practice were painstakingly created by a local committee that carefully drafted each point of doctrine. By the 1850s there was growing sentiment in favor of adopting statements of faith and practice originating from major urban publishing centers. Presumably, copies of the articles would then be purchased and

5. Cortland First Baptist Church, Record Book, February 15, October 15, 1851, October 18, 1852, June 18, October 15, 1853, June 14, 1856, June 20, 1857, and April 14, 1860, April 11, 1859.

distributed to members. The first known attempt to adopt mass-produced doctrinal statements was rejected by the Cortland Baptists in 1854.[6] Six years later, a similar proposal was made and eventually adopted in the Virgil Baptist Church.[7] As the wealth of members increased, more supplementary religious materials were purchased. The Truxton Congregationalists bought new hymnals in 1845 as did their Homer brethren in 1849.[8] The Union Congregationalists began to use *The Christian Manual* in 1851 and bought $100 worth of Sabbath School books nine years later.[9] By 1860 the Cortlandville and Cincinnatus Baptist churches not only averaged fifty subscriptions each to *The Young Reaper* but had established church libraries.[10] Mass-produced religious materials made worship easier and more enjoyable but reduced congregations' use of their own personal spiritual resources. With new wealth at their disposal, county fellowships sought the best religious services that money could buy.

The increased religious influence of prosperous men led to a minimized role for evangelical women. This shift in power between the sexes most likely led to altered congregational priorities and may explain the low evangelism rates of the 1850s. In the frontier era, devout females were able to break through the male hierarchy because churches were fragile instruments of grace that required the help of all who were willing. As a result, women often played important, if unofficial, roles. Women initiated the founding of the county's first Congregational church as well as the county's first major revival. Eventually women spoke regarding the qualifications of prospective members, served on discipline committees, and occasionally even voted on the retention of the minister. The early role of women can be linked to the desperate need of cash-poor congregations for financial contributions. Through individual giving and organized benevolence, women provided evangelical denominations with invaluable monetary assistance.

6. Ibid., June 17, 1854.
7. Virgil Baptist Church, Minutes, December 1, 1860, March 2, 1861.
8. Truxton First Presbyterian Church, Records, March 19, 1845, Accession No. 6241, CUA. Homer Congregational Church, Minutes, June 1849.
9. Cincinnatus and Solon, Union Congregational Church, Records, May 2, 1851, June 30, 1860.
10. *Minutes of the Cortland Baptist Association*, 1860.

After 1830 women became less important in church financial affairs. Powerful statistical evidence of this trend is contained in the Cortland Baptist Association's donor lists for benevolent projects. In 1828–29, 52 percent of the giving for benevolence came from women. By the late 1850s known female contributions fell to only 4 percent of all benevolence (Table D.1).

During this thirty-year period, female contributions to the Cortland Baptist Association declined in both absolute and relative terms. Much of the absolute decline can be traced to changing economic conditions. Improved transportation and the development of a regional market destroyed demand for homemade textiles. Since much of what women gave (87 percent in 1828–29) was clothing, blankets, and other handicrafts made at home or in church sewing circles, the changing market largely destroyed their ability to contribute to benevolent projects. By the early 1850s female donations in the form of domestic goods was only 14 percent of 1828–29 levels (percentages derived from Table D.1). The doubling of cash contributions was not enough to offset the sharp decline in product donations, which meant that, overall, female giving in the 1850s was roughly half of what it had been in the late 1820s.

The relative decline in female giving to the association was far more important than the absolute decline. Even if women's contributions had remained the same as in the early 1830s, the proportion of their donations would have fallen from one-half to one-eleventh of all giving by the beginning of the Civil War. The key variable in shifting gender contributions was unprecedented male affluence fostered by a strong cash economy. Despite the absolute decline in female contributions, total Baptist benevolence contributions rose from 16 cents per member in 1828–39 to 60 cents in 1850–59.[11] Among Presbyterians and Congregationalists, whose female contributors were presumably suffering from the same adverse economic forces, per capita giving to the presbytery's benevolence funds rose from 39 cents between 1824 and 1838 to $1.31 between 1852 and 1859.[12] As men grew more prosperous and entered the weakened corporate church, women's financial gifts were no longer needed.

11. Ibid., 1828–39, 1850–59.
12. *Minutes of the General Assembly*, 1824–38, 1852–59.

As women were displaced from their position as economic partners, they probably lost influence in other aspects of church life as well. Although there is no evidence that women lost privileges gained in earlier decades, the 1850s brought no advances either. Official church policy, however, may not reveal all of the relevant internal dynamics. Women's work in evangelical congregations had always been primarily informal and usually went unrecognized by male leaders.

The flaccid evangelism indexes of the 1850s among Calvinist churches suggest that women were losing informal influence within the churches in that decade. Females, whether working through voluntary religious societies or extended kin networks, had traditionally been at the heart of county revivals. The county's greatest revivals occurred at a time when women were significant financial contributors to evangelical projects and thus had informal influence over church funds and activities. By the 1850s, women had lost their economic clout. At the same time, organizational and material concerns (traditionally male preoccupations) dominated congregational attention, replacing the traditional female focus on evangelizing family and kin. Not surprisingly, county evangelism indexes reached record lows in the 1845–59 era. Baptists annually had only 4.63 converts per 100 members in this fifteen-year period; the Presbyterian-Congregational rate fell to 3.35 during the same span. Both figures were far below the evangelism rates of the 1816–44 period (Table B.3). In short, as wealthy men grew powerful enough to ignore female religious advice and influence, the ability of evangelical churches to evangelize fell proportionately.

The low levels of religious conversion do not represent a total male disregard for evangelism, however. When men came to dominate congregational affairs, the emphasis shifted from personal to bureaucratic evangelism. Instead of converting their neighbors, churches now sought to raise funds to save the world.

Benevolence, of course, had long been a feature of evangelical life, but in the 1850s religious fund-raising proliferated far beyond earlier proportions. At an 1860 business meeting, the Homer Congregational Church noted that the church was currently contributing to the American Board of Foreign Missions, the American Tract Society, the Bible Society, the Bethel Cause, Sabbath Schools, the American and Foreign Christian Union, the

Education Cause, the home mission church in Cedar Falls, Iowa, the Reverend Mr. Loquen of Syracuse, the Publication Cause, the American Missionary Association, and the home mission church in Richmond, Illinois. Because of the growing sums of money spent in religious philanthropy, the Homer church had two treasurers, one to handle regular church finances and one who dealt only with benevolent contributions.[13] The Truxton Congregationalists responded to the myriad pleas for financial help by resolving to "take 6 collections during the year for many of the prominent objects of benevolence which come before the churches."[14] The burden of benevolence grew so great that Baptists began to complain. In 1852 Hezekiah Harvey bemoaned that the typical Baptist association had become "a merely fiscal organization."[15] Six years later, the Cortland Baptist Association urged the consolidation of benevolence efforts because "we have too many Societies."[16] Calvinist churches everywhere were flooded with pleas for money.

By the 1850s the local evangelical churches were losing their place as the locus of evangelistic effort. Instead of supplementing local efforts, national organizations now viewed themselves as being all-important, with local congregations serving as their auxiliaries. Once the servant of local churches, the numerous missionary, tract, and Bible societies now sought the position of master.

Of all of the major evangelical groups, only the Methodists appear to have avoided the penchant for bureaucratic over personal evangelism in the 1850s. There are several reasons why the Methodists retained older evangelical habits. First, the Methodists were antiformal in orientation and hence were more skeptical than Presbyterians and Congregationalists about the utility of major organized efforts. Second, unlike the Calvinists, the Methodists had been Arminian from the very beginning of Cortland County history. As a result, they did not undergo conversion to Arminianism by way of Finneyite theology, which emphasized organized benevolence as the fruits of salvation. Local Methodists could, as they had in the past, emphasize personal salvation to the

13. Homer Congregational Church, Minutes, March 29, 1860.
14. Truxton First Presbyterian Church, Records, February 15, 1859.
15. Harvey, *Memoir*, p. 104.
16. *Minutes of the Cortland Baptist Association*, 1858, p. 6.

exclusion of other issues. Never having experienced the impact of the New Measures, Methodists placed little faith in Finney's formulas but rather adapted to changing conditions. Several revivals occurred among local Methodists in the 1850s without the aid of protracted meetings.[17] Third, Methodists remained the least wealthy major evangelical group up to the Civil War (Tables B.7 and B.8). As a result, they were less distracted by the need to maintain elaborate churches or raise funds for national organizations and by the secular values of wealthy male minimalists. As a result, Methodists had to rely more on their own individual spiritual resources and devoted more energy to personal than to bureaucratic evangelism. Not surprisingly, county Methodist membership increased over 60 percent between 1850 and 1860 while the collective membership of the three major Calvinist groups declined.

Overall, the balance of power within Cortland County's evangelical churches shifted remarkably between the early 1840s and 1860. The ultraists had been the primary proponents for expanding the power of the corporate church over members' private and political lives. Most ultraists, however, bolted the Calvinist churches when their pleas for greater church activism went unheeded. Women, because of their vulnerable social position, had also favored a strong corporate church, partly to restrain male behavior. But they had lost considerable economic clout between 1830 and 1860. The vacuum created by declining ultraist and female influence was filled by the growing presence of wealthy and prestigious men, who advocated a modified form of minimalism. Unlike those who dominated early religious societies, the new male elite was willing to retain religious conversion as a requirement of membership. Once accepted into membership, however, prosperous males demanded that the church exert minimal influence over the public and private lives of its members.

In 1873 the parishioners of Homer Congregational Church received a most unexpected pleasure. Jedediah Barber—wealthy merchant, longtime religious society member, scourge of the Reverend John Keep, and resister of ecclesiastical authority—walked to the front of the church to request that he be admitted to

---

17. Davis, *History of the Methodist Episcopal Church*, pp. 136–39.

membership. The event no doubt created a great stir. His wife, Matilda Barber, had experienced saving grace during the county's first major revival in 1813. For sixty years, Jedediah Barber had resisted the supplications of his wife, his son Paris, and numerous friends and relatives to repent, give his life to God, and formally enter the Homer fellowship. Now, at the age of eighty-six, the crusty old merchant finally yielded to family pressure and willingly entered the Kingdom of God.[18]

Most in the audience that day probably interpreted Barber's membership vows as a triumph for the Homer congregation. The old man had finally given in. In terms of individual versus ecclesiastical power, however, Barber's entry was not a congregational victory but a sign of its defeat. The Homer Congregational Church that Barber joined was vastly different from the evangelical churches of 1813, 1831, or even 1845. After a long struggle, the minimalists, riding on a wave of prosperity, had emerged victorious. The corporate church had been stripped of its claws. Jedediah Barber no longer had reason to fear ecclesiastical meddling in his private and public life. There was no longer any reason to resist conversion and, once he had experienced saving grace, Barber joined. Homer Congregational Church now fit Barber's image of what a church should be and, accordingly, the victory was his. As in the rest of the county's Calvinist congregations, minimalists could rest easy. The corporate church was dead, and a "modern" church had taken its place.

18. Howe, *Barber*, p. 172.

13

Cortland County Churches
as "Modern" Churches

Cortland County's churches had changed considerably since their founding in the early 1800s. H. Richard Niebuhr's typology regarding the church and culture can be used to interpret this spiritual migration. Niebuhr argued that the church had the choices of standing against the dominant culture, seeking to transform wider culture, or simply confirming existing culture.[1] Cortland's evangelical churches progressed through all three modes. In the 1810s county fellowships stood as islands of holiness in a community perceived to lack religious seriousness. By the 1830s churches sought to transform Cortland society through religious revivalism, social reform, or both. By the 1850s mainstream evangelicalism was largely conformist as churches mimicked the middle-class culture of that era. As today, mainstream and evangelical churches of the 1850s fit the confirming mode much more clearly than either the oppositional or transforming postures. In short, the chaos of the 1830s and early 1840s destroyed the corporate church and paved the way for the "modern" church.

The term *modern* has been deliberately enclosed with quotation marks. In other studies, this term has often been equivalent to "whatever exists today." Although such a definition lacks analytical content, it is sufficient for the purpose of this study. Cortland County's evangelical churches abandoned traditional corporate

1. H. Richard Niebuhr, *Christ and Culture* (New York, 1951), esp. pp. 39–44.

structure in the late 1840s and 1850s and adopted the church structure now familiar to contemporary Americans. In that sense, county religion had indeed become "modern."

One of the most striking features of Cortland's congregations of the 1850s is that they were no longer islands of holiness. In most ways, church members acted and behaved as their neighbors because they shared the same primary sources of information and socialization. Cases involving worldliness nearly disappeared from church dockets as members became far less interested in separating Christian from non-Christian behavior. In this sense, the Cortland County churches of the 1850s were closer to Protestant congregations in twentieth-century America than to the fellowships of only three decades earlier. Today, mainstream Protestant behavior and thought so closely mirror national norms that one school of church scholars has concluded that their inability to identify distinctive central beliefs that are beyond compromise is the primary reason for their falling membership over the past several decades.[2] Evangelical Protestants, on the other hand, work hard at maintaining doctrinal and behavioral standards. Even so, contemporary evangelicals generally confirm culture as their list of traditional taboos steadily shrinks and they adopt widespread but questionably Christian business, social, and political ideas and practices.

Cortland County congregations were "modern" in where they placed ultimate religious authority. Matters of individual belief and practice were increasingly left to church members to decide, and the individual replaced the gathered church as the locus of religious power. Discipline was seen as undemocratic and was reserved for only the most serious offenses. Contemporary Protestant congregations have continued this shift toward individual autonomy. Today church discipline is rarely invoked, except by

2. For an overview of the debate, see Dean R. Hoge and David A. Roozen, eds. *Understanding Church Growth and Decline, 1950–1978* (New York, 1979). Dean Kelley's *Why Conservative Churches Are Growing* (New York, 1972) argues that a lack of mainstream Protestant "strictness" regarding doctrine and practice led to mainstream decline in the 1960s while conservative churches, clear about their mission and purpose, continued to grow. Others have cited demographic factors as being more important in producing church growth. See William McKinney and Dean R. Hoge, "Community and Congregational Factors in the Growth and Decline of Protestant Churches," *Journal for the Scientific Study of Religion* 22 (1983): 51–66.

certain fundamentalist groups, and its future is made doubtful by recent court decisions.[3] Rigid standards of behavior are passé, and some mainline groups do not require agreement with denominational statements of faith.[4] In doctrine and daily practice, the contemporary Protestant is basically unencumbered by ecclesiastical authority.

As secularization undermined the island mentality and as individualism undercut congregational authority, the symbolic importance of church membership was devalued. In 1810 joining a church meant "leaving the world" and adhering to a "holy community." Fifty years later, church membership meant that one was merely joining another local voluntary association. When Cortland County was founded, joining a church meant submitting oneself to the authority of one's fellow believers. By the Civil War, rigid codes of behavior were loosened and activities that once brought rebuke were tolerated. The sacrifice of personal autonomy that once inhibited many from formal membership was now largely absent. As a result, by the late 1850s membership hovered between 25 and 30 percent of the adult population (Table B.1). Since that time, Protestantism has continued to relax admission requirements (a few informal meetings with the minister usually suffice) and to reduce behavioral standards for those already admitted. Generally, membership involves little personal commitment, a condition readily appreciated by the American public, as now about 70 percent of all adults formally belong to a church or synagogue.[5]

During the 1850s both formal and antiformal denominations in the county gravitated toward increased fund-raising, bureaucracy, and organizational complexity. Maintaining church buildings became more important than maintaining high levels of spirituality. Standardized hymnals, prayer books, devotionals,

3. *New York Times*, March 16, 1984, sec. 1, 13:2.
4. Two notable examples are the United Church of Christ and the United Methodist Church.
5. In 1981 58.7 percent of the United States population belonged to a church, down slightly from the 60.5 percent reporting membership in 1980. See Constant H. Jacquet, Jr., ed., *Yearbook of American and Canadian Churches, 1982* (Nashville, Tenn., 1982), p. 236. If the percentages are restricted to adults, the contemporary percentage of church members is higher. In 1982 68 percent of those interviewed by the Gallup Poll identified themselves as church members. See *Religion in America: The Gallup Report*, No. 201–2, June–July 1982.

and Sabbath School materials could be purchased, thus reducing the need for intense private spirituality. The preoccupation with programs, budgets, and building maintenance continues to dominate both mainline and evangelical Protestantism. Even those groups that emphasize "religion of the heart" largely do so through prepackaged Bible studies, simplistic formulas such as the "Four Spiritual Laws," and evangelistic tape recordings. These materials may encourage conversion and provide the rudiments of Christian theology, but they fail to address the existential questions of belief and meaning posed by thoughtful churchgoing Americans. As in nineteenth-century Cortland County, wealthy congregations often pursue program at the expense of religious purpose. Encouraging personal spiritual growth has become a casualty.

Early in Cortland County history, evangelical churches offered the greatest opportunities for women outside of the household. Women prayed together, encouraged the salvation of their kin, organized to raise money for benevolence, and, in many ways, were the heart of the church. They made tentative gains within the congregational power structure. By the 1850s, however, women had lost their economic clout and new opportunities for service did not arise. Nineteenth-century feminism, which in many ways had its origins in the evangelical subculture, shifted its attention increasingly to the secular arena as religious opportunities shriveled. Today, Protestantism still lags behind the larger culture in providing professional opportunities for women. Despite the preponderance of females among church members, women find it hard to rise above entry-level positions in the ministry. The contemporary Protestant record on women's rights no doubt has contributed to the desire of many radical feminists to abandon orthodox Christianity.[6]

In sum, the collapse of Cortland County's corporate church structure in the 1850s led to the formation of churches that were modern in organization, orientation, and values. The supremacy of the individual, the celebration of commercial values, a penchant for program, a dearth of personal spirituality, fewer opportunities for women than for men, and a lack of commitment to

6. A quick orientation to feminist theology can be found in Rosemary Radford Ruether, *Womanguides: Readings toward a Feminist Theology* (Boston, 1985), and Janet Kalvin and Mary I. Buckley, eds., *Women's Spirit Bonding* (New York, 1984).

that which involves personal sacrifice characterized Cortland County society then as it reflects American society now—whether one is within the Protestant church or without.

Despite the capitulation of American Calvinism to individualism during the Second Great Awakening, the battle between church authority and individual autonomy continues today. Sonja Johnson, the Mormon feminist excluded from the Church of the Latter Day Saints, and Charles Curran, the Catholic academic, are fighting battles for individual conscience that resemble those fought by Oren Cravath and Stephen Brewer in long-ago Cortland County.[7] The assertion of American individualism within the Mormon and Catholic hierarchies presents the two denominations with the same dilemma that Cortland County evangelicals faced in the early nineteenth century. If the Mormon and Catholic churches choose to deny the sovereignty of the individual conscience, they will run against the dominant stream of contemporary thought and experience, create cognitive dissonance for their members, and alienate their larger American audience. Hierarchism is out of fashion in this egalitarian age. Ardent defenders of ecclesiastical authority face the same consequences as rigid predestinarians faced a century ago—faithfulness to outdated doctrine leads to reduced membership and declining social influence.

Yet compromise with dominant cultural values does not appear to be the answer either. The experience of Cortland County's evangelical congregations cautions against total capitulation to individual autonomy. When church discipline collapsed between 1845 and 1860 in the face of rising individualism, doors were opened to further secularization, reduced religious standards, and a blurring of the evangelical message. Such history warns contemporary religionists that when the church is no longer able to direct its members, but merely follows what a majority wants at any given time, it loses its character, its message, its identity, and its very reason for existence. Instead of improving society, the church merely reflects the secular trends of its time. The dilemma over whether and when to compromise is real. The Catholic and Mormon churches of today must walk the tightrope between losing their audience and diluting their message.

Some hope for churches caught in the struggle between indi-

7. *New York Times*, August 19, 1986, sec. 1, 1:2, December 6, 1979, 26:1.

vidualism and church authority can be gained from the experience of Cortland County's Methodists. Despite adverse conditions in the early 1800s, the Methodists rode out the theological storms of the antebellum era to become the county's largest denomination by the Civil War. A strict religious hierarchy assured the Methodists' success. Within the Methodist system, "disagreements had to be formally resolved or generally agreed to be unimportant."[8] As a result, all Methodists were required to accept the essentials of faith but were given considerable latitude in matters of individual conscience. Thus the sons and daughters of John Wesley were able to steer a middle path between uncontrollable individualism on one hand and suffocating church authority on the other.

The approach of balancing competing claims of church and individual rights was enhanced by the Methodist emphasis on personal spirituality. As antiformalists, Methodists had always been skeptical of organized programs, especially those directed to changing society. Less wealthy and less Whiggish than antiformal Baptists, Methodists were both less able and less tempted to seek organizational solutions to either social or religious problems. Instead, the relatively poor Methodists used their own spiritual resources to foster personal religion among their members. By emphasizing the life of the spirit, Cortland County Methodists maintained the religious style of the frontier era when religion was not the best money could buy—it was the genuine article.

8. Ahlstrom, *Religious History*, 2:107. Although this hierarchic system tended to increase personal freedom at the local level, it could severely divide the denomination at the national level when controversial topics such as slavery arose.

Conclusion

The Second Great Awakening was an intellectual watershed in American history. In the tumultuous decades of the early nineteenth century, the citizens of the United States threw off the vestiges of the colonial communitarian ethos and embraced republican individualism. Economic, political, and social institutions were restructured in a "democratic" direction. Northern Protestantism felt the impact of this transformation as Calvinist orthodoxy and corporate church authority were challenged by the message and methods of the evangelical Arminians. By the time the revivals had run their course, Protestant churches were very different institutions than they had been just thirty years earlier.

Although religious enthusiasm in upstate New York ebbed in the 1850s, the process of religious renewal and revitalization continues within American Christianity. As Frances FitzGerald argues in *Cities on a Hill*, the process of reworking one's worldview is an integral part of contemporary American culture. Americans are always seeking to reinvent themselves, to "start over," to be "born again." FitzGerald notes, "The history of the religious revivals of the 1830s and 1840s throws a good deal of light on the events of the 1960s and 1970s."[1] The Burned-over District is unique in this process as "upstate New York was an analogue to Southern California in the 1960s," and the Oneida Community,

1. Frances FitzGerald, *Cities on a Hill: A Journey through Contemporary American Cultures* (New York, 1986), p. 390.

the Mormons, and perfectionist revivalists serve as nineteenth-century parallels to contemporary retirement communities, Rajneeshees, gay activities, and Protestant fundamentalists.[2]

Because of the role of the Second Great Awakening and the Burned-over District in our "usable past," it is important that we understand early nineteenth-century New York evangelicalism. To this end, I offer the principal conclusions of this study as seven propositions.

First, *antebellum American religion must be analyzed in the context of rural, as well as urban, environments.* Contemporary historians have a tendency to read the urbanized present back into the past. "Urban" often appears to represent modern values; "rural" represents traditional and perhaps "backward" mores. Scholars seeking to understand "how we came to what we are" must, of course, study nineteenth-century cities, where markets expanded, factories grew, immigrants settled, power was centralized, and culture was transformed. As a result, studies of antebellum religion have had a decided urban cast. Although we see much of ourselves in the cities of a century ago, we must not overemphasize the city's impact on antebellum America. In 1800 about 80 percent of America's population farmed; in 1860 the proportion was still well over half. Thus history written with an urban bias fails to address the lives of over half the nation's population. Urban studies are extremely important but one must go beyond this approach to gain a full understanding of American culture.

Perhaps one of the worst errors that scholars can make is to interpret the Second Great Awakening solely on the basis of urban revivals. The historiography of the 1950s and 1960s produced vivid but now somewhat dated portraits of rural revivalism, but studies of the awakening produced in the 1970s and 1980s, using the latest social science methods and theory, focus almost exclusively on citified religion. Generalizations from these investigations do not apply to a rural setting. Paul Johnson's class analysis cannot be employed to explain Cortland County's revivals of the 1830s because factories and industrial wage labor did not arrive in significant numbers until the 1850s. Likewise, it is difficult to transfer Mary Ryan's analysis of Utica to Cortland County. Women were as important to Cortland revivals as they

2. Ibid., pp. 383–414; quotation on p. 397.

were to those in Oneida County, but Cortland women were not shocked into action by hordes of directionless young people flooding into the county's largest villages, nor did they express their religious concerns primarily through female voluntarist organizations. Instead, rural women were driven to evangelism by a spiritual republicanism, a desire to see their congregations maintained in the face of heavy out-migration, and an overwhelming concern that their offspring find God before abandoning the county for the West. In pursuing their religious goals, Cortland women channeled their efforts primarily through the traditional institutions of church and family. Overall, the motivations of Cortland evangelicals were quite different from those of their coreligionists in nearby urban locales.

Second, *ideology played a greater role in promoting rural revivalism than did broad-based economic and demographic factors.* Changing religious ideas played the central role. Evangelism rates increased as evangelicals came to believe that personal salvation was vitally important and became convinced that they had a role in promoting the salvation of themselves and others.

A number of social factors promoted belief in the vital importance of salvation—the need for women to control aggressive male behavior by bringing men under the domain of the local church, the need for congregations to gain or maintain institutional viability by attracting new members, the need for women to convert offspring before they left home and were lost to parental influence, and, most important, the overriding evangelical assumption that a personal salvation experience was necessary for anyone seeking the blessing of eternal life. As long as these factors pressured county Protestants into evangelistic activity, revivals were common and the number of souls saved remained high. Once these pressures eased and material concerns replaced religious desires during the late 1840s and 1850s, evangelism rates plummeted.

Economic and demographic conditions had some impact on the perceived importance of salvation but relatively little on the debate over free will. During the early decades of the nineteenth century, Cortland Calvinists were meeting increasing resistance to their predestinarian doctrine, which was out of step with the popular republican values of self-determination and self-reliance. Women, in particular, abandoned strict Calvinism by encouraging their friends and relatives to "accept Jesus" even though Calvinist doctrine ordained that such efforts did not bring salvation. Despite such behavioral wandering, Calvinist congregations upheld official church teaching in the face of Arminian encroachments until the early 1830s. At that point, John Keep and Jedediah Burchard, borrowing heavily from Charles Finney, introduced Arminianized Calvinism (which stressed the individual's responsibility for his or her salvation) and the New Measures (which emphasized human ability to promote the salvation of others) into the Homer Congregational Church. Other Calvinist fellowships quickly followed, and the Arminian belief that people could influence the salvation of themselves and others expanded beyond the Methodists to all evangelical groups in the early 1830s. Correspondingly, with belief in both the attainability and the importance of salvation at record levels, local Protestants evangelized more successfully in the early 1830s than at any time between settlement and the Civil War.

Economic and demographic factors are less important than ideology because during the great revivals of the 1820s and 1830s, evangelicals differed little (except for the preponderance of females) from their neighbors. Male evangelical church members had about the same wealth and occupational profiles as did male household heads across the county.

Third, *women played a central role in spreading evangelical values and religious enthusiasm.* From the very beginning, evangelical women were deeply involved in Cortland County religion. They provided leadership that led to the county's first church, helped spark the first major local revival, raised surprising sums of money for benevolent causes, and supported efforts to Arminianize Calvinism in the 1830s. The reasons for this female support are manifold. Spiritual republicanism was nearly the only part of the republican self-definition that women were allowed. The churches offered some protection against male abuse. Local congregations offered significantly more opportunities for service than did other social institutions. Most important, local churches were the medium through which women, their husbands, and their children could hear the message of saving grace. As long as women were able to operate with relative freedom in the county's evangelical churches, evangelism rates remained high. During the 1850s, when women were displaced from their position as agents of the gospel message, evangelistic success declined drastically.

Fourth, *wealthy men had a negative impact on evangelical values generally and on revivalism in particular.* Between 1812 and 1835, when revivalism rates were high, the economic profiles of church members were not much different from those of others in the community. As institutions, churches were generally small and needed the personal spiritual resources of all members. These needs opened the doors of service to evangelical women, who provided a large percentage of the church's energy and financial support. In this era, wealthy men—fearful of the corporate church's power over their personal and public lives—generally participated only in religious societies, if at all.

After corporate church power was broken by the divisions of the late 1830s and early 1840s, wealthy males entered the county's evangelical churches in ever-increasing numbers. As society members, such men had long fought temperance, abolitionist, and revivalistic efforts. Once affluent men had assumed even more crucial positions as church members, their influence was pervasive. Women were displaced because their gifts were no longer essential to the financial health of congregation and denomination. Personal religious knowledge became less important because churches were able to buy articles of faith, hymnals, devotionals, and Sabbath School materials for their members. Church meetings of the 1850s mirrored the commercial values of their wealthiest members. Instead of promoting evangelism, wealthy males brought attitudes and practices into county churches that dropped evangelism rates between 1845 and 1860 to very low levels. Only the Methodists, the least wealthy of the four major evangelical groups, were able to sustain successful evangelism and high levels of growth.

Fifth, *evangelical Protestants were clearly a minority in Cortland County, as they were throughout the United States, during the antebellum period.* A majority of Cortlanders probably identified themselves with a religious denomination. Some went a step further and provided financial support to a congregation through membership in a religious society. The motivations for such identification and participation varied from feelings of civic duty, to seeking social companionship, to shared political values. But identification with a religious denomination or membership in a religious society did not make a person an evangelical. Cortland County's antebellum evangelicals believed that individuals crossed over from the world to the gathered church only after having experienced saving grace. Until individuals—no matter how respectable and financially benevolent—had joined the ranks of the redeemed they were held suspect by Cortland's islands of holiness and were denied church membership. In every decade, only a minority of those who identified with a denomination and fewer of the county's adult population ever had the requisite salvation experience to ascend to full church membership.[3]

The minority status of evangelical church members has enormous implications for historical scholarship. One cannot analyze antebellum behavior and pre–Civil War social structure simply by observing evangelical churches—the church is not a proxy for the rest of society. It has been suggested, for example, that public morality in early New York communities was upheld in forums such as church trials.[4] Such an idea assumes that most early New Yorkers fell under church authority, which is not the case.

In actuality, evangelical churches could enforce standards only on the minority who chose to join the church. Everyone, both within the church and without, recognized that evangelical churches held their members to much higher standards than were required by the rest of the community. Therefore, excommunication from an evangelical church was no disgrace in the larger society. A number of excommunicants joined nonevangelical churches and some were elected to public office.[5] Obviously,

3. The *Census of the State of New York for 1855* reveals that the minority status of church members in Cortland County is typical of the entire state. Communicants of all denominations made up 21.9 percent of the total population in Cortland County versus 20.2 percent statewide. On a typical Sunday, 32.5 percent of Cortland County's total population attended church compared to 32.4 percent statewide. Clearly, church members generally, and evangelicals specifically, were in the minority in the Empire State before the Civil War.

4. Ryan, *Cradle of the Middle Class,* p. 233.

5. The Episcopal and Universalist churches often accepted those excluded from evangelical congregations. For example, Asa Austin was excommunicated by the Homer Congregationalists in 1813 and joined the Homer Episcopal Church in 1831 (Homer Congregational Church, Minutes, August 12, 1813; Homer Calvary Episcopal Church, Record Book, Record of Members of the Congregation, Accession No. 6251, CUA). In 1838 Augustus Hitchcock was disfellowshipped from the Homer Congregational Church; six years later his name appeared on the Calvary Episcopal membership list (Homer Congregational Church, Minutes, Exclusions List; Homer Calvary Episcopal Church, Record Book, 1844 Roster). Reuben

equating evangelical church standards with community standards can lead to unwarranted conclusions. Historians would be well advised to remember that when they describe antebellum evangelical churches, they are portraying a group set apart from the larger worldly community. The minority status of evangelicals does not detract from their historical significance. Evangelicals were influential, not because they were numerous but because they were mobilized. In an era when the traditional external constraints on human behavior dissolved in the spirit of republicanism, the Arminianized doctrines of Calvinists and Methodists called for a new constraint, the Holy Spirit, that would control the otherwise directionless, undisciplined, and totally free individual. Finney and other New Measures men explained that God wanted the recently redeemed to turn their efforts toward redeeming the nation both spiritually and socially. In an atomistic society, in which other individuals were moving in random directions seeking personal gain, evangelicals, inspired by perfectionist visions of the common good, focused their efforts in a specific direction. Their unifying vision of national redemption enabled evangelical perfectionists to have an impact on society that far exceeded their number, both in Cortland County and in the nation.

The small percentage of church members also raises an inter-

Clough was forced out of the Homer Congregational Church in 1828 but was a charter member of the Cortland Universalist Church seven years later (Homer Congregational Church, Minutes, Exclusions List; *History: All Souls' Universalist Church*, p. 29).

Numerous excommunicants were politically active after exclusion. For example, John Hooker, excluded from the Truxton Congregational Church in 1831, was elected delegate to the Whig county convention in 1834. Enos Stimson, who was excommunicated from the Homer Congregational Church in 1828, served as a delegate to the county Jacksonian convention in 1832 (Truxton First Presbyterian Church, Record Book, January 19, 1831; *Cortland Republican*, October 18, 1834; Homer Congregational Church, Minutes, List of Exclusions; *Cortland Advocate*, February 3, 1832).

Perhaps the best evidence that the community held individuals to less stringent standards than did evangelical churches is the election of excommunicants to positions of public trust. For example, in 1834, two (Gilmore Kinney and Isaac Kinney, Jr.) of the three constables elected in the town of Cortlandville were excluded church members. Obviously, the rest of the town found the two Kinneys morally fit to enforce local laws even though each had been excluded from an evangelical congregation. See the *Cortland Democrat*, March 6, 1834; Homer Congregational Church, Minutes, List of Exclusions; Truxton Baptist Church, Record Book, October 23, 1830.

esting, if difficult, historical problem—what were religious behaviors and attendance of the 70 percent of the population that never joined a church? For Cortland County's first two decades, this group can be studied because many of its members participated in religious societies. As the New England communitarian ethos was replaced by Jacksonian era individualism, however, fewer nonmembers joined religious societies. After 1820 most Cortlanders used their republican freedom to pursue political and economic goals independent of religious organizations. The degree to which the unchurched occasionally attended worship services is impossible to ascertain. Likewise, because the unchurched had no occasion to produce religious documents, it is very difficult to determine the extent to which they were influenced by evangelical ideas. About all that can be said with certainty is that after 1820 the unchurched were less likely to participate in voluntary organizations, less likely to stay in the community for an extended period of time, and, by 1850, less likely to have property and high-status occupations.[6] In a sense, Cortland County's churches served as islands of social stability while streams of detached, unchurched (and hard to study) citizens flowed through the county over the decades.

Sixth, *historians must be very careful when generalizing about the impact of evangelicalism on American antebellum society because evangelicalism was a diverse and divided movement.* Evangelicals influenced the surrounding community in contradictory ways. They agreed on the necessity of a salvation experience and a personal, ongoing relationship with God but were sharply divided on a host of other issues. Early on, Cortland County evangelicals were split between Calvinists and Arminians. When Calvinism was Arminianized in the 1830s, traditional Calvinists stormed out of their former congregations.

Splits between formalists and antiformalists also had an awesome effect on the way religious groups related to the larger society. The formal Calvinists (Presbyterians and Congregationalists) were quick to organize for the salvation of souls and the purification of American society. For these people, the appeal of Finneyite theology went beyond resolution of the conflict be-

6. These tentative conclusions are arrived at by subtracting weighted aggregate data on church members from data covering the entire county.

tween predestinarianism and republican self-determination. The New Measures appealed to formal Calvinists because Methodist revivalist techniques had now been reduced to a formula guaranteed to bring results any time, any place. Formalists also had a passion for changing society. Congregationalists and Presbyterians dominated local temperance, antislavery, and other reformist organizations and were the most ardent supporters of the Whig party. By contrast, antiformal Arminians (Methodists) distrusted human efforts to redeem society. For these religionists, only the Holy Spirit could change society as individuals were converted one by one. Methodists thus gravitated toward the Democratic party and paid scant attention to most reform movements. Antiformal Calvinists (Baptists) stood between the two other evangelical groups. They were influenced by New Measures theology yet traditionally emphasized personal piety rather than social action. Politically, antiformal Calvinists fell between the other two groups, leaning slightly to the Whigs but not much inclined to voluntarist reform activities.

The divisions in the evangelical camp go even deeper. Congregations often felt pressure from internal countervailing forces. Before 1830 evangelicals generally advocated maintaining traditional controls over the public and private behavior of members, even as religious society members sought to minimize congregational authority. Between 1831 and 1846, the religious configuration became even more confused as minimalists, traditionalists, moderates, and ultraists battled for ideological control of the county's churches. Not until the 1850s, after traditionalists and ultraists had left the churches, did consensus return to local evangelical congregations. A modified minimalism, which required a conversion experience for membership but reduced the congregation's governing role over the lives of its members, finally restored a measure of unity by 1860.

Seventh, *if Cortland County is at all representative of northern antebellum communities, the Second Great Awakening was central in shifting evangelical congregations from a corporate to a "modern" orientation.* Between 1801 and 1830, religious fellowships in all four denominations were traditional in their orientation. As corporate churches, they saw themselves as separate communities, islands of holiness, which had to maintain sharp distinctions between themselves and the world. To maintain doctrinal and behavioral purity, all evangelical denominations demanded that individuals yield a large share of their autonomy to the will of the group. Church discipline was employed rigorously as church trials delineated acceptable from unacceptable behavior, thus clarifying the line between the "saved" and the "lost." In this early period, women played an important, if often uncelebrated, role in the church. By contrast, wealthy men, who were fearful of corporate authority over their lives, chose religious society involvement over church membership.

Among Calvinists, the Second Great Awakening was clearly an ideological watershed. Finney's Arminianized Calvinism brought Baptist, Presbyterian, and Congregational doctrine in line with dominant republican values. Once the genie of free will was released, however, it could not be returned to the bottle. According to New Measures doctrine, humans were free to choose God or the Devil. Furthermore, the perfectionist theories accompanying New Measures teaching weakened the theoretical basis for church discipline. If humans could be guided by the Holy Spirit in matters of personal behavior, why was church discipline necessary? Individuals now sought to choose for themselves the proper boundaries for Christian living. Ultraists came to believe that their spirituality was superior to that of the established denominations, which also undermined the concept that the gathered church was the proper judge of Christian and non-Christian activities. The years between 1835 and 1846 formed the most crucial period in the battle between individual Calvinists and church authority.

After 1846 Calvinists desperately sought to restore unity to their torn congregations. The simplest way to accomplish this goal was to jettison the concept of the corporate church. Church discipline procedures were relaxed because members were less willing to submit to congregational rulings. In particular, cases involving worldliness diminished as the line separating the church and the rest of society became blurred. As local congregations abandoned ecclesiastical authority, the threat to male autonomy lessened, and wealthy men began to join in larger numbers. Calvinist congregational wealth soared to new levels. As affluent men joined the county's Calvinist congregations, women—the guardians of personal piety and reflective evangelism—were displaced. Commercial values overrode those of personal piety, organization was emphasized over spirituality, fund-raising superseded soul-winning, and the church building became more important than building the church. Rather than remaining separate from the dominant culture or seeking to transform secular society, county Calvinists were now confirming the commercial ethics and values of 1860. In short, these evangelical churches had become "modern."

One major evangelical group did not fit the above pattern. Local Methodists managed to avoid much of the tumult of the 1830s and 1840s. Already Arminian, Methodists saw little new or instructive in Finney's message. Since Methodists had strong antiformal leanings and paid scant attention to New Measures teaching, they were relatively unaffected by ultraism. Furthermore, their episcopal structure limited the ability of church members to reorient local church policy and doctrine to fit societal opinion. As a result, Cortland County Methodists did not experience major doctrinal shifts or widespread rebellion against church authority. Their traditional powers still intact, Methodists did not experience the influx of wealthy men as did the Calvinists. As a result, the older values of personal piety and determined evangelism were still strong in 1860.

By the coming of the Civil War, Cortland County's corporate churches were fading into the past and modern institutions were taking their place. There was more freedom and liberty within the newer structures, but some no doubt felt a sense of loss. The clarity of vision and the strong sense of identity when local congregations were islands of holiness was gone forever. Yet most church members did not wish to turn back. Personal liberty was too precious and memories of virulent controversy too recent.

The ideological change that occurred during the Second Great Awakening had transformed not only the churches but those who sat in the pews. Even though the Cortland County faithful identified themselves as Christians, they were also nineteenth-century Americans who sought to extend freedom of the will to all aspects of life. Institutions that impinged on individual rights had no place on the American landscape. As good republicans, Cortland County's evangelicals preferred to have all aspects of their destiny—economic, political, social, and spiritual—resting in their own hands.

APPENDIXES

A

Methodological Notes

When historians grapple with the social complexities of ante-bellum religion, they frequently match membership lists of religious organizations with census data in an effort to understand where competing religious groups stood in relation to each other and to the larger society. In so doing, it is easy for scholars to make one or more of the following four errors.

The first common mistake is to confuse religious society membership with church membership. Since household heads who were members of the societies were generally wealthier than those in the churches they supported, using society membership rosters in the absence of congregational membership lists can lead to inflated estimates of the wealth of church members. As a result, society lists were not substituted for church rosters in this study (with the exception of political analysis, an area in which there were no large differences between church and society viewpoints).

A second error is the temptation in the face of scarce ecclesiastical records to make maximum use of any indicators of denominational affiliation. As a result, in some studies, individuals who are known to have joined a given church in a given year are classified as members and treated as members twenty years earlier or later. Such an approach inflates the total number of members in a given community and distorts the ethnic, economic, and demographic composition of a particular church at any given time.

Congregational membership was treated as temporary, not lifelong, in this inquiry. For example, a young man who joined a

Presbyterian church in 1843 but was excluded in 1849 was not included on the list of Presbyterians matched with the 1840 or 1850 censuses. Data on members covering the years before admission or after departure were not included in denominational calculations of wealth, occupation, or other variables.

A third temptation, when examining wealth, occupation, or other social variables, is to sum the data on all evangelical denominations to create a composite. This technique would work if the records of each denomination had an equal rate of survival. In Cortland County, Presbyterian and Congregational records survived at a much higher rate than Baptist and Methodist records. Simply to total all wealth information on all known members of the four denominations would lead to skewed results because the formal (and wealthier) evangelicals are clearly overrepresented.

This problem was minimized in this investigation by weighting the data so as to create the same denominational distribution as existed in nineteenth-century Cortland County. The completeness of each denominational sample was determined by comparing local church records with denominational records. If lists of local Congregationalists covered 90 percent of county Congregationalists, all Congregational data were weighted by a factor of 1.1. If Baptist lists were about 50 percent complete, all Baptist data were weighted by a factor of 2.0. Once the denominational data were weighted to indicate the true strength of each group within the county, all denominational data were totaled to get wealth, occupational, and other profiles of evangelicals.

The last mistake commonly made when working with church rosters and census data is to confuse the impact of age with that of class. For a number of reasons, including incomplete church records, the mean age of Cortland County household heads who can be identified as church members was somewhat higher than the mean age of all county household heads. As a result, the typical churched household head had several more years to accumulate property. All other factors being equal, male church members were likely to have more property than their unchurched neighbors simply because they were older. A failure to recognize this peculiarity in the data could have led to an overstating of genuine class and wealth differences between church members and other local residents.

To avoid this error, lists of church members used in calculating denominational wealth distributions were weighted so that the age distributions of household heads in the churched population matched the age distributions of household heads in the county at large. After this procedure was completed, wealth differences between evangelicals and their neighbors no longer reflected the age differences between the two populations, thus making it much easier to evaluate the independent impact of class and/or social standing.

B

Evangelicalism in Cortland County

Table B.1. Cortland County church membership as a percentage of the county's adult population (10 years old and older)

Years	Major evangelical*	Other evangelical†	Non-evangelical‡	All churches
1810	9.5	0.0	0.0	9.5
1814	17.1	0.0	0.0	17.1
1820	23.2	0.4	0.0	23.6
1825	18.4	0.9	0.0	19.3
1830	18.8	1.4	0.1	20.4
1835	26.7	2.0	0.9	29.5
1840	24.1	2.2	0.9	27.3
1845	24.3	2.2	1.1	27.5
1850	21.2	2.3	1.4	24.9
1855	23.8	2.0	3.0	28.7
1860	21.7	1.5	2.4	25.6

*Includes Methodists, Baptists, Congregationalists, and Presbyterians.
†Includes Seventh Day Baptists, Free Will Baptists, Wesleyan Methodists, and antislavery evangelicals.
‡Includes Christians, Episcopalians, Catholics, and Universalists.

Table B.2. Date and membership of Cortland County congregations at the time of worship house construction, 1801–1838

Church	Date	Membership
Homer Congregational	1805	49
Homer Baptist	1811	76
Preble Presbyterian	1815	unknown
Preble Methodist	1820	unknown
Cortland Methodist	1821	25–30
Virgil Congregational	1821	67
Truxton Baptist	1822	252
Truxton Congregational	1822	108
Homer Baptist	1827	136
Scott Baptist	1827	114–123
Cortland Presbyterian	1828	119
Marathon Presbyterian	1830–1	64
Cincinnatus Baptist	1831	112
McGrawville Baptist	1831	55–73
Virgil Baptist	1831	75–85
Virgil Universalist	1831	unknown
Homer Calvary Episcopal	1832	30–35
Union Congregational	1832	123
McGrawville Presbyterian	1833–4	unknown
McGrawville Methodist	1834	unknown
Taylor Methodist	1835	unknown
Cortland Universalist	1837	101
Scott Congregational	1838	68
Virgil Free Baptist	1838	unknown

Table B.3. Evangelism indexes, 1816–1859 (annual number of converts added per 100 members)

Years	Baptist	Congregational/ Presbyterian	Evangelism index needed to maintain current membership
1816–19	11.60	9.61	−.44*
1820–24	7.93	5.21	2.65
1825–29	6.61	5.07	3.25
1830–34	10.07	13.01	7.55
1835–39	7.31	4.19	6.21
1840–44	7.05	4.83	6.11
1845–49	2.28	2.11	5.31
1850–54	4.69	2.65	5.71
1855–59	7.28	5.20	3.91

*The negative figure indicates that even if a church had no converts, congregational membership would rise because of in-migration.

Table B.4. Wealth of male evangelical household heads compared to all Cortland County household heads, 1825 and 1835

1825 (acres of improved land, distributions in percent)

	N	0	1–20	21–50	51–100	101+	Median
A. Male evangelical household heads*	486	14	32	41	13	1	25ia
B. Male evangelical household heads (after adjusting for age)†	485	15	32	40	13	1	–
C. County male household heads	1965	17	40	32	10	1	20ia

Eta between B and (C minus B) = .09

1835 (acres of improved land, distributions in percent)

	N	0	1–20	21–50	51–100	101+	Median
A. Male evangelical household heads*	906	19	22	37	20	1	29ia
B. Male evangelical household heads (after adjusting for age)†	912	25	21	35	17	2	–
C. County male household heads	4075	23	31	28	15	3	20ia

Eta between B and (C minus B) = .12‡

*Data are weighted to reflect the strength of each denomination within Cortland County.

†Data are weighted so that the age distributions of evangelical household heads mirror those of household heads throughout Cortland County.

‡The statistic "Eta" reveals differences in distribution among the five categories and has no sensitivity to the direction of those differences. When the data show that one group (evangelicals) are wealthier than another group (the remainder of the county), Eta can also be used as an indicator of wealth differences. In 1835, however, evangelicals were less wealthy than the rest of the county in two categories (0 acres, 101+ acres). A true measure of relative wealth would subtract these differences, since they reduce the overall wealth difference between evangelicals and the rest of the county. Eta adds these differences and thus is misleadingly high as a wealth indicator for 1835.

Table B.5. Wealth of male evangelical household heads compared to all Cortland County household heads, 1850 and 1860

1850 (value of real property, distributions in percent)

	N	$0	$100–$1,000	$1,100–$2,000	$2,100–$5,000	over $5,100	Median
A. Male evangelical household heads*	839	16	27	26	24	6	$1,300
B. Male evangelical household heads (after adjusting for age)†	841	18	30	25	22	5	–
C. County male household heads	4,522	24	32	23	18	3	$ 900

Eta between B and (C minus B) = .10

1860 (value of real property, distributions in percent)

	N	0	$100–$1,000	$1,100–$2,000	$2,100–$5,000	over $5,100	Median
A. Male evangelical household heads*	975	12	21	19	31	17	$2,000
B. Male evangelical household heads (after adjusting for age)†	976	16	19	20	29	16	–
C. County male household heads	5,086	21	24	19	26	9	$1,300

Eta between B and (C minus B) = .15

*Data are weighted to reflect the strength of each denomination within Cortland County.

†Data are weighted so that the age distributions of evangelical household heads mirror those of household heads throughout Cortland County.

Table B.6. Occupations of male evangelical household heads compared to all Cortland County household heads, 1840, 1850, and 1860 (in percent)

1840	N	Farmers	Mechanics/ manufacturers	Professionals	Merchants	Unskilled
A. Evangelical household heads*	860	80	18	2	1	1
B. Cortland County household heads	4,128	80	18	1	1	2
Eta between A and (B minus A) = .01						

1850	N	Farmers	Mechanics/ craftsmen	Small commercial/ white collar	Professionals	Merchants/ bankers/ manufacturers	Unskilled
A. Evangelical household heads*	841	76	13	2	4	3	1
B. Cortland County household heads	4,424	76	15	2	3	2	2
Eta between A and (B minus A) = .08							

1860	N	Farmers	Mechanics/ craftsmen	Small commercial/ white collar	Professionals	Merchants/ bankers/ manufacturers	Unskilled
A. Evangelical household heads*	973	67	17	6	3	3	3
B. Cortland County household heads	4,935	64	17	2	3	2	12
Eta between A and (B minus A) = .17							

*Data are weighted to reflect denominational strength within the county.

Table B.7. Median wealth of male household heads by denomination, 1825–1860

Category	1825 (improved acres)	1835 (improved acres)	1850 (real estate)	1860 (real estate)
Congregational	30	35	$1,500	$3,000
Presbyterian	28	17½	$1,800	$2,500
Baptist	30	30	$1,300	$2,500
Methodist	5½	27½	$1,200	$1,500
Antislavery evangelicals*	25	10	$ 900	$1,300
All evangelicals†	25	29	$1,300	$2,000
Cortland County	20	20	$ 900	$1,300

*Antislavery evangelicals include the Scott Seventh Day Baptists in 1825 and 1835 and members of the Scott Seventh Day Baptist, Cortland Free Congregational, and Preble Free churches in 1850 and 1860.
†Data weighted to reflect denominational strength within Cortland County.

Table B.8. Percentage of male household heads in top wealth quintile by denomination, 1825–1860

Denomination	1825	1835	1850	1860
Congregational	27.1	32.0	34.2	43.3
Presbyterian	32.8	26.9	32.7	33.3
Baptist	25.0	32.5	34.6	38.4
Methodist	10.0	15.6	21.7	20.8
Antislavery evangelicals	21.5	10.0	18.8	18.4
All evangelicals*	21.9	26.2	29.8	30.9

*Data weighted to reflect denominational strength within Cortland County.

C

Church Discipline

Table C.1. General charges brought against church members in religious trials, 1801–1859 (in percent)

Ecclesiastic domain (religious thought and practice)	1801–9	1810–19	1820–29	1830–39	1840–49	1850–59
Violations of church covenant	38.1 (8)*	45.7 (80)	45.2 (128)	52.0 (128)	44.1 (130)	62.5 (95)
Violations of articles of faith	9.5 (2)	1.7 (3)	8.1 (23)	4.9 (12)	5.8 (17)	7.2 (11)
Violations of church practice	9.5 (2)	4.6 (8)	2.8 (8)	8.5 (21)	6.8 (20)	11.2 (17)
Charges in the ecclesiastic domain as a percentage of all charges	57.2 (12)	52.0 (91)	56.2 (159)	65.4 (161)	56.6 (167)	80.9 (123)

Public domain (behavior outside of church)	1801–9	1810–19	1820–29	1830–39	1840–49	1850–59
Broken commandments	28.6 (6)	22.3 (39)	19.4 (55)	13.4 (33)	25.4 (75)	9.9 (15)
Interpersonal conflicts	4.8 (1)	12.6 (22)	7.4 (21)	7.3 (18)	7.5 (22)	3.9 (6)
Worldliness	9.5 (2)	13.1 (23)	17.0 (48)	13.8 (34)	10.5 (31)	5.3 (8)
Charges in the public domain as a percentage of all charges	42.9 (9)	48.0 (84)	43.8 (124)	34.6 (85)	43.4 (128)	19.1 (29)
Total number of general charges	21	175	283	246	295	152

*All percentages show the type of charge as a percentage of all charges. The figure in parentheses is the number of charges.

Table C.2. Selected specific charges brought against church members in religious trials as a percentage of all charges, 1801–1859

Charge	1801–9	1810–19	1820–29	1830–39	1840–49	1850–59
Refusal to support the church financially	0.0 (0)*	2.3 (4)	0.0 (0)	3.7 (9)	4.7 (14)	3.9 (6)
Commercial wrongdoing	14.3 (3)	9.7 (17)	4.6 (13)	4.1 (10)	8.5 (25)	2.0 (3)
Alcohol-related offenses	4.8 (1)	5.7 (10)	9.5 (27)	7.7 (19)	5.4 (16)	1.3 (2)
All charges	21	175	283	246	295	152

*Figures in parentheses refer to the number of charges.

Table C.3. Excommunication rates by denomination, 1801–1859 (annual exclusions per 100 members)

Years	Baptist	Congregational	Presbyterian	All churches
1801–4	0.96	0.00	–	0.48
1805–9	0.96	0.00	–	0.36
1810–14	0.69	0.08	–	0.37
1815–19	1.05	0.24	–	0.67
1820–24	1.68	0.12	–	1.05
1825–29	2.11	0.66	0.22	1.44
1830–34	1.62	0.25	0.06	0.98
1835–39	1.49	0.35	0.30	0.97
1840–44	2.03	0.57	0.42	1.44
1845–49	1.29	0.33	0.22	0.89
1850–54	1.14	0.22	0.12	0.74
1855–59	0.72	0.21	0.06	0.49
1801–59	1.46	0.31	0.21	0.96

Table C.4. Conviction rates by denomination, 1801–1859 (percentage of cases ending in exclusion)

Years	Baptist	Congregational	Presbyterian	All churches
1801–14	23.0 (61)*	22.2 (9)	–	22.9 (70)
1815–24	35.2 (244)	43.8 (43)	–	36.2 (287)
1825–34	29.6 (226)	26.2 (42)	37.5 (8)	29.3 (276)
1835–44	53.0 (168)	60.9 (46)	32.6 (46)	50.8 (260)
1845–59	50.9 (159)	58.1 (31)	17.9 (39)	46.3 (229)
1801–59	39.3 (858)	43.8 (171)	26.9 (93)	39.2 (1122)

*The number of cases are in parentheses.

Table C.5. New cases per year per church by denomination, 1801–1859

Years	Baptist	Congregational	Presbyterian	All churches
1801–14	2.10	.23	–	1.03
1815–24	8.00	.68	–	3.68
1825–34	9.04	1.33	.56	3.78
1835–44	6.72	1.66	2.30	3.54
1845–59	3.53	.69	1.30	1.91
1801–59	5.64	.84	1.37	2.71

D

Religious Voluntarism

Table D.1. Average annual giving by women to Cortland Baptist Association benevolence, 1828–1859

Years	Giving traceable to women	Cash	Goods	Association's average annual benevolence
1828–29	$87 (52)*	$11 (7)	$76 (46)	$167
1830–34	$114 (30)	$56 (15)	$58 (16)	$374
1835–39	$113 (20)	$37 (7)	$76 (14)	$554
1840–44	$111 (12)	$46 (5)	$64 (7)	$913
1845–49	$75 (8)	$44 (5)	$31 (3)	$955
1850–54	$38 (3)	$24 (2)	$14 (1)	$1,155
1855–59	$46 (4)	NA	NA	$1,217

*Giving by women as a percentage of total benevolence is presented in parentheses. Distinctions between giving in cash and in goods are not recorded after 1854.

Table D.2. Denominational representation in reform organizations (in percent)*

Denomination	Cortland County Temperance Society 1829–40 N = 134	Cortland County Anti-Slavery Society 1837–41 N = 107	Liberty party "call" 1841 N = 222
Congregational	22–28†	25–31	14–19
Presbyterian	8–9	30	16–21
Methodist	10	6–9	9
Baptist	5–7	10–19	10–15
Seventh Day Baptist	1	2	5–6
Episcopal	4	3	1
Universalist	0	1	0
All churches	50–60	81–97	55–71

*Percentages show the portion of each organization's membership that were church members of a given denomination. Data are weighted to reflect the strength of each denomination within Cortland County.

†Ranges are used because of uncertain identifications in matching names across lists.

Table D.3. Male members of each denomination that joined the Cortland County Temperance Society, 1829–1840

Formal denominations	Church members at some point between 1829 and 1840	Members who joined the society	Percent of all male members
Episcopal	44	6	13.6
Congregational	676	38	5.6
Presbyterian	312	9	2.9
Total	1,032	53	5.1

Antiformal denominations	Church members at some point between 1829 and 1840	Members who joined the society	Percent of all male members
Methodist	35	1	2.9
Baptist	746	7	0.9
Seventh Day Baptist	109	1	0.9
Universalist	81	0	0.0
Christians	19	0	0.0
Total	990	9	0.9

Table D.4. Male members in each denomination who signed the Liberty party "call" in 1841

Formal denominations	Members in 1841	Members who signed the call	Signers as a percent of all male members
Presbyterian	293	33	11.3
Congregational	472	40	8.5
Episcopal	32	2	6.3
Total	797	75	9.4

Antiformal denominations	Members in 1841	Members who signed the call	Signers as a percent of all male members
Seventh Day Baptist	101	13	12.9
Methodist	37	4	10.8*
Baptist	616	15	2.4
Universalist	75	0	0.0
Christian	18	0	0.0
Total	847	32	3.8

Formal and antiformal denominations with ultraist churches removed†	Members in 1841	Members who signed the call	Signers as a percent of all male members
Formal	739	50	6.8
Antiformal	746	19	2.5
Ultraist	161	40	24.8

*Most of the Methodist data come from one group in Cincinnatus. A broader sample of Methodist churches would drop this percentage dramatically.

†Scott Seventh Day Baptist, Cortland Free Congregational, and Preble Free Church.

Table D.5. Wealth of male antislavery evangelical household heads, 1850 (value of real property, distributions in percent)

Category	N	0	$100–$1,000	$1,100–$2,000	$2,100–$5,000	over $5,100
Cortland Free Congregational	11	0	9	73	0	18
Preble Free Church	16	38	19	13	25	6
Scott Seventh Day Baptist	43	23	42	21	12	2
Antislavery evangelical household heads	70	23	31	27	13	6
Evangelical household heads	839	16	27	26	24	6
Cortland County household heads	4,522	24	32	23	18	3

Table D.6. Occupations of male antislavery evangelical household heads, 1850 (in percent)

Category	N	Farmers	Mechanics/craftsmen	Small commercial/white collar	Professionals	Merchants/bankers/manufacturers	Unskilled
Cortland Free Congregational	10	80	0	0	10	0	10
Preble Free Church	15	87	7	0	0	0	7
Scott Seventh Day Baptist	43	65	23	0	2	7	2
Antislavery evangelical household heads	68	72	16	0	3	4	4
Evangelical household heads	841	76	13	2	4	3	1
Cortland County household heads	4,424	76	15	2	3	2	2

Bibliography

PRIMARY SOURCES

Unpublished Church and Denominational Records

Cincinnatus First Congregational Church, Records, 1809–40. In "Presbyterian Church, Freetown, New York. Records, 1809–1885." Accession No. 6238, CUA.
Cincinnatus Methodist Class Book, 1825–27. Cincinnatus Town Collection, 1825–65, CCHS.
Cincinnatus and Solon Union Congregational Church, Record Book, 1819–39. In "Union Congregational Church, Cincinnatus and Solon, New York. Record Book, 1819–1839." Accession No. 6235 (pt. 1), CUA.
———. Records, 1839–72. In "Union Congregational Church, Cincinnatus and Solon, New York. Record Book, 1819–1839." Accession No. 6235, (pt. 2), CUA.
Cincinnatus and Solon Union Congregational Society, Records, 1822–1972. In "Union Congregational Church, Cincinnatus and Solon, New York. Record Book, 1819–1839." Accession No. 6235, (pt. 2), CUA.
Cold Brook Methodist Class, 1851–62. Cortland County Churches Collection, CCHS.
Cortland First Baptist Church, Record Books, 1801–35, 1835–76. In "First Baptist Church, Cortland, New York. Records, 1801–1876." Accession No. 6239, CUA.
Cortland First Methodist Society, Minutes, 1821–66. In "First Methodist Episcopal Church, Cortland, New York. Records, 1821–1905." Accession No. 6250, CUA.
Cortland Presbyterian Church, Records, 1825–60. In "Presbyterian

Church, Cortland Village, New York. Records, 1824–1901." Accession No. 6260, CUA.

Cuyler Methodist Church, Records, 1858–1929. In "Methodist Episcopal Church, Cuyler, New York. Record Book, 1858–1929." Accession No. 6246, CUA.

Freetown Presbyterian Society, Book, 1809–86. In "Presbyterian Church, Freetown, New York. Records, 1809–1885." Accession No. 6238, CUA.

Harford Christian Church of Christ, Minutes, 1839–61. In "Christian Church of Christ, Harford, New York. Meeting minutes, 1839–1861." Accession No. 6243, CUA.

Homer Calvary Episcopal Church, Record Book, 1831–76. In "Calvary Episcopal Church, Homer, New York. Record Book, 1831–1876." Accession No. 6251, CUA.

Homer Congregational Church, Minutes, 1801–34, 1840–55, 1856–1910. In "Congregational Church of Homer, New York. Records, 1799–1910." Accession No. 6236, CUA.

——. Roster of Pastors, Deacons, and Members, 1801–57. In "Congregational Church of Homer, New York. Records, 1799–1910." Accession No. 6236, CUA.

Homer First Baptist Society Minutes, 1810–75. In "First Baptist Church, Homer, New York. Record Book, 1810–1875." Accession No. 6253, CUA.

Homer, First Religious Society of, Minutes, 1799–1856. In "Congregational Church of Homer, New York. Records, 1799–1910." Accession No. 6236, CUA.

Keeney Settlement Methodist Church, Records, 1854–1916. In "Methodist Episcopal Church, Keeney Settlement. Cuyler, New York. Records, 1854–1916." Accession No. 6247, CUA.

Marathon Baptist Society, Minutes, 1831–89. In "First Baptist Church, Marathon, New York. Meeting Minutes, 1831–1889." Accession No. 6249, CUA.

Marathon Presbyterian Church, Records, 1813–53. CCHS.

McGraw Presbyterian Church, Records, 1859–1913. Town of McGraw Collection, CCHS.

Methodist Episcopal Church of East Homer Society, Records, 1841–1933. CCHS.

Minutes of the Cortland Presbytery. PHS.

Preble First Presbyterian Church, Book of Discipline, 1827–40. In "First Presbyterian Church, Preble, New York. Records, 1827–1875." Accession No. 6256, CUA.

——. Records, 1827–40, 1841–75. In "First Presbyterian Church, Preble, New York. Records, 1827–1875." Accession No. 6256, CUA.

Scott Baptist Church, Record Book, 1808–33. In "Seventh Day Baptist Church, Scott, New York. Records, 1808–1927." Accession No. 6237, CUA.

Scott Methodist Episcopal Church, Minutes. Handwritten transcription of original record by Leonard P. Hackney. Cottrell Papers, CCHS.

Scott Methodist Episcopal Society, Minutes. CCHS.

Scott Seventh Day Baptist Church, Minutes, 1834–50. In "Seventh Day Baptist Church, Scott, New York. Records, 1808–1927." Accession No. 6237, CUA.

——. Treasurer's Book, 1833–48. In "Seventh Day Baptist Church, Scott, New York. Records, 1808–1927." Accession No. 6237, CUA.

Scott Seventh Day Baptist Church, Trustee Meeting Minutes, 1831–83. In "Seventh Day Baptist Church, Scott, New York. Records, 1808–1927." Accession No. 6237, CUA.

Solon First Baptist Church, Minutes, 1807–22. In "First Baptist Church, Solon, New York. Meeting Minutes, 1807–1872." Accession No. 6248, CUA.

Truxton Baptist Church, Record Book, 1829–41. In "Baptist Church, Truxton, New York. Records, 1820–1914." Accession No. 6242, CUA.

——. Book of Records, 1841–1878. In "Baptist Church, Truxton, New York. Records, 1820–1914." Accession No. 6242, CUA.

Truxton Baptist Society, Minutes, 1820–53. In "Baptist Church, Truxton, New York. Records, 1820–1914." Accession No. 6242, CUA.

Truxton First Presbyterian Church, Record Book, 1811–40. In "First Presbyterian Church, Truxton, New York. Records, 1811–1840." Accession No. 6241, CUA.

——. Records, 1840–76. In "First Presbyterian Church, Truxton, New York. Records, 1811–1840." Accession No. 6241, CUA.

Virgil Baptist Church, Minutes, 1833–98. In "Baptist Church, Virgil, New York. Meeting Minutes, 1833–1898." Accession No. 6244, CUA.

Virgil Methodist Society, Minutes, 1831–1921. In "Methodist Episcopal Church, Virgil, New York. Meeting Minutes, 1831–1921." Accession No. 6245, CUA.

Virgil Presbyterian Church, Church Book of Virgil, 1805–23. In "Presbyterian Church, Virgil, New York. Record Book, 1805–1823." Accession No. 6234, CUA.

Voluntary Association Records

Cortland County Anti-Slavery Society, Records, 1837–41. CCHS.

Cortland County Temperance Society. Records, 1829–40. CCHS.

Female Branch Bible Society, Homer, New York. Records, 1822–71. Accession No. 6240, CUA.
Sons of Temperance, Division No. 152, McGrawville. Minutes. CCHS.
Temperance Society of Homer, New York. Meeting Minutes, 1841–42. Accession No. 6252, CUA.

Newspapers

Cortland Advocate, 1831–34, CUMMN.
Cortland County Republican, 1855–60, CUMMN.
Cortland Democrat, 1840–42, 1844–49, CUMMN.
Cortland Observer, 1825–32, CCHS.
Cortland Republican, 1832–36, CUMMN.
Cortland Republican and Eagle, 1836–40, CUMMN.
New York Times, 1979–86.

Published Nineteenth-Century Sources

Bouton, Nathan. *Festal Gathering of the Early Settlers and Present Inhabitants of the Town of Virgil, Cortland County, New York, Held at Virgil Village on Thursday, the 25th of August, 1853.* Dryden, N.Y.: A. M. Ford, 1878.
Census of the State of New York for 1825. Senate Journal, 49th sess., 1826, Appendix A.
Census of the State of New York for 1835. Albany: Croswell, Van Benthuysen, and Burt, 1836.
Census of the State of New York for 1845. Albany: Carroll and Cook, 1846.
Census of the State of New York for 1855. Albany: Charles Van Benthuysen, 1857.
Census of the State of New York for 1865. Albany: Charles Van Benthuysen, 1867.
Child, Hamilton. *Gazetteer and Business Directory of Cortland County, N.Y. for 1869.* Syracuse: Printed at the Journal Office, 1869.
Cravath, Oren. *A Case of Withdrawal from the Presbyterian Church with the Reasons for So Doing.* Cortland: Eels and Goodwin, 1845.
Davis, L. D. *The History of the Methodist Episcopal Church in Cortland.* Syracuse: William T. Hamilton, Bookseller, 1855.
DeBow, J. D. B. *Statistical View of the United States.* Washington, D.C.: A. O. P. Nicholson, Public Printer, 1854.
The Extracts of the Minutes of the General Assembly of the Presbyterian Church. 1825. PHS.
Fowler, Philemon H. *Historical Sketch of Presbyterianism within the Bounds of Central New York.* Utica, N.Y.: Curtiss and Childs, 1877.

French, John H. *Gazetteer of the State of New York*. Syracuse: R. Pearsall Smith, 1860.

Goodwin, Herman C. *Pioneer History, or Cortland County and the Border Wars of New York*. New York: A. B. Burdick, 1859.

Gordon, Thomas F. *Gazetteer of the State of New York*. Philadelphia: Thomas F. Gordon, 1836.

Halsey, Lewis. *History of the Seneca Baptist Association with Sketches of Churches and Pastors*. Ithaca: Journal Association Book and Job Printing House, 1879.

Harvey, Hezekiah. *The Memoir of Alfred Bennett*. New York: Edward Fletcher, 1852.

Hotchkin, James H. *A History of the Purchase and Settlement of Western New York, and of the Rise, Progress and Present State of the Presbyterian Church in That Section*. New York: M. W. Dodd, 1848.

Keep, John. *A Narrative of the Origin and Progress of the Congregational Church in Homer, N.Y., with Remarks*. Homer, N.Y.: Kinney and Aikin, Printers, 1833. Typescript, CCHS.

A Manual of the Congregational Church in Homer, Cortland Co., N.Y. Homer, N.Y.: Joseph R. Dixon, 1856.

The Minutes of the Annual Conferences of the Methodist Episcopal Church, vols. 1–3, 1800–1853. SU.

Minutes of the Berkshire Baptist Association. 1826–34. ABHS.

Minutes of the Cayuga Baptist Association. 1816–26. ABHS.

Minutes of the Chenango Baptist Association. 1833–48. ABHS.

Minutes of the Cortland Baptist Association. 1828–60. ABHS.

The Minutes of the General Assembly of the Presbyterian Church in the U.S.A. 1826–29, 1830–35, 1836–41, 1842–47, 1848–52, 1853–57, 1858–60, and (New School) 1838–51, 1852–60. PHS.

Minutes of the Madison Baptist Association. 1808–30. ABHS.

Minutes of the Monroe Baptist Association. 1829–40. ABHS.

Minutes of the Oneida Conference of the Methodist Episcopal Church. 1854–60. SU.

Minutes of the Seneca Baptist Association. 1808–30. ABHS.

Peck, George. *Life and Times of George Peck, D.D.* New York: Nelson and Phillips, 1874.

Proceedings of the First Annual Meeting of the New York State Anti-Slavery Society. Utica, N.Y.: Published for the Society, 1836.

Proceedings of the Trial of Stephen Brewer before the Presbyterian Church of Cortland Village. Cortland: Van Slyke and Hitchcock, 1859.

Reed, Andrew, and James Matheson. *A Narrative of the Visit to the American Churches by the Deputation from the Congregational Union of England and Wales*. New York: Harper and Brothers, 1835.

Second Annual Report of the New-York State Society for the Promotion of Temperance. Albany: Packard and Van Benthuysen, 1831.

Smith, Henry P. *History of Cortland County.* Syracuse: D. Mason and Company, 1885.

Spafford, Horatio Gates. *Gazetteer of the State of New York.* Albany: H. C. Southwick, 1813.

——. *Gazetteer of the State of New York.* Albany: B. D. Packard, 1824.

U.S. Census Office. *The Eighth Census of the United States, 1860.* Washington, D.C.: U.S. Government Printing Office, 1866.

——. *Fifth Census. Enumeration of the Inhabitants of the United States, 1830.* Washington, D.C.: Duff Green, 1832.

——. *Fourth Census, Book One. Census for 1820.* Washington, D.C.: Gales and Seaton, 1821.

——. *Second Census. Return of the Whole Number of Persons within the Several Districts of the United States.* Washington, D.C.: Duane, 1801.

——. *Seventh Census of the United States, 1850.* Washington, D.C.: Robert Armstrong, Public Printer, 1853.

——. *Sixth Census, Book One. Enumeration of the Inhabitants of the United States, 1840.* Washington, D.C.: Blair and Ives, 1841.

——. *Third Census, Book One. Aggregate Amount of Each Description of Persons within the United States of America, and Territories Thereof, Agreeably to Actual Enumeration Made According to Law, in the Year, 1810.* Washington, D.C., 1811.

——. *Twelfth Census of the United States, Taken in the Year 1900.* Vol. 5. Washington, D.C.: U.S. Census Office, 1902.

Ward, Samuel Ringgold. *Autobiography of a Fugitive Negro.* 1855. Reprint. New York: Arno Press, 1968.

SECONDARY SOURCES

Books

Ahlstrom, Sydney E. *A Religious History of the American People.* 2 vols. Garden City, N.Y.: Image Books, 1975.

Altschuler, Glenn C., and Jan M. Saltzgaber. *Revivalism, Social Conscience, and Community in the Burned-over District: The Trial of Rhoda Bement.* Ithaca: Cornell University Press, 1983.

Barkun, Michael, *Crucible of the Millennium: The Burned-over District of New York in the 1840s.* Syracuse: Syracuse University Press, 1986.

Barron, Hal. *Those Who Stayed Behind: Rural Society in Nineteenth-Century New England.* Cambridge: Cambridge University Press, 1984.

Bell, Marion L. *Crusade in the City: Revivalism in Nineteenth-Century Philadelphia.* Lewisburg, Pa.: Bucknell University Press, 1977.

Bilhartz, Terry. *Urban Religion and the Second Great Awakening: Church and*

Society in Early National Baltimore. Rutherford, N.J.: Fairleigh Dickinson University Press, 1986.

Blodgett, Bertha E. *Stories of Cortland County for Boys and Girls.* 1932. Reprint. Cortland: Cortland County Historical Society, 1952.

Blumin, Stuart M. *The Urban Threshold: Growth and Change in a Nineteenth-Century American Community.* Chicago: University of Chicago Press, 1976.

Bodo, John R. *The Protestant Clergy and Public Issues, 1812–1848.* Princeton: Princeton University Press, 1954.

Brumberg, Joan Jacobs. *Mission for Life: The Judson Family and American Evangelical Culture.* New York: New York University Press, 1984.

Bushman, Richard L. *Joseph Smith and the Beginnings of Mormonism.* Urbana: University of Illinois Press, 1984.

Cole, Charles C., Jr. *The Social Ideas of the Northern Evangelists, 1820–1860.* New York: Octagon, 1954.

Cott, Nancy F. *The Bonds of Womanhood: "Women's Sphere" in New England, 1780–1835.* New Haven: Yale University Press, 1977.

Cross, Whitney R. *The Burned-over District: The Social and Intellectual History of Enthusiastic Religion in Western New York.* Ithaca: Cornell University Press, 1950.

Curti, Merle. *The Making of an American Community: A Case Study of Democracy in a Frontier County.* Stanford: Stanford University Press, 1959.

Dawley, Alan. *Class and Community: The Industrial Revolution in Lynn.* Cambridge: Harvard University Press, 1976.

Dollar, Charles M. and Richard Jensen. *Historian's Guide to Statistics.* Huntington, N.Y.: Robert E. Krieger, 1971.

Douglas, Ann. *The Feminization of American Culture.* New York: Knopf, 1977.

Ellis, David M., James A. Frost, Harold C. Syrett, and Harry J. Carmen. *A History of New York State.* Ithaca: Cornell University Press, 1967.

Epstein, Barbara L. *The Politics of Domesticity: Women, Evangelism, and Temperance in Nineteenth-Century America.* Middletown, Conn.: Wesleyan University Press, 1981.

Erikson, Kai. *Wayward Puritans: A Study in the Sociology of Deviance.* New York: John Wiley, 1966.

Faler, Paul G. *Mechanics and Manufacturers in the Early Industrial Revolution: Lynn, Massachusetts, 1780–1860.* Albany: State University of New York Press, 1981.

FitzGerald, Frances. *Cities on a Hill: A Journey through Contemporary American Cultures.* New York: Simon and Schuster, 1986.

Foster, Charles I. *An Errand of Mercy: The Evangelical United Front, 1790–1837.* Chapel Hill: University of North Carolina Press, 1960.

Fox, Dixon Ryan. *Yankees and Yorkers*. New York: New York University Press, 1940.

Frisch, Michael H. *Town into City: Springfield, Massachusetts, and the Meaning of Community, 1840–1880.* Cambridge: Harvard University Press, 1972.

Gaustad, Edwin Scott. *Historical Atlas of Religion in America*. Rev. ed. New York: Harper & Row, 1976.

Genovese, Eugene. *Roll, Jordan, Roll: The World the Slaves Made*. New York: Vintage Books, 1976.

Griffin, Clifford S. *Their Brothers' Keepers: Moral Stewardship in the United States, 1800–1865.* New Brunswick, N.J.: Rutgers University Press, 1960.

Hansen, Klaus J. *Mormonism and the American Experience*. Chicago: University of Chicago Press, 1981.

Hewitt, Nancy A. *Women's Activism and Social Change: Rochester, New York, 1822–1872.* Ithaca: Cornell University Press, 1984.

Hoge, Dean R., and David A. Roozen, eds. *Understanding Church Growth and Decline, 1950–1978.* New York: Pilgrim Press, 1979.

Howe, Herbert Barber. *Jedediah Barber, 1787–1876.* New York State Historical Association Series, 8. New York: Columbia University Press, 1939.

——. *Paris Lived in Homer*. Cortland: Cortland County Historical Society, 1968.

Jacquet, Constant H., Jr., ed. *Yearbook of American and Canadian Churches, 1982.* Nashville: Abingdon, 1982.

Johnson, Paul E. *A Shopkeeper's Millennium: Society and Revivals in Rochester, New York, 1815–1837.* New York: Hill and Wang, 1979.

Kalvin, Janet, and Mary I. Buckley, eds. *Women's Spirit Bonding*. New York: Pilgrim Press, 1984.

Katz, Michael. *The People of Hamilton, Canada West: Family and Class in a Mid-Nineteenth Century City.* Cambridge: Harvard University Press, 1972.

Kelley, Dean. *Why Conservative Churches Are Growing*. New York: Harper & Row, 1972.

Kerber, Linda K. *Women of the Republic: Intellect and Ideology in Revolutionary America.* Chapel Hill: University of North Carolina Press, 1980.

McKivigan, John R. *The War against Proslavery Religion: Abolitionism and the Northern Churches, 1830–1865.* Ithaca: Cornell University Press, 1984.

McLoughlin, William G. *Modern Revivalism: Charles Grandison Finney to Billy Graham.* New York: Ronald Press, 1959.

——. *New England Dissent, 1630–1833: The Baptists and the Separation of Church and State.* Cambridge, Mass.: Harvard University Press, 1971.

——. *Revivals, Awakenings, and Reform: An Essay on Religion and Social Change in America, 1607–1977.* Chicago: University of Chicago Press, 1978.

Mathews, Donald G. *Religion in the Old South.* Chicago: University of Chicago Press, 1977.

——. *Slavery and Methodism: A Chapter in American Morality, 1780–1845.* Princeton: Princeton University Press, 1965.

Miller, Roberta Balstad. *City and Hinterland: A Case Study of Urban Growth and Regional Development.* Westport, Conn.: Greenwood, 1979.

Miyakawa, T. Scott. *Protestants and Pioneers: Individualism and Conformity on the American Frontier.* Chicago: University of Chicago Press, 1964.

Niebuhr, H. Richard. *Christ and Culture.* New York: Harper & Row, 1951.

Norton, Mary Beth. *Liberty's Daughters: The Revolutionary Experience of American Women, 1785–1800.* Boston: Little, Brown, 1980.

Norwood, Frederick A. *Church Membership in the Methodist Tradition.* Nashville: Methodist Publishing House, 1958.

Oberholzer, Emil, Jr. *Delinquent Saints: Disciplinary Action in the Early Congregational Churches of Massachusetts.* New York: Columbia University Press, 1956.

Quarles, Benjamin. *Black Abolitionists.* New York: Oxford University Press, 1969.

Religion in America: The Gallup Report. No. 201–2. June–July 1982.

Reuther, Rosemary Radford. *Womanguides: Readings toward a Feminist Theology.* Boston: Beacon Press, 1985.

Rorabaugh, W. J. *The Alcoholic Republic: An American Tradition.* New York: Oxford University Press, 1979.

Rowe, David L. *Thunder and Trumpets: Millerites and Dissenting Religion in Upstate New York, 1800–1850.* Chico, Calif.: Scholars Press, 1985.

Ryan, Mary P. *Cradle of the Middle Class: The Family in Oneida County, New York, 1790–1865.* Cambridge: Cambridge University Press, 1983.

Smith-Rosenberg, Carroll. *Religion and the Rise of the American City: The New York City Mission Movement, 1812–1870.* Ithaca: Cornell University Press, 1971.

Sorin, Gerald. *The New York Abolitionists: A Case Study of Political Radicalism.* Westport, Conn.: Greenwood, 1971.

Spaulding, E. Wilder. *New York in the Critical Period, 1783–1789.* New York State Historical Association Series, 1. New York: Columbia University Press, 1932.

Wallace, Anthony F. C. *Rockdale: The Growth of an American Village in the Early Industrial Revolution.* New York: Norton, 1980.

Walters, Ronald G. *American Reformers, 1815–1860.* New York: Hill and Wang, 1978.

Weber, H. C. *Evangelism: A Graphic Survey.* New York: Macmillan, 1929.

Weisberger, Bernard. *They Gathered at the River: The Story of the Great Revivalists and Their Impact upon Religion in America.* Chicago: Quadrangle Books, 1966.

White, Philip L. *Beekmantown, New York: Forest Frontier to Farm Community.* Austin: University of Texas Press, 1979.

Wilentz, Sean. *Chants Democratic: New York City and the Rise of the American Working Class, 1788–1850.* New York: Oxford University Press, 1984.

Zuckerman, Michael. *Peaceable Kingdoms: New England Towns in the Eighteenth Century.* New York: Knopf, 1970.

Articles and Pamphlets

Banner, Lois. "Religious Benevolence as Social Control: A Critique of an Interpretation." *Journal of American History* 60 (June 1973): 23–41.

Boylan, Anne M. "Women in Groups: An Analysis of Women's Benevolent Organizations in New York and Boston, 1797–1840." *Journal of American History* 71 (December 1984): 497–523.

Brumberg, Joan Jacobs. "Benevolent Beginnings: Volunteer Traditions among American Women, 1800–1860." In *Women, Volunteering, and Health Policy: Historical Perspectives and Contemporary Viewpoints,* pp. 1–16. New York: United Hospital Fund, 1982.

Centennial Anniversary, First Baptist Church, Cortland, New York. 1901. CCHS.

Cott, Nancy F. "Young Women in the Second Great Awakening in New England." *Feminist Studies* 3 (1975): 15–29.

Cushing, John D. "Notes on Disestablishment in Massachusetts, 1780–1833." *William and Mary Quarterly,* 3d ser. 26 (1969): 169–90.

Easterlin, Richard A. "Population Change and Farm Settlement in the Northern United States." *Journal of Economic History* 36 (March 1976): 46–75.

Ellis, David M. "The Yankee Invasion of New York." *New York History* 32 (January 1951): 3–17.

Faler, Paul. "Cultural Aspects of the Industrial Revolution: Lynn, Massachusetts, Shoemakers and Industrial Morality, 1820–1860." *Labor History* 15 (Summer 1974): 367–94.

First Presbyterian Church, One Hundredth Anniversary, Cortland, N.Y., April 16–19, 1925. Accession No. 1151M, CUA.

Goodman, Paul. "A Guide to American Church Membership Data before the Civil War." *Historical Methods Newsletter* 10 (November 1977): 183–90.

Hammond, John L. "The Reality of Revivals." *SA Sociological Analysis* 44 (Summer 1983): 111–15.

History (in part): All Souls' First Universalist Church, Cortland, New York: First 100 Years. 1937. CCHS.

Lerner, Gerda. "The Lady and the Mill Girl: Changes in the Status of Women in the Age of Jackson." In Jean E. Friedman, William G. Shade, and Mary Jane Capozzoli, eds., *Our American Sisters; Women in American Life and Thought*, pp. 125–38. Lexington, Mass.: D. C. Heath, 1987.

McKinney, William, and Dean R. Hoge. "Community and Congregational Factors in the Growth and Decline of Protestant Churches." *Journal for the Scientific Study of Religion* 22 (March 1983): 51–66.

Pritchard, Linda. "The Burned-over District Reconsidered." *Social Science History* 8 (Summer 1984): 243–65.

Van Hoesen, David W. *History of the Presbyterian Church of Preble, N.Y.* September 26, 1915. PHS.

Unpublished Works

Johnson, Curtis D. "Islands of Holiness: Rural Religion in Cortland County, New York, 1790–1860." 2 vols. Ph.D. dissertation, University of Minnesota, 1985.

Ralston, Leonard. "Migration and Settlement: Cortland County, 1855." Paper delivered before the New York State Studies Group Meeting, Brockport, New York, June 1978.

Roth, Randolph A. "Whence This Strange Fire? Religious and Reform Movements in the Connecticut River Valley of Vermont, 1791–1843." 2 vols. Ph.D. dissertation, Yale University, 1981.

Wadsworth, Maud Bingham (Mrs. Frank). "History of the Solon Baptist Church, Cortland Association, N.Y." September 26, 1954. Typescript. Accession No. 1482M, CUA.

Wellman, Judith. "The Burned-over District Revisited: Benevolent Reform and Abolitionism in Mexico, Paris, and Ithaca, New York, 1825–1842." Ph.D. dissertation, University of Virginia, 1974.

Index

Church of the Latter Day Saints, 9n, 163
Cincinnatus and Solon Union Congregational Church, 57n, 58n, 61, 153; discipline, 104, 107; New Measures, 49, 123; Sabbath regulations, 25; and temperance, 117–18, 126; women in, 60
Cincinnatus Baptist Church, 153
Cincinnatus Congregational Church, 56. *See also* Freetown Congregational Church
Cincinnatus Methodists, 91
Cleveland, John, 56
Clough, Reuben, 170n, 171n
Cole, Charles, 9
Collins, Charlotte, 95
congregational finances, 28, 109–10, 114, 148–49, 152–57, 161–62
Congregationalists, 19, 21, 23, 27, 57n, 58n, 97–100, 153; and antislavery, 120–24, 126–31; benevolence, 114, 154–56; discipline, 91–93, 104–12, 142–43, 157–58; as formalists, 67–71, 78n, 172–73; membership growth, 50, 70–71, 155; struggle against Arminianism, 43–52; and temperance, 115–18; voting, 83, 173. See also *entries for individual churches*
congregational size, 26–27, 39, 73–76
conviction rates, 93, 111, 142–43; defined, 91
corporate churches, 71–72, 82, 94, 115–16; collapse of, 140–58, 173–75; defined, 24–26, 89; discipline, 89–93, 103–12; and gender relations, 55–57, 60–61
Cortland Academy, 147
Cortland Advocate, 38
Cortland All Souls' First Universalist Church, 98–100
Cortland Baptist Association, 106n, 141; and antislavery, 124; benevolence, 114, 156; New Measures, 75; and temperance, 119; women, 54, 65, 154
Cortland Baptist Church, 57n, 58n, 61, 65n, 66n, 73, 119n, 125; and discipline, 107, 110–11, 123, 143n. *See also* Cortlandville Baptist Church; Homer Baptist Church
Cortland Baptist Society, 57n, 58n, 80

Cortland County, 46; formation of, 15; historical sources on, 6; typicality of, 3–6
Cortland County Agricultural Society, 38
Cortland County Anti-Slavery Society, 120, 125
Cortland County Temperance Society, 117–18
Cortland Free Congregational Church, 130–31
Cortland Methodist Church, 81, 125
Cortland Methodist Society, 81, 125
Cortland Presbyterian Church, 61, 73, 110, 146n; and antislavery, 130–32; discipline, 61, 128; influence of wealth upon, 58; revivals in, 49n, 50n, 62–63; and temperance, 118–19, 126; transfers, 39
Cortland Presbytery, 98, 114, 118, 122–23, 126–29, 131–32, 154
Cortland Republican, 110, 146n
Cortland Republican and Eagle, 38, 125
Cortlandville Baptist Church, 49, 65, 153. *See also* Cortland Baptist Church, Homer Baptist Church
Cortlandville Christian Church, 101
Cott, Nancy F., 9, 41, 54
covenants, 24–25, 99–100, 142
Crandall, Brother, 92
Cravath, Austin, 128
Cravath, Oren, 130
Crosby, Parker, 110
Cross, Whitney, 2, 7, 38
Curran, Charles, 163

Darling, Electa, 143n
Davis, L. D., 39n, 40n, 48, 81
Democratic party, 82–83, 126n, 173
discipline, 24–27, 55–56, 123, 160–61, 173–75; and commercial activities, 56–57; denominational variation in, 91–92, 170n, 171n; and intemperance, 115–16, 118–19; opposition to, 103–12, 140–44, 149–51; procedures, 90; role of, 89–90, 170–71; and ultraism, 127–29; and women, 59–61; and worldliness, 95, 146–47
Downs, Lucy, 109
Dunbar, Miles, 95
Duncan, George, 128
Dyer, John, 47, 96

Library of Congress Cataloging-in-Publication Data

Johnson, Curtis D., 1949–
    Islands of holiness : rural religion in upstate New York.
1790–1860/Curtis D. Johnson.
        p. cm.
    Bibliography: p.
    Includes index.
    ISBN 0–8014–2275–2 (alk. paper)
    1. Cortland County (N.Y.)—Religious life and customs. 2. Cortland County
(N.Y.)—Church history. I. Title.
BR555.N72C674   1989   277.47'72081—dc19   88–43436